Futures & Options For Dummies®

Cheat Sheet

P9-CMU-522

Rules to Keep You Sane in the Futures and Options Markets

- Trust in chaos.
- Avoid undercapitalization.
- Be patient when setting up trades.
- Believe in the charts and the markets, not the talking heads.
- Diversification is protection.
- Set realistic goals.
- Remember that bragging is a sign of trouble.
- Have low expectations.

Making Sense of Technical Analysis

Technical analysis, discussed in Chapters 7 and 8, can be intimidating. These tips should help:

- Charting isn't meant to replace fundamental analysis. Charts are meant to complement and enhance it, enabling you to make better decisions.

- Understanding the fundamentals of supply and demand in your particular segment of the market is necessary for you to be able to trade futures and options based on charted technical signals. Knowing the fundamentals and the technical analysis makes investing your hard-earned money easier.

- Becoming familiar with more than one set of indicators and being able to combine them gives you more than one perspective from which to view the markets. Narrow-minded traders don't go too far.

- Learning the basics of following moving averages, identifying trend reversals, and drawing trend lines is important for you to be able to add new layers of analysis, such as moving average crossover systems, Fibonnacci retracements, and other more sophisticated techniques as you gain more experience.

- Continuing to expand your knowledge of technical analysis is important. You can do so by reading books and magazines like *Technical Analysis of Stocks and Commodities* and *Active Trader* magazine, which are excellent sources of interesting articles. *Investor's Business Daily,* either the print or the digital version of the paper on its Web site, is a chart reader's paradise for stock and futures traders.

- Exercising care so that you avoid clutter in your charts, even as you become more sophisticated in your approach to trading futures and options. The simpler your charts, the better the picture you get and the better your decisions will be.

Wiley, the Wiley Publishing logo, For Dummies, the Dummies Man logo, the For Dummies Bestselling Book Series logo and all related trade dress are trademarks or registered trademarks of John Wiley & Sons, Inc. and/or its affiliates. All other trademarks are property of their respective owners.

For Dummies: Bestselling Book Series for Beginners

Futures & Options For Dummies®

Cheat Sheet

Essential Economic Reports to Monitor as a Futures Trader

- ✔ The monthly employment report
- ✔ The Consumer Price Index
- ✔ The Producer Price Index
- ✔ ISM and regional purchasing manager's reports
- ✔ The Beige Book from the Federal Reserve
- ✔ Housing Starts
- ✔ Index of Leading Economic Indicators
- ✔ Gross Domestic Product
- ✔ Oil Supply Data

Essential Requirements of an Online Charting Service

- ✔ **Accessibility:** The service needs to be available to you virtually anywhere, either online or by the use of a convenient online interface.
- ✔ **Support:** Make sure that the service offers a toll-free telephone number to call for support and that it provides online support.
- ✔ **Charting tools:** The charts provided by your charting service must be easy-to-read and user-friendly. You shouldn't have to punch five or ten keys or toggle your mouse for 10 minutes while trying to make your chart look right.
- ✔ **Real-time quotes:** Trading futures without real-time quotes is a sure path down the road to ruin.
- ✔ **Live charts:** If you're going to trade, you need access to *live charts* that actually change with every tick (up or down movement) of the market.
- ✔ **Time-frame analysis:** Make sure that your charting service enables you to produce intraday charts. You want to be able to look at different time frames simultaneously.
- ✔ **Multiple indicators:** Make sure that the service to which you subscribe lets you plot price charts and multiple indicators at the same time.

Three Reasons to Use Candlestick Charts

- ✔ **Trends are easier to spot.** For example, a sea of rising green (or white), meaning a large grouping of bullish candles on a candlestick chart is hard to mistake for anything other than a strong uptrend. Because candlesticks tend to have a body in most cases, the overall trend of the market often is easier to identify.
- ✔ **Trend changes are easier to spot.** Candlestick patterns can be dramatic and can help you identify trend changes before you can recognize them on bar charts. Some candlestick patterns are reliable at predicting future prices.
- ✔ **Shifts in momentum are as easy to spot.** Conditions in which a security is oversold and overbought, along with trends and other kinds of indicators, might be easier to spot on candlestick charts as they are on bar charts due to the presence of doji candles and color. For example, an engulfing pattern, which can be either negative or positive, is easier to spot in a candlestick chart.

Copyright © 2006 Wiley Publishing, Inc. All rights reserved. Item 5283-5. For more information about Wiley Publishing, call 1-800-762-2974.

For Dummies: Bestselling Book Series for Beginners

Futures & Options
FOR DUMMIES®

by Joe Duarte, MD

WILEY

Wiley Publishing, Inc.

Futures & Options For Dummies®

Published by
Wiley Publishing, Inc.
111 River St.
Hoboken, NJ 07030-5774
www.wiley.com

Copyright © 2006 by Wiley Publishing, Inc., Indianapolis, Indiana

Published by Wiley Publishing, Inc., Indianapolis, Indiana

Published simultaneously in Canada

No part of this publication may be reproduced, stored in a retrieval system, or transmitted in any form or by any means, electronic, mechanical, photocopying, recording, scanning, or otherwise, except as permitted under Sections 107 or 108 of the 1976 United States Copyright Act, without either the prior written permission of the Publisher, or authorization through payment of the appropriate per-copy fee to the Copyright Clearance Center, 222 Rosewood Drive, Danvers, MA 01923, 978-750-8400, fax 978-646-8600. Requests to the Publisher for permission should be addressed to the Legal Department, Wiley Publishing, Inc., 10475 Crosspoint Blvd., Indianapolis, IN 46256, 317-572-3447, fax 317-572-4355, or online at http://www.wiley.com/go/permissions.

Trademarks: Wiley, the Wiley Publishing logo, For Dummies, the Dummies Man logo, A Reference for the Rest of Us!, The Dummies Way, Dummies Daily, The Fun and Easy Way, Dummies.com and related trade dress are trademarks or registered trademarks of John Wiley & Sons, Inc. and/or its affiliates in the United States and other countries, and may not be used without written permission. All other trademarks are the property of their respective owners. Wiley Publishing, Inc., is not associated with any product or vendor mentioned in this book.

LIMIT OF LIABILITY/DISCLAIMER OF WARRANTY: THE PUBLISHER AND THE AUTHOR MAKE NO REPRESENTATIONS OR WARRANTIES WITH RESPECT TO THE ACCURACY OR COMPLETENESS OF THE CONTENTS OF THIS WORK AND SPECIFICALLY DISCLAIM ALL WARRANTIES, INCLUDING WITHOUT LIMITATION WARRANTIES OF FITNESS FOR A PARTICULAR PURPOSE. NO WARRANTY MAY BE CREATED OR EXTENDED BY SALES OR PROMOTIONAL MATERIALS. THE ADVICE AND STRATEGIES CONTAINED HEREIN MAY NOT BE SUITABLE FOR EVERY SITUATION. THIS WORK IS SOLD WITH THE UNDERSTANDING THAT THE PUBLISHER IS NOT ENGAGED IN RENDERING LEGAL, ACCOUNTING, OR OTHER PROFESSIONAL SERVICES. IF PROFESSIONAL ASSISTANCE IS REQUIRED, THE SERVICES OF A COMPETENT PROFESSIONAL PERSON SHOULD BE SOUGHT. NEITHER THE PUBLISHER NOR THE AUTHOR SHALL BE LIABLE FOR DAMAGES ARISING HEREFROM. THE FACT THAT AN ORGANIZATION OR WEBSITE IS REFERRED TO IN THIS WORK AS A CITATION AND/OR A POTENTIAL SOURCE OF FURTHER INFORMATION DOES NOT MEAN THAT THE AUTHOR OR THE PUBLISHER ENDORSES THE INFORMATION THE ORGANIZATION OR WEBSITE MAY PROVIDE OR RECOMMENDATIONS IT MAY MAKE. FURTHER, READERS SHOULD BE AWARE THAT INTERNET WEBSITES LISTED IN THIS WORK MAY HAVE CHANGED OR DISAPPEARED BETWEEN WHEN THIS WORK WAS WRITTEN AND WHEN IT IS READ.

For general information on our other products and services, please contact our Customer Care Department within the U.S. at 800-762-2974, outside the U.S. at 317-572-3993, or fax 317-572-4002.

For technical support, please visit www.wiley.com/techsupport.

Wiley also publishes its books in a variety of electronic formats. Some content that appears in print may not be available in electronic books.

Library of Congress Control Number: 2005935160

ISBN-13: 978-0-471-75283-7

ISBN-10: 0-471-75283-5

Manufactured in the United States of America

10 9 8 7 6 5 4 3 2

1B/SS/QT/QW/IN

About the Author

Dr. Joe Duarte is a widely read market analyst, writer, and an active trader. His daily Market IQ column is read by thousands of investors, futures and stock traders, information seekers, intelligence aficionados, and professionals around the world.

Dr. Duarte is well recognized as a geopolitical and financial market analyst combining a unique set of viewpoints into an original blend of solutions for his audience. His daily columns appear at www.joe-duarte.com and are syndicated worldwide by FinancialWire.

He is author of *Successful Energy Sector Investing, Successful Biotech Investing,* and coauthor of *After-Hours Trading Made Easy.*

He is a board certified anesthesiologist, a registered investment advisor, and President of River Willow Capital Management.

Dr. Duarte has appeared on CNBC and appears weekly on *The Financial Sense Newshour with Jim Puplava* radio show, where he comments on the energy markets and geopolitics. He has logged appearances on Biz Radio, Wall Street Radio, JagFn, WebFN, KNX radio in Los Angeles, and WOWO radio.

One of CNBC's original Market Mavens, Dr. Duarte has been writing about the financial markets since 1990. An expert in health care and biotechnology stocks, the energy sector, as well as financial market sentiment, his daily syndicated stock columns have appeared on leading financial Web sites, including Reuter's e-charts, afterhourtrades.com and MarketMavens.com.

His articles and commentary are regularly featured on Marketwatch.com. He has appeared in *Barron's, U.S.A. Today, Smart Money, Medical Economics,* Rigzone.com, and in *Technical Analysis of Stocks and Commodities* magazine.

Dr. Duarte published the critically acclaimed market timing newsletter "The Wall Street Detective," from 1990-1998, when it became an exclusively electronic publication. His daily market commentary 'Joe Knows' appeared on Financialweb.com from 1998-2000. Dr. Duarte served as senior columnist for Investorlinks.com from 1998-2001.

Dedication

This one goes to the usual suspects. Without you, life wouldn't be as interesting. You know who you are. No matter what, you continue to do that voodoo that you do . . . so well. . . .

Author's Acknowledgments

A book is as much about environment, accidents, incidents, and circumstances as it is about research. This group of people fits the bill for creating all of the above, and I'd like to offer my sincere gratitude, because it is the sum of their interactions with me that often leads to interesting ideas and observations that make their way onto the written page.

I'd like to thank the subscribers and sources of `Joe-Duarte.com` for their continued interest and support.

My wife, Lourdes, my son, Metheny, my mother and father, Raquel and Jose, and Angela, the book maven, are always there, no matter how grumpy I get near manuscript deadlines. Thanks to them.

Sal, Lib, and the office gangs, this one was harder on all of us than I would have expected. Thanks as usual.

Frank Kollar is as good a partner as anyone could have. Thanks, and enjoy that kafi.

Greg Morris, thank you for lunch, and all kinds of intangibles.

John Duke, for all the e-mails . . . and stuff.

Marty, thanks for the annual pilgrimage to Starplex, where the soul gets renewed.

And especially Grace, without whom there would be no book gigs. Keep them coming.

And thank you for your ongoing support to:

Jim, Mary, John, and Liz at Financial Sense News Hour.

Tom Bemis at MarketWatch.com.

Gail Essary at Financial Wire.

Charly Butcher and the gang at WOWO.

Jill Woerner at CNBC.

A very special thanks to the new gang at Wiley — Stacy, Tim, Neil, and company. It's good to be back in the saddle.

Very special thanks to Thom Calandra, whose early support allowed my writings to go farther and wider than I could have ever imagined. Stay well, and no worries.

Coffee and tea . . . fuel for life . . . and writing books.

Publisher's Acknowledgments

We're proud of this book; please send us your comments through our Dummies online registration form located at www.dummies.com/register/.

Some of the people who helped bring this book to market include the following:

Acquisitions, Editorial, and Media Development

Senior Project Editor: Tim Gallan

Acquisitions Editor: Stacy Kennedy

Copy Editor: E. Neil Johnson

Editorial Program Coordinator: Hanna K. Scott

Technical Editor: Noel M. Jameson

Editorial Manager: Christine Meloy Beck

Editorial Assistants: David Lutton, Nadine Bell, Erin Calligan,

Cover Photo: © Steven Hunt/Getty Images

Cartoons: Rich Tennant (www.the5thwave.com)

Composition Services

Project Coordinator: Jennifer Theriot

Layout and Graphics: Carl Byers, Lynsey Osborn, Alicia B. South

Proofreaders: Leeann Harney, Joe Niesen, Techbooks

Indexer: Techbooks

Publishing and Editorial for Consumer Dummies

    Diane Graves Steele, Vice President and Publisher, Consumer Dummies

    Joyce Pepple, Acquisitions Director, Consumer Dummies

    Kristin A. Cocks, Product Development Director, Consumer Dummies

    Michael Spring, Vice President and Publisher, Travel

    Kelly Regan, Editorial Director, Travel

Publishing for Technology Dummies

    Andy Cummings, Vice President and Publisher, Dummies Technology/General User

Composition Services

    Gerry Fahey, Vice President of Production Services

    Debbie Stailey, Director of Composition Services

Contents at a Glance

Table of Contents

Part II: Analyzing the Markets *89*

Chapter 6: Understanding the Fundamentals of the Economy 91

Chapter 7: Getting Technical Without Getting Tense 111

Introduction

*R*isk and uncertainty go hand in hand with opportunities to make money.

Goods, services, and basic materials probably will undergo major price swings, up and down, at one time or another during the next 20 years. The volatility of the markets is only going to increase. And the chances for sustainable trends that last for decades, the way the stock market rallied in the 1980s and 1990s, are less likely than they were a few years ago.

If global warming doesn't get you, then politicians, militants, or dictators are almost certain to try. That's why learning how to trade futures and options is important for investors who not only want to diversify their own portfolios but also want to find ways to protect and grow their money when times are hard in traditional investment venues such as the stock market.

The world has changed since the events of September 11, 2001. And the December 2004 tsunami and the New Orleans disaster with Hurricane Katrina are more proof of what's in store.

Whereas in the past, investors could afford the luxury of buying and holding stocks or mutual funds for the long term, the post September 11, 2001, world calls for a more active and even a speculative investor. The new world calls for a trader. And futures and options markets, although high risk, offer some of the best opportunities to make money trading in volatile times.

So you need to get ready to work as a stock trader, a geopolitical analyst, a money manager, and an expert in the oil markets. I have to keep up with news about the economy, disruptions in the supply of oil, the weekly trends of oil supply, weather patterns, and the stock market, both in a macro and micro universe. As a futures and options trader, you have to do the same with your contract of choice, and you have to pay attention to time factors, especially expiration dates and how much time you have left to decide whether you have to exercise your option.

Remember that successful traders

- Have a plan, follow it, and adjust it to changing conditions.
- Look at trading as a business.
- Are disciplined in their personal and professional lives.
- Understand the risks and the game they're playing.

✔ Know and accept that they will make mistakes.

✔ Never forget their mistakes and learn from them.

✔ Never enter into a trade without knowing their exit strategy — how they'll get out of the market.

✔ Never risk money that they aren't willing to or can't afford to lose.

✔ Never allow a bad trade to lead to a margin call.

Trading futures and options isn't gambling; it's speculating. It's also gathering information and making judgment calls about situations that are unfolding, and it's a process of self-protection and an ongoing education.

You may think of yourself as a dummy. But after you read this book, you'll know how trading futures and options is done and how to stay in the game as long as you want, not necessarily by hitting home runs but rather by showing up to work everyday, getting your uniform dirty, and playing good, consistent, fundamental baseball.

About This Book

Futures markets are resurging and are likely to be hot for several decades, given the political landscape. Changing world demographics and the emergence of China and India as economic powers and consumers, coupled with changing politics in the Middle East, are likely to fuel the continued prominence of these markets.

I take you inside these markets and give you tools that you can use for

✔ **Analyzing, trading, or just gaining a better understanding of how money works and affects your daily life.**

✔ **Starting fresh in your views of how the markets work.** A traditional buy and hold mind-set is a recipe for trouble in futures and options trading, while profit taking or hedging a position before the weekend is normal operating procedure.

✔ **Discovering that time is on your side in the stock and bond markets, but it's your enemy in futures and options.** You've got to be on top of how much time you have left before your trading position expires worthless or when you have a load of something delivered with a bill for a large sum of money.

✔ **Reading a sentence just the way it's written.** No tricks, hidden clues, political agendas, or attempts to make you look foolish. If you don't get it, I didn't do a good job of writing it.

✔ **Remembering that measuring the return of your money is more important than measuring the return on your money.**

Conventions Used in This Book

To help you make the best use of this book, I use the following conventions:

- *Italics* are used for emphasis and to highlight new words or terms.
- **Boldfaced text** is used to indicate key words in bulleted lists or the action parts of numbered steps.
- `Monofont` is used for Web addresses.

What I Assume about You

I had to start somewhere, so I assumed some things that may or may not apply to you. I'm not trying to offend you or to be condescending. So here's what I've assumed about you:

- You're curious about the futures and options markets, but you don't know enough to trade them and want to find out how to do it without losing your shirt.
- You've been a stock trader, but you'd like to know more about using charts, indicators, and trading psychology.
- You want to find out how to decrease the risk within your portfolio.
- You want to become a more active trader and make money more consistently by letting your profits run and cutting your losses short.
- You want to know how to make sense of the big picture in the markets and to try your hand at trading currencies, bonds, and commodities.
- You like the idea of trading on margin, and you're not afraid of leveraging additional money.
- You aren't afraid of being wrong five or six times in a row when trading, but you're willing to try again until you succeed.
- You want to investigate more about how politics, wars, weather, and external events can be used as opportunities to trade.

If these assumptions describe you, you've picked up the right book. Nevertheless, I also assume that you have some tools and resources at your disposal. Here's what you need to get started in futures and options trading:

- **Plenty of money and a cast-iron stomach to boot.** You need to have at least twice the amount that your broker/advisor lists as a minimum for opening an account. And you have to be ready to lose it all, fast.
- **Your head screwed on straight before you start.** Futures and options trading is really dangerous and can wither away your trading capital fast.

✔ **A quiet place to prepare, set up your trading station, and make sure you know your market stuff really well.** Exchange hours, what brokers do and don't do, what trading terms like bid and offer mean, and how to read a brokerage statement are only some of what you need to know.

✔ **A fast computer with a fast Internet connection.**

✔ **Access to good charts.** You can gain access to charts either through the Web or a good trading software program and the ability to test your strategies before you commit to them.

✔ **Subscriptions to newsletters, books, magazines, and software.** Be ready to spend some money for these important information resources. You can also take courses, and you need to get used to paper trading (practicing without money) before jumping into the deep end.

How This Book Is Organized

I've organized *Futures & Options For Dummies* into six parts. Parts I and II introduce you to the futures markets and market analysis — technical and fundamental. Parts III through V take you into the nuts and bolts, the exchanges, the contracts, trading strategies, and indicators. Part VI is the now famous *For Dummies* Part of Tens, in which you can discover a little about a lot of different futures and options information.

Part 1: Understanding the Financial Markets

Sure, this sounds like a lot to swallow, but if you don't understand how the pieces fit together, you won't get the finer points that can make you a better trader.

This part shows you three things:

✔ Where money comes from and why markets move the way they do

✔ What the function and role of futures and options markets are

✔ How the financial markets work together

Part II: Analyzing the Markets

This part is where you get your basic training. It's all about fundamental and technical analyses, and it gives you details about supply and demand, how to use economic reports, and how to take advantage of seasonal and chart patterns and market sentiment.

Part III: Financial Futures

Most stock investors think the stock market is the center of the universe. After you read this part, you'll see things differently, because I look at the role of the bond market, and how it's really the tail that wags the dog.

Part IV: Commodity Futures

Yeah baby! We finally get to pork bellies, soybeans, and wheat. But more important, this part is about trading oil, natural gas, steel, copper, gold, you name it — all of which are affected by strange things like weather, pollution, and electricity, thrown in for good measure.

Part V: The Trading Plan

This part is a big case of the nuts and bolts of trading. Relax, it isn't catching, but it is likely to get you a bit more organized. Who can't use a little discipline, eh?

This part details how you can set up, organize, execute, and operate a trading business, starting with the trading calendar and working your way all the way to deciding what your best markets and surefire strategies are and how to mix and match approaches while trading and hedging.

Part VI: The Part of Tens

Here I give you lists of rules and resources that can help you make money and keep you from losing big chunks of it whenever the markets turn on you.

Icons Used in This Book

For Dummies books use little pictures, called icons, to flag certain chunks of text and information that are of particular interest. Here's what they actually mean to you, the reader:

Yup, this one is important. Don't forget the stuff marked with this icon.

The bull's-eye gives you info that you can put to use right away, such as when to trade or how to engage a specific strategy.

I like this one best, because it reminds me of Inspector Clouseau of *The Pink Panther* fame. The "bemb," as Clouseau would say, is a sign that you need to read the information highlighted by it carefully. If you ignore this icon, you can end up in a world of hurt.

Although you can skip this important, but not necessarily essential, information without repercussion, you may not be able to impress your friends at the water cooler as much as you otherwise would.

Where to Go from Here

For Dummies books are set up so you can start reading anywhere. Don't feel as though you have to read everything from beginning to end. If you're a true beginner, I recommend that you read Parts I and II carefully before you start skipping around. Here's to profitable futures and options trading.

Part I
Understanding the Financial Markets

In this part . . .

You'll get a handle on where money comes from and the important details about how the futures and options markets work in this part of *Futures & Options For Dummies*. I start you out with the key relationship between central banks and the bond markets and take you on a tour of the futures markets, while offering a little history lesson along the way. That leads you into an overview of today's markets — how they work with and depend on one another. And before moving on, I tell you about option strategies that are designed to help you get the most out of your trading.

Chapter 1

The Ins and Outs of Trading Futures and Options

*I*f you're one of those people who look at their mutual fund portfolios once a year and wonder how the results came about, futures trading isn't for you — at least until you make some changes in how you view the financial markets, your knowledge base, and in general, how the world works.

No, you don't have to live in a monastery and wear a virtual-reality helmet that plugs into the Internet, has satellite TV, and features real-time quotes and charts. You are, however, going to have to take the time to review your current investing philosophy and find out how futures trading can fit into your day-to-day scheme of things without ruining your family life and your nest egg.

Trading is not investing; it's speculating. *Speculating* is defined as assuming a business risk with the hope of profiting from market fluctuations. Successful speculating requires analyzing situations, predicting outcomes, and putting your money on the side of the trade on which way you think the market is going to go, up or down. Speculating also involves an appreciation of the fact that you can be wrong 70 percent of the time and still be a successful futures trader if you apply the correct techniques for analyzing trades, managing your money, and protecting your account.

Basically that means you have to chuck all your preconceptions about buy-and-hold investing, asset allocation, and essentially all the strategies that stock brokerages put out for public consumption.

And just so you don't call your brother-in-law the broker and get the publisher and me in trouble, what I mean is that buy-and-hold doesn't work in the futures markets. They're designed for trading.

Futures trading is risky business and requires active participation. It can be plied successfully only if you're serious about it and committed to it.

That means you must be able to develop your trading craft by constantly reviewing and modifying your plan and strategies.

To be a successful futures and options trader, you're going to have to become connected with the world through the Internet, television, and other news sources so you can be up-to-date and intimately knowledgeable with regard to world events. And I don't mean just picking up on what you get from occasionally watching the evening or headline news shows.

You're also going to have to spend some time and money setting up for this endeavor. You'll need a computer, trading program, and brokerage account of some sort, not to mention how much money you need or how well capitalized you have to be to be able to survive.

In essence, you must either make some changes, or your foray into trading futures and options will be nothing more than a quick endeavor.

Who Trades Futures and Options?

Aside from professional speculators and hedgers, whose numbers are many, the ranks of futures traders essentially are made up of people like you and me who are interested in making money in the markets — the wide variety of people who trade futures and options contracts at the retail level.

In his book *Starting Out in Futures Trading* (McGraw-Hill), author Mark Powers cites a study by the Chicago Mercantile Exchange (CME) that described the profile of a futures trader in the 1970s as a male between 35 and 55 years of age with middle- to upper-class income. The study indicated that

- Fifty-four percent were professionals, including doctors, lawyers, dentists, and white-collar workers, especially upper-management types.
- Sixty-eight percent were college graduates.
- Their overall tendency was toward short-term trading.

By 1999, *Futures Industry* magazine surveyed futures brokers regarding online futures trading. A summary of the results identified

- Some general tendencies but couldn't settle on a description for a typical online futures trader.

- Account sizes ranging from $14,000 to $30,000 at brokerages aimed at retail investors, with average transaction sizes within that group ranging from 1.6 to 5 contracts.

- Account sizes ranging from $40,000 to millions of dollars at brokerages with mostly institutional clienteles, with average transaction sizes within that group ranging from 17 contracts to even larger transactions.

The bottom line seems to be that to be able to trade futures and options, you need to have a certain amount of education and the necessary technological and financial means to get started.

Who Is a Successful Futures Trader?

Everyone knows that it helps to know a few things about the financial markets and that you need the ability to at least consider online trading and, of course, some finances to trade futures contracts.

But how do you become good at it? How do you manage to survive, even when you're not particularly good at it?

The answer is simple. You must have enough money and be able to develop a trading plan that enables you to keep making trades in the markets long enough to make enough money so you capitalize on your next big trade.

Simply put: If you don't have enough money, you won't last. And if you don't have a good trading plan, your money quickly disappears.

Indeed, your success depends more than anything else on how you prepare yourself financially, intellectually, technologically, and personally through the development of a detailed and easy-to-implement trading plan.

What You Need to Trade

You need money, knowledge, patience, and technology to be able to trade futures and options contracts.

In terms of money, many experienced traders say that you need $100,000 to get started, but the figures from the previous section show that retail investors rarely have that much money in their accounts — at least as of 1999.

The truth is that there are many talented traders who have made fortunes after starting out with significantly less than $100,000. However, it would be irresponsible for me to lead you astray and give you the false impression, as some would, that the odds are very much in your favor if you start trading at a very low equity level.

The reality is that different people fare differently depending on their trading ability, at any level of experience. A trader with a million dollars in equity can lose large amounts just as easily as you and I with $10,000 worth of equity in our account.

My only point here is to make sure that you understand the risk involved and that you go into trading with realistic expectations.

If you don't have that much money and are not sure how to proceed, you need to either reconsider trading altogether, develop a stout trading plan and the discipline required to heed its tenets, or consider managed futures contracts. I discuss these topics in detail in Chapter 17. Would-be traders who have less than $30,000 should also consider the managed futures opportunities like the ones I tell you about in Chapter 17.

When it comes to technology, you need an efficient computer system that has enough memory to enable you to look at large numbers of data and run either multiple, fully loaded browsers or several monitors at the same time.

You also need a high-speed Internet connection. If you get serious about trading, you also need to consider having two modes of high-speed Internet access. For a home office, a full-time trader often has high-speed Internet through the cable television service and through DSL (digital subscriber line), with one or the other serving as a backup.

Trading Modalities

Trading futures and options contracts is truly a hybrid that lies somewhere between the types of trading that are separately based on technical analysis and fundamental analysis.

The fundamental side of trading (see Chapter 6 for all the details) involves your getting to know the following:

✔ The industry in which you're making trades

✔ Contract specifications

✔ Seasonal tendencies of the markets

✔ Important reports on which you need to keep an eye

The technical side of trading (at least that part that I concentrate on) focuses on what the market is doing in response to fundamentals. When you use technical analysis, you'll be looking at jargony-sounding things, such as trading volume, price charts, and open interest, and how they respond to factors like the global economy, interest rates, and politics — just a few influences on prices. To do that you need to have access to and be able to read charts and to know how to use indicators, such as trend lines, moving averages, and oscillators. (I show you how in Chapters 7, 8, and 20.) Without these instruments and indicators, your trading is likely to suffer significantly, because they help you to keep track of prices and guide you in choosing when and how best to place your trades — getting in and out of the markets.

To be sure, there are other approaches to technical analysis ranging from those listed in this book to rather esoteric techniques that are not mentioned, such as using astrology, or rather precise but not so commonly seen chart patterns. My goal here is to give you methods and examples that you can begin to see and use immediately. See Chapter 7 for more on technical analysis.

It's always better to make money than to be right. The key is not what you think should happen, but rather what the market does in response to events and fundamental information and how you manage your trade. Success comes from letting winning positions go as long as possible and cutting losses short before they wipe you out.

Getting Used to Going Short

The concept of going short usually troubles stock investors. *Going short* means that you're trying to make money when prices fall. It involves borrowing a marketable asset from someone so you can sell it at a high price, wait for prices to fall, buy it back at the lower price, return the asset to the lender, and pocket the difference between what you sold it for and what you had to pay for it.

Although this may sound confusing, trading software simplifies the concept by giving you a button choice for short selling. Chapters 7 and 8 offer nice examples, including illustrations of what short selling is and when it's the correct strategy to follow.

In futures trading, every transaction involves a trader who's trading short and one who's trading long.

You can also bet on the market falling by using options called *put options*. These instruments let you decide whether you want to sell something at a predetermined price before a certain future date when the put option contract expires. For more about puts and their counterparts known as calls, turn to Chapters 4 and 5.

If this confuses you, you definitely need to read this book carefully before you consider trading futures contracts, or aggressively trading stocks, for that matter.

Managing Your Money

To be a successful trader, you must have a successful money management system that includes a minimum of these three components:

- **Having enough money to start:** You need enough money to get a good start and to keep trading. Undercapitalization is the major reason for failure. See "What You Need to Trade," earlier in this chapter.

- **Setting appropriate limits:** You need to set attainable limits on how much you'll risk, how you'll diversify your account, how much you're willing to lose, and when and how you take profits. Knowing your limits and sticking to them with regard to all these factors is important to successful trading. You'll get there by doing things like developing and regularly reviewing your trading plan, and using techniques such as placing stop-loss orders under your trades, to limit losses if you're wrong. See Chapters 17, 18, 19, and 20 for trading strategies.

- **Avoiding margin calls:** Margin calls will come if your account's equity falls below critical levels. Margin levels are different for each contract that you trade. A *margin call* is what happens when you hold a position that is falling in value beyond a limit set by the exchange. For example, if you were trading widgets with a margin set at $1,000, and your widget contracts fell below $1,000, your broker would call you and ask you for more money. If you can't put more money in the account, either by wiring it or by selling what's left of your widgets, the broker sells the widgets to raise the money, and your account is inactive until you raise the amount of money needed to meet future margins. Margin calls are explained in detail in Chapter 12.

Analyzing the Markets

One of the most important steps you can take toward being a good trader is developing a knack for analyzing the markets. That means you need to understand the technical and fundamental aspects of the market with respect to the underlying asset that you're trading.

The two basic ways for choosing what you'll trade are

- ✔ **Monitoring different markets to see which ones are moving or are likely to move.** Assuming that you have an understanding of the environment and the variables that move the markets, you can then trade them. The advantage to knowing these factors is that you're likely to have more activity in your account. The disadvantage is that when you're just getting started, you certainly won't be an expert in too many markets. Chapters 6 through 8 focus on technical and fundamental analyses of the economy, the futures markets, and basic speculating strategies.

- ✔ **Becoming an expert (on the technical and fundamental aspects) in at least one or two markets, and then trading them exclusively.** The advantage is that you get a good feeling for the subtleties of these markets and that your chances of success are likely to increase. The disadvantage is that you may have a good deal of dead time or dull stretches if the markets you choose don't move much. Chapters 10 through 16 cover the major mainstream futures markets in detail, including trading strategies.

Enjoying Your Trading Habit

I trade regularly, based on my time commitments to other activities and based on market conditions.

What I've discovered through years of trading, though, is that few times have I not enjoyed the process of analysis and decision-making that is involved in trading.

To me, trading is just about as good as it gets. Maybe it's something that's programmed into my DNA, personality, or mojo that just keeps me coming back.

As you progress through this and other books about trading futures and options, you'll discover whether your connection to the force (your karma) is good for trading.

Just remember that when you're ready to trade, you're going to be excited. That's okay, because the thrill of the hunt is one of the reasons everyone trades. However, you need to temper that excitement and hone it to your advantage. If you can manage the exhilaration of trading and turn it into an awareness of what is happening, you're likely to be more successful.

Welcome to one of the final frontiers left on the planet Earth.

If you start trading and you're not enjoying it, you need to revise your trading plan or find another way to put your investment capital to work.

Chapter 2

Where Money Comes From

Money doesn't grow on trees. But the truth isn't far from that. In fact, money is manufactured inside the world's central banks, especially the United States Federal Reserve System, essentially from thin air.

Okay, so there is some method to the madness. But the global monetary system mostly seems like madness that is far from leading to any certain outcomes, which, of course, is what makes trading a potentially profitable occupation — as long as you know what to look for.

If you know how the system works and how to use it, you can turn it to your advantage. In this chapter, I tell you how the Federal Reserve System in the U.S. (the Fed — the central bank of the United States) and other central banks around the world have branch offices throughout their respective countries, where economists directly monitor economic activity by going out into the community and talking to businesses, by designing and refining models, and by compiling reports based on all the data collected.

I also let you in on what happens when the Fed and its branch chiefs meet a few times every year to look at all this economic information so they can make informed decisions about how much money to pump into the system and how easy (or hard) they're going to make it to borrow that money.

You can't get into the inner workings of the Fed without knowing about the interactions between money supply, interest rates, and inflation, so I also include these topics and tie them together with the Federal Reserve, central banks, and money and the markets in general.

When I talk about the Federal Reserve, unless I say otherwise, I also refer to other central banks, because they all work in similar fashion. When there are important differences in the way they go about their business, I also let you know.

How Money Works: The Fiat System

The global monetary system is what's called a Fiat system in which *money* is a storage medium for purchasing power and a substitute for barter. Each dollar bill, euro, yen, gold ingot, or whatever currency you choose enables you to buy things as the need or want arises, thus making the barter system (trading one service or product for another) mostly obsolete.

Money then enables enterprises to development and societies to establish subspecializations, thus fostering a sort of dynamic progression toward the future.

For example, before there was money, anyone who owned land produced their own necessities and traded the surplus with other people for the things they needed.

Money changed that system by its inherent ability to store purchasing power, thus giving people the opportunity to make plans for the future and to specialize. In other words, if you're a good wheat farmer, then you can specialize in wheat, and buy your equipment, hire workers, and look for neighbors' land to buy to expand your wheat farm.

Markets and central banks then value the relative worth of the paper (currency) based on the perception of how a particular country is governing itself, the current state of its economy, and the effects the interplay of those two factors have on interest rates.

Money's money because we say it's money

Most of the world's money is called *fiat money,* meaning it is accepted as money because a government says that it's legal tender, and the public has enough confidence and faith in the money's ability to serve as a storage medium for purchasing power. A *fiat system* is based on a government's mandate that the paper currency it prints is legal tender for making financial transactions. *Legal tender* means that the money is backed by the full faith and credit of the government that issues it. In other words, the government promises to be good for it. I know how it sounds. But that's what the world's financial system is based on.

Fiat money is the opposite of *commodity money,* which is money that's based on a valuable commodity, a method of valuation that was used in the past. At times, the commodity itself actually was used as money. For instance, the use of gold, grain, and even furs and other animal products as commodity money preceded the current fiat system.

Where money comes from

Central banks create money either by printing it or by buying bonds in the treasury market. When central banks buy bonds, they usually buy their own country's treasury bonds, and their purchases are made from banks that own bonds. The money from the central banks goes to the bank vaults, and becomes loan-making capital.

When the Fed wants to increase the money supply in the U.S., it buys bonds from banks in the open market and uses a pretty simple formula to calculate how much money it actually is creating.

Instead of using gold as the basis for the monetary system — as was the custom until 1971, the Fed requires its member banks to keep certain specific amounts of money on reserve as a means of keeping a lid on the uncontrolled expansion of fiat money — in other words, to keep the money supply from exploding. These reserve requirements are the major safeguard of the system.

When the economy slows down, the Fed attempts to jump-start it by lowering interest rates. The Fed lowers interest rates by injecting money into the system. The monetary injection is sort of like a flu shot for an ailing economy. But instead of a vaccine, the Fed injects money into the system by buying bonds from the banks.

To keep the system from becoming inflationary, the Fed keeps a lid on how much banks can actually lend by using a bank reserve management system. The reserve management system, to be sure, is not an exact science, but over the long haul, it tends to work as long as the public buys the validity of the system, which in the United States, it does.

Here's how the reserve requirements work:

- ✔ If the current formula calls for a 10 percent reserve ratio, it means that for every dollar that a bank keeps in reserve, it can lend ten dollars to its clients.

- ✔ At the same time, if the Fed buys $500 million in bonds in the open market, it creates $5 billion in new money that makes its way to the public via bank loans.

- ✔ The reverse, or opposite, is true when the Fed wants to tighten credit and slow down the economy. It sells bonds to banks, thus draining money from the system, again based on the reserve formula.

Fiat money is created (and gotten rid of) out of thin air, but the process isn't by hocus-pocus from some wizard's wand. Its power comes from its use as accurate storage for purchasing power that is based on

- ✔ The public's acceptance of the legal-tender mandate. See the earlier section on "Money's money because we say it's money."

- ✔ The market's expectations that a government's promise to make its currency legal tender, by law, will hold.

Understanding Central Banks (Including the Federal Reserve)

Central banks are designed to make sure that their respective domestic economies run as smoothly as possible. In most countries, central banks are expected at the very least to combat inflationary pressures.

The overarching goal of the central banks is to repeal (or keep in check) the boom and bust cycles in the global economy. So far this goal is only an intention, because boom and bust cycles remain in place and are now referred to as the *business cycle*.

One good impact has come from the actions of the Fed and other central banks. They've been able to lengthen the amount of time between boom and bust cycles to the extent that they've smoothed out volatile trends and created an environment in which the futures markets offer a perfect vehicle for hedging and speculation.

Prior to the advent of central banks, booms and busts in the global economy came about as often as every harvest season. Because money was hard to come by prior to the centralization of the global economies, a bad harvest, a spell of bad weather, or just a bad set of investment decisions by a local bank in a farming community could devastate the economy in an area or even a country.

The central bank of the United States (and the world): The Federal Reserve

The Fed is the prototype central bank, because of its relative success, not because it was the first central bank. Created in 1913 to stabilize the activities of the money and credit markets, it administers the Federal Reserve Act, which mandated the creation of an agency intent on "improving the supervision" of banking and "creating an elastic currency."

The current objectives of the Fed are to fight inflation and maintain full employment to keep the consumption-based U.S. and global economies moving.

Under Chairman Alan Greenspan (whose appointment as a member of the Fed Board of Governors expired on January 31, 2006), the Federal Reserve became the most important financial institution in the world. In reality, the Fed is the central bank to the world, especially having grown in prestige and deeds during Greenspan's more than 18 years as chairman.

The fact that Greenspan's term expired and he can't be reappointed may offer up a considerable amount of volatility in the markets and give futures traders a nice chance to make some money.

How central banks function

The Fed has two official mandates: keeping inflation under control and maintaining full employment. However, it has some leeway and in many ways has outgrown its mandates, becoming lenders of last resort and sources of money in times of crises. In many speeches, especially after September 11, 2001, Greenspan and other Fed governors made it clear that their perception of the Fed's duties included maintaining the stability of the financial system and containing systemic risk.

Some central banks, such as the European Central Bank (ECB), use inflationary targets to gauge their successes. Unlike the Fed (which didn't set such targets under Chairman Alan Greenspan, but may do so in the future), the ECB must keep raising interest rates until the target is achieved, even if unemployment is high in Europe and inflation is above the central bank's target.

The positive side of inflation targeting is that it gives the market a sense of direction with regard to what the central bank's actions may be toward interest rates. The negative side, as is evident in Europe, is that the use of inflation targets often prevents the ECB from moving on interest rates. As a result, the European economy has lagged in its ability to grow. In other words, the dogma of adhering to the target set by the central bank has hurt the European economy. In contrast, despite frequent criticism, the U.S. economy, albeit in fits and starts, has continued to be the leading economy in the world. Much of that is because of the relatively good management of interest rates by the Fed.

The ECB's mandate opens up opportunities for trading currency, interest rates, and commodity futures, because after a central bank starts down a certain policy route, it usually stays with it for months, creating an intermediate-term trend on which to base the direction of trading.

For example, after September 11, 2001, the Fed lowered interest rates an amazing 14 times, which also shows that the Fed generally tends to raise or lower rates in a series of moves (except for the period between 1995 and 1998).

The Fed reversed its course and began raising interest rates in June 2003. As of November 2005, the Fed had raised interest rates 12 times, with the rate rising four-fold from 1 percent to 4 percent as measured by the Fed's official short-term rate, the *Fed funds rate,* which governs overnight loans between banks.

Understanding Money Supply

Money supply is how much money is available in the economy to buy goods, services, and securities. The money supply is as important as the supply of goods in determining the direction of the futures and options markets.

The four money supply figures to watch are

- **M0:** The *M0* is the money supply figure that's mentioned least often, but it's as important as any other, because it's all the cash and coins in circulation.

- **M1:** The *M1* money supply is M0 plus the amount of money housed in all checking and savings accounts.

- **M2:** The *M2* money supply is M1 plus money housed in other types of savings accounts, such as money market funds and certificates of deposit (CDs) of less than $100,000.

- **M3:** The *M3* money supply is M2 plus all other CDs, deposits held in euros, and all *repurchase agreements* (Repos), in which one party sells securities to another party and agrees to buy them back at a later date. A *Repo* is essentially a secured loan.

Money supply and inflation: The inevitable equation

I don't like equations, and you don't either, but this one is important. It's called the *monetary exchange equation,* and it explains the relationship between money supply and inflation as:

$$\text{Velocity} \times \text{Money Supply} = \text{Gross Domestic Product (GDP)} \times \text{GDP Deflator}$$

Velocity is a measure of how fast money is changing hands, because it records how many times per year the money actually is exchanged. *GDP* is the sum of all the goods and services produced by the economy. The *GDP deflator* is a measure of inflation, or a sustained rise in prices. *Inflation* is usually defined as a monetary phenomenon in which prices rise because too much money is in circulation, and that money's chasing too few goods.

Here's what's important about the money supply as it applies to futures and options trading:

- ✔ Money supply is related to inflation because of the number of times it actually changes hands (see the definition of velocity in the previous paragraph).

- ✔ More money in the system — chasing goods and services at a faster rate — is inflationary.

- ✔ A rising money supply tends to spur the economy and eventually fuels demand for commodities.

- ✔ A rising money supply usually is spawned by lower interest rates.

- ✔ Whenever the money supply rises to a key level, which differs in every cycle, eventually inflationary pressures begin to appear, and the Fed starts reducing the money supply.

- ✔ *Deflation* is when money supply shrinks because nobody wants to buy anything. Deflation usually results from *oversupply,* or a glut of goods in the marketplace. The key psychology of deflation is that in contrast to inflation, consumers put off buying things, hoping that prices will fall further — as opposed to times of inflation when consumers are willing to pay high prices in fear that they will rise further.

- ✔ *Reflation* is when central banks start pumping money into the economic system, hoping that lower borrowing costs will spur demand for goods and services, create jobs, and create a stronger economy.

- ✔ The more money that's available, the more likely that some of it will make its way into the futures and options markets.

As a general rule, futures prices respond to inflation. Some tend to rise, such as gold, and others tend to fall, such as the U.S. dollar (see Chapters 11 and 14). Each individual area of the futures market, though, at any time, is more responsive to its own fundamentals and its own supply-and-demand equation. Otherwise, here is a quick-and-dirty guide to general money supply/commodity tendencies:

- ✔ Metals, agricultural products, oil, and livestock contracts generally tend to rise along with money supply. This tendency is not a daily occurrence but rather one that you can see over an extended period of time if you compare graphs and charts of economic indicators with futures prices. The overall trend is toward higher consumer prices, which have resulted from higher commodity prices.

- ✔ Bonds and other interest-rate products do the opposite. Generally, bond prices fall, and interest rates or bond yields rise in response to inflation (see Chapter 10).

✔ Stock index futures are more variable in their relationship with the money supply, but eventually, they tend to rise when interest rates — either from the Fed or market rates in the bond and money markets — are falling, and they tend to fall when interest rates reach a high enough level. In other words, the relationship of money supply to the stock market and stock index futures is indirect and has more to do with how effective the Fed and the bond market are bringing about the desired effect on the economy, whether slowing it down or speeding it up. However, during some periods, such as 1994 and most of 2005 when the Fed raised interest rates, stocks and stock index futures stayed in a trading range.

✔ Currencies tend to fall in value during times of inflation.

In a global economy, many of these dynamics occur simultaneously or in close proximity to each other, which is why an understanding of the global economy is more important when trading futures than when trading individual stocks.

Something from something is something more

The wildest thing about money is how one dollar counts as two dollars whenever it goes around the loop enough times in an interesting little concept known as the *multiplier effect.*

For example, if the Fed buys $1 worth of bonds from Bank X, then Bank X lends it to Person 1. Person 1 then buys something from Person 2, who then deposits the dollar in Bank 2. Bank 2 then lends the money to Person 3, who then deposits it in Bank 1, where the $1, in terms of money supply, is now $2, because it's been counted twice.

By multiplying this little exercise by billions of transactions, you can arrive at the massive money supply numbers in the United States, where as of late 2004, the M0 alone was $688 billion.

As of March 21, 2005, M1 was $1.38 trillion, M2 was $6.41 trillion, and M3 was $9.5 trillion.

Getting a handle on money supply from a trader's point of view

Although you and I can use money supply data in many ways from an academic point of view, believe me, it won't make you the life of the dinner party.

The key to making money by using money supply information is to have a good grip on whether the Fed actually is putting money into the system or taking it out. What's even more important is how fast the Fed is doing whatever it's doing at the time.

Still another equation

I have a quick-and-dirty formula that I use to figure out how fast the money supply is growing or shrinking. Every week I check Barron's Web site (www.barrons.com) for a Money Supply table that can be found under "Economic Indicators" in the Market Laboratory. Figure 2-1 is a reproduction of one of the tables.

Because I'm not an economist, I ignore the seasonal adjustments and go straight to the raw data in the table, calculating a ratio of the growth rate. Although it isn't scientific, it works.

For example, I plug the M2 numbers for the same time frame this year and last into this simple equation:

$$[(\text{This year's M2} \div \text{Last year's M2}) - 1] \times 100 = \text{percentage growth}$$

With the numbers from Figure 2-1 plugged in, the equation looks like this:

$$[(6{,}471.4 \div 6{,}176.8) - 1] \times 100 = 4.7 \text{ percent}$$

The 4.7 percent growth rate is what I care about, because that's how fast the M2 money supply grew during the past year and that means that on a yearly basis, as of the date in the figure, 4.7 percent more money was in circulation than the year before.

Sifting through the data

I have about ten years worth of money-supply data, so I can look through my spreadsheets and get an idea of how the money supply has fluctuated over various longer-term time frames.

For example, I checked the growth rate for October 11, 2004, and found that it was 4.8 percent. In December 2004, it was 5.4 percent, and on October 10, 2003, the growth rate was 6.3 percent.

Although the Fed was raising interest rates during this period, the money supply was still showing an upward rate of growth, despite the fact that it was at a lower rate of growth in November 2004 than in October 2003, 5.4 percent versus 6.3 percent. The message to take away is that the Fed still had a long way to go in its quest to decrease the growth rate of the money supply. My analysis proved correct, because by November 2005, the Fed was still raising interest rates and telling the market in its statement after the Federal Open Market Committee (FOMC) met on November 1 that "monetary policy accommodation, coupled with robust underlying growth in productivity, is providing ongoing support to economic activity."

Money Supply

Money Supply (Bil. $ sa)		Latest	Prev.	Yr. Ago
Week ended 3/21				
M1	(seas. adjusted)	1380.1	1352.9	1343.5
M1	(not adjusted)	1382.1	1338.7	1341.1
M2	(seas. adjusted)	6477.6	r6447.4	6183.3
M2	(not adjusted)	6471.4	r6472.9	6176.8
M3	(seas. adjusted)	9509.8	r9491.9	9001.0
M3	(not adjusted)	9530.7	r9547.5	9019.3
Monthly Money Supply				
Month Ended February				
M1	(seas. adjusted)	1366.9	1358.5	1311.9
M2	(seas. adjusted)	r6456.4	6442.2	6129.0
M3	(seas. adjusted)	r9502.6	9485.3	8930.6

Figure 2-1: Money Supply Weekly Summary.

From a trading standpoint, the only thing that can be surmised is that the Fed was being careful in its handling of the economy. And if the Fed is being careful, you and I need to be careful in our trading.

What the market is saying

Look at other markets and indicators during the time frame of your analysis to make use of the information when setting up your trading. I like to use the CRB Index as an overall gauge of inflation, knowing that it is limited by its heavier weight toward grains, not metals. The combination of rising commodity prices and year-over-year growth in money supply is a recipe for higher interest rates because prices for commodities, as measured by the CRB Index, were rising.

When the Fed is being careful, you need to be careful, but you also need to be monitoring the markets. For example, both the S&P 500 Index and the December 2005 crude oil complex had big rallies in the 2003–2004 period. The connection was the money supply, which had been growing steadily since the Fed began lowering interest rates after the events of September 11, 2001. By 2003, the economy began to grow, demand for oil picked up, and the S&P 500 Index began to indicate an economic recovery.

The money supply growth rate, when put together with other market indicators such as consumer prices and the CRB Index, likewise can be a useful set of trading tools.

Putting Fiat to Work for You

The average person may find the fiat concept difficult to grasp. But as a futures trader, it is the center of your universe. If you can figure out which way interest rates are headed and where money is flowing, most of what happens in the markets in general will fall into place, and you can make better decisions about which way to trade. Keep these relationships in mind:

✔ Futures markets often move based on the relationship between the bond market and the Fed, which means that when either the Fed or the bond market moves interest rates in one direction, the other eventually will follow. See Chapters 6 and 10.

✔ Higher interest rates tend to eventually slow economic growth, while lower interest rates tend to spur economies.

A perfect example of how the system works occurred after the events of September 11, 2001. In response to the catastrophe, the Fed lowered key official interest rates, such as the Fed funds and discount rates, but it also bought massive amounts of government treasuries, thus making much more money available to the banking system.

Currency traders, who are not well-known for their patriotism, sold dollars, and bought euros, yen, and other currencies, and effectively moved money out of the United States.

Much of the money that the Fed injected into the system made its way to China and ended up fueling the major economic boom in that country that marked the post September 11, 2001, economic recovery.

China used the infusion of foreign money to finance a building boom that, in turn, led to increased demand for oil and raw materials, such as copper, steel, and lumber.

This major change in the flow of money spread to all the major futures markets and led to a bull market in commodities, because China bought increasing amounts of steel, copper, and the fuel needed to power the boom — oil.

When the Fed began to raise interest rates, it did so partially with the intention of cooling off the growth in China and diverting the flow of dollars away from Beijing and back to the U.S.

Get in the habit of watching all the markets together. When the Fed starts lowering interest rates, it is doing so because it wants the economy to grow and jobs to be created. When the Fed starts to ease rates, as a trader, you want to start looking at what happens to commodities like copper, gold, oil, and so on. The commodities markets provide you with confirmation of what the markets in general are starting to expect as the Fed makes its move.

Normally, you begin to see these markets come to life at some point before or after the Fed makes a move. For example, if you see the copper market starting to move, you want to check on what the bond and stock markets are doing, because smart money starts pricing in expectations of a change in trend by the Fed.

Bonding with the Fed: The Nuts and Bolts of Interest Rates

If you want to make money in futures, you need to become intimately familiar with what the Fed does and how it goes about it.

Credit makes the world go around. Credit enables everyone to have the things they want now and to pay for them later. How much stuff you can buy depends on how easy the Fed makes it for you to borrow the money. The Fed wants to create an environment that prompts consumers to buy as much stuff as they want without letting them create inflation.

One way the Fed raises and lowers interest rates is by buying or selling U.S. Treasury bonds in the open market. In past decades, the market had to guess what the Fed was trying to do with interest rates where the bond market was concerned.

In the latter years of Alan Greenspan's terms as Fed chairman, the central bank became more open in its communications with the markets, but a fair amount of *Fedspeak,* the often-difficult-to-decipher language from the central bank, still was in use. In some cases it was even conjecture.

No matter what you think of the Fed and central banks in general, they're a fact of life, and the better you can understand them and decipher some of the things they say and do, the better you can trade and make other decisions about your money.

Finding out how central banks work is easier than trying to decipher what they say and do. They buy and sell bonds and inject or extract money from the banking system they control. When the Fed buys bonds, it gives the markets and the economy money. When the Fed sells bonds, it takes money out of the markets and the economy. Pretty simple, right?

The amount of money that the Fed uses to buy bonds can signal which way the Fed's Board of Governors wants interest rates to go. This relationship is pretty simple any more, because the Fed rarely goes into the bond market — other than for routine maintenance of the money supply — without making a statement. Routine maintenance is conducted by the New York Fed. An example is when the Fed adds more reserves than usual during holiday periods, such as Christmas, to make sure banks have enough money on hand to handle the shopping season. In the new year, the Fed drains the extra reserves from the system. This maneuver usually isn't meant as a major economic action by the Fed.

When an announcement about interest rates is made, however, the Fed usually follows the announcement with a market action, either buying or selling bonds to agree with its statement.

Relating Money Flows to the Financial Markets

Central banks have convinced the world's population that money and its wonderful extension, credit, are the centerpieces of the world's economic system. And the easier it is to borrow money, the more things get done and the bigger things get built.

When central banks buy bonds from banks and dealers, they're putting money into circulation, making it easy for people and businesses to borrow. At the juncture where money becomes easier to borrow, the potential for commodity markets to become explosive reaches its zenith.

Commodity markets thrive on money, and their actions are directly related to

✔ Interest rates

✔ Underlying supply

✔ The perceptions and actions of the public, governments, and traders, as they react to

• **Supply** — how much is available and how fast it's going to be used up

• **Demand** — How long this period of rising demand is likely to last

Demand is not as important for most of the business cycle as the supply side of the equation.

The higher the money supply, the easier it is to borrow, and the higher the likelihood that commodity markets will rise. As more money chases fewer goods, the chances of inflation rise, and the central banks begin to make it more difficult to borrow money.

If you keep good tabs on the rate of growth of the money supply, you'll probably be ahead of the curve on what future trends in the markets are going to be.

To make big money in all financial markets, futures and options included, you have to find out how to spot changes in the trend of how easy or difficult it is to borrow money. The perfect time to enter positions is as near as possible to those inflection points in the flow of money — when they appear on the charts as changes in the direction of a long-standing trend.

These moves can come before or after any changes in money supply or adjustments to borrowing power appear. However, when a market trends in one direction (up or down) for a considerable amount of time and suddenly changes direction after you notice a blip in the money supply data, you know that something important is happening, and you need to pay close attention to it.

Chapter 3

The Futures Markets

A futures contract is a security, similar conceptually to a stock or a bond, while being significantly different. For example, when you buy a stock, you're buying part of a company, while a bond makes you a lender to a government or a corporation.

Whereas a stock gives you equity and a bond makes you a debt holder, a futures contract is a legally binding contract that sets the conditions for the delivery of commodities or financial instruments at a specific time period in the future.

Futures markets are the hub of capitalism, because they provide the bases for prices at wholesale and eventually retail markets for commodities ranging from gasoline and lumber to key items in the food chain, such as cattle, pork, corn, and soybeans.

Futures contracts are available for more than just mainstream commodities, including stock index futures, interest rate products — bonds and treasury bills — and lesser known commodities like propane. Some futures contracts are even designed to hedge against weather risk and for trading electricity.

Futures markets emerged and developed in fits and starts several hundred years ago as a mechanism through which merchants traded goods and services at some point in the future, based on their expectations for crops and harvest yields.

Now virtually all financial and commodity markets are linked, with futures and cash markets functioning as a single entity on a daily basis. Thus, as a successful trader, you need to understand the basics of all major markets — bonds, stocks, currencies, and commodities — and their relationships to each other and the economic cycle.

In this chapter, you gain an understanding of who the major players are, how the futures markets evolved to their prominent role in the global economy, and what basic rules and regulations keep the markets as fair and reasonable as possible.

Who Trades Futures?

The futures and options markets serve two major constituencies, hedgers and speculators, two groups with differing interests, but without whose participation the markets would not function.

Hedgers, in general, are major companies that actually produce the commodities, or others (like farmers) who have an inherent interest in the market. Exxon Mobil is a perfect example of a hedger in the oil markets, because the company must gauge the potential risk of weather, politics, and other external factors on future oil production.

Hedgers may employ professional traders to use options and futures contracts on commodities and related products to decrease the company's risk of loss. Their goal is not to profit from futures trading, but rather to cover their risk of losses and keep company operations moving forward.

Considering the effects of a crash

The stock market crash of 1987 had one positive result. It ushered in the era of the one market. After that fateful day, October 19, 1987, anyone who'd ever invested in any market understood that all markets are linked, regardless of the underlying securities traded on them, and that money can and does flow at the speed of light from one type of market to another. In fact, the futures markets, according to Mark Powers, in his book *Starting Out In Futures Trading* (McGraw-Hill), are like "convenient laboratories" for conducting market analysis.

After the 1987 crash, the Brady Commission coined and defined the concept that all markets were linked, because the action in one or more of them had an influence on one or several others. But the commission did little to dissuade the media's and the public's perception that the futures markets were not to blame for the crash — something the Federal Reserve concluded in its post-crash study released in 1988.

Another positive of the post-crash environment was the implementation of *circuit breakers,* or intraday limits on trading that slow or stop trading in specific products when the markets for those products are moving too fast. The Board of Governors of the Federal Reserve System (the Fed), the Securities and Exchange Commission (SEC), and the various exchanges (see the "Futures Exchanges: Where the Magic Happens," section later in this chapter for a list of exchanges) also developed better techniques for monitoring position sizes and overall market liquidity after the crash.

Speculators, the second constituency (you and I), trade futures and options contracts with a goal of making money from market trends and special situations. In other words, the speculator's job is to see where the big money is going and follow it there, regardless of whether prices are going up or down.

So although hedgers may actually take delivery or receive products specified in a futures contract, speculators are trying to ride the price trend of those products as long as possible, while always intending to cash in before the delivery date.

Contract and Trading Rules

Futures contracts are by design meant to limit the amount of time and risk exposure experienced by speculators and hedgers, those traders who use them. As a result, futures contracts have several key characteristics that enable traders to trade them effectively.

I briefly list them and describe them in the sections that follow and use these explanations to expand on how the contracts work throughout the book.

Expiration

All futures contracts are time-based; they *expire,* which means that at some point in the future they will no longer exist. From a trading standpoint, the expiration of a contract forces you to make one of the following decisions:

- Sell the contract and roll it over by buying the contract for next front month or another that's further into the future.
- Sell the contract (taking your profits or losses) and just stay out of the market.
- Take delivery of the underlying commodity, equity, or product represented by the contract.

Daily price limits

Because of their volatility and the potential for catastrophic losses, limits are placed on futures contracts that freeze prices but do not freeze trading. Limits are meant to let markets cool down during periods of extremely active trading. It's important to remember that the market can trade at the limit price but not beyond it. Some contracts have variable limits, which means that the limits are changed if the market closes at the limit. For example, if the cattle markets close at the limit for two straight days, the limit is raised on the third day.

Size of account

Most brokers require individuals to deposit a certain amount of money in a brokerage account before they can start trading. A fairly constant figure in the industry is $5,000.

For most people, depositing only $5,000 with the brokerage firm probably is not enough to provide you with a good trading experience. Some experienced traders will tell you that $100,000 is a better figure to have on hand, and $20,000 is probably the least amount you can actually work with.

These are no hard and fast rules, though. The bottom line is that to be a successful trader, you should know yourself and your risk tolerance, get a good handle on your trading plan, let your winners ride, and cut your losses short.

You Can't Just Swipe a Card: Exploring the Uniqueness of the Futures Markets

Futures contracts are nothing like credit-card transactions. Buying something and promising to pay for it later, the way you do when you go shopping with a credit card, doesn't make a futures contract. True futures contracts must meet these six criteria, which have developed since the inception of the futures markets:

✔ Trading must be conducted on an organized *exchange,* a physical place where trading actually takes place either by open-cry trading in a trading pit, which is what you always see on television when you turn on the business channels, or by electronic means, which is an increasing phenomenon, especially in Europe, where trading already is done electronically.

✔ Common rules govern all transactions. The two most important ones are as follows:

  • Trading occurs in one designated place, the ring or pit of the exchange, by open outcry during specific trading hours, with every participant having equal access to the bids and offers and the flow of trading.

  • No exchange member can offer to fill or match an order without first offering it to the crowd. A *member* is a firm or an individual that buys a *seat on the exchange,* or the privilege to trade directly for his own account and to be an intermediary for other traders. When a floor broker *fills an order,* he is fulfilling your request from his own inventory of futures contracts. When a floor broker *matches an order,* he is fulfilling your request by finding a buyer or seller in the trading crowd and matching the buyer with the seller.

✔ Contract sizes, delivery dates, mode of delivery, and procedure are standardized.

✔ Traders negotiate only the original transaction with each other. Beyond the original agreement, the exchange becomes a clearinghouse, and the obligation of the parties to a futures contract transaction is with the exchange.

✔ Futures contracts are canceled, or closed out, by offset. When a trader sells a contract to deliver a specific amount of a marketable product for December delivery, he has an obligation to deliver that product to the exchange by December. If he buys a contract for the same amount of that product before December, then he has met his obligation; he has *offset* the original sale with an equivalent buy and is out of the market.

✔ The exchange clearinghouse acts as a guarantor, or guardian, for each transaction, requiring its members to have minimum amounts of working capital and enough funds to meet their outstanding debts. Exchange members that are not clearinghouse members must associate with exchange members that are to guarantee and verify all contracts.

Futures Exchanges: Where the Magic Happens

Several active futures and options exchanges are open for business in the United States. Each has its own niche, but some overlaps occur in the types of contracts that are traded. In this section, I cover the basics of three of the more frequently used Chicago exchanges. The names of the exchanges are as follows:

✔ **Chicago Board Options Exchange** (www.cboe.com): The premier options exchange market in the world, the CBOE specializes in trading options on individual stocks, stock index futures, interest rate futures, and a broad array of specialized products such as exchange-traded mutual funds. The CBOE is not a futures exchange but is included here to be complete, because futures and options can be traded simultaneously, as part of a single strategy.

✔ **Chicago Board of Trade** (www.cbot.com): Trades are made in futures contracts for the agriculturals, interest rates, Dow Indexes, and metals. Specific contracts traded on the CBOT include

- **Agricultural futures:** Corn, the soybean complex, wheat, ethanol, oats, rough rice, and mini contracts in corn, soybeans, and wheat

- **Interest rate–related futures:** Treasury bonds, spreads, Fed funds, municipal bonds, swaps, and German debt

- **Dow Jones Industrial Average:** Dow Jones Industrial mini contracts
- **Metals futures:** Gold and silver and e-mini contracts for gold and silver

✔ **Chicago Mercantile Exchange (www.cme.com):** The CME is the largest futures exchange in North America. It trades a wide variety of instruments, including commodities, stock index futures, foreign currencies, interest rates, TRAKRS, and environmental futures. Among the contracts traded on the CME are

- **Commodities:** Live cattle, milk, lean hogs, feeder cattle, butter, pork bellies, lumber, the Goldman Sachs Commodities Index (and associated futures contracts), and fertilizer
- **Stock index futures:** S&P 500, S&P 500 Midcap, S&P Small Cap 600, NASDAQ Composite, NASDAQ 100, Russell 2000, and the corresponding e-mini contracts for all the major indexes traded
- **Other important stock-related contracts:** Single stock futures, futures on exchange-traded funds (ETFs), and futures on Japan's Nikkei 225 index
- **Options:** Options on the futures contracts the CME lists

✔ **Kansas City Board of Trade (KCBT, www.kcbt.com):** The KCBT is a regional exchange that specializes in wheat futures and offers trading on stock index futures for the Value Line Index, a broad listing of 1,700 stocks.

✔ **Minneapolis Grain Exchange (MGEX, www.mgex.com):** MGEX is a regional exchange that trades three kinds of seasonally different wheat futures, and offers futures and options on the National Corn Index and the National Soybeans Index.

✔ **New York Board of Trade (NYBOT, www.nybot.com):** A major international exchange, the NYBOT offers a broad array of products, including

- **Commodities:** Sugar, cocoa, cotton, frozen orange juice, ethanol and pulp, and the Reuters/Jefferies CRB Index
- **Currencies:** U.S. dollar index and a wide variety of foreign currency pairs and cross rates
- **Stock index futures:** Russell Equity Indexes and NYSE Composite Index

✔ **New York Mercantile Exchange (NYMEX, www.nymex.com):** The NYMEX is the hub for energy trading in

- **Energy futures:** Light sweet crude, natural gas, unleaded gasoline, heating oil, electricity, propane, and coal
- **Metals:** Gold, silver, platinum, copper, palladium, and aluminum

Futures contracts for the Goldman Sachs Commodity Index and options on the futures contracts that the CME lists also are traded on the CME.

E-mini contracts are smaller-value versions of the larger contracts, and they trade for a fraction of the price of the full value instrument and thus are more suitable for small accounts. The attractive feature of e-mini contracts is that you can participate in the market's movements for lesser investment amounts. Be sure to check commissions and other prerequisites before you trade, though.

The Trading Floor: How Trading Actually Takes Place

The United States still uses the open-cry system of futures trading, where traders on a trading floor or in a trading pit shout and use hand signals to make transactions or trades with each other. Futures contracts are traded in a clear, albeit nonlinear order.

When you call your broker, he relays a message to the trading floor, where a runner relays the message to the floor broker, who then executes the trade. The runner then relays the trade confirmation back to your broker, who tells you how it went. The order is just about the same when you trade futures online, except that you receive a trade confirmation via an e-mail or other online communiqué.

Trade reporters on the floor of the exchange watch for executed trades, record them, and then transmit these transactions to the exchange, which, in turn, transmits the price to the entire world almost simultaneously.

Shifting sands: Twenty-four-hour trading

Around the world, most futures exchanges have converted from open-cry to electronic trading. In the U.S., physical commodities, such as agriculturals and oil, are still traded primarily by an open-cry system; however, most futures markets also offer electronic models of trading because they provide

- ✔ A more level playing field
- ✔ More price transparency
- ✔ Lower transaction costs

Globex, the electronic data and trading system founded in 1992, extends futures trading beyond the pits and into an electronic overnight session. Globex is active 23 hours per day, and contracts are traded on it for Eurodollars, S&P 500, NASDAQ-100, foreign exchange rates, and the CME e-mini futures. You can also trade options and spreads on Globex.

When you turn to the financial news on CNBC before the stock market opens, you see quotes for the S&P 500 futures and others taken from Globex as traders from around the world make electronic trades. Globex quotes are real, meaning that if you kept a position open overnight, and you place a sell stop under it, or you place a buy order with instructions to execute in Globex, you may wake up the next morning with a new position, or out of a position altogether.

Globex trading overnight tends to be thinner than trading during regular market hours (usually from 8:30 a.m. to 4:15 p.m. eastern time), and it tends to be more volatile in some ways than trading during regular hours.

You can monitor Globex stock index futures, Eurodollars, and currency trades on a delayed basis overnight free of charge at www.cme.com/trading/dta/del/globex.html.

Here are a few questions that you'll want to ask your futures broker about trading via Globex:

- ✔ Does the brokerage firm that you're using provide access to Globex? If so, what kind of an interface, front-end system or link to Globex does it supply? You want to know whether the system is compatible and how smoothly it works.

- ✔ Are the commissions for Globex trading different than the commissions charged for using the firm's regular trade routing?

- ✔ Are there any other rule or requirement changes, such as limits on the number of contracts that you can trade, margin requirements, or other particulars?

- ✔ You may want to put in an order by phone. Does the firm offer customer support in after-hours trading?

You can find out more details about what you need to ask your broker about using Globex at www.cme.com/files/Questionstoaskyourbroker5-9.pdf.

Talking the talk

If you're going to trade futures, you have to know trader talk. Knowing several key terms helps you get the job done and helps you understand what reporters and advisors are talking about.

Some key terms that refer to your expectations of the market include

✔ **Going long,** which means that you're bullish, or positive on the market, and that you want to buy something. When I say I'm long oil, in the context of futures trading, it means that I own oil futures.

✔ **Being short,** which means that you're bearish, or negative on the market, and that your goal is to make money when the price of the futures contract that you choose to short falls in price. If you deal in the stock market, you know that you have to borrow stocks before you can sell them short. In the futures market, you don't have to borrow anything; you just post the appropriate margin and instruct your broker that you're interested in selling short.

I know this can be confusing, so it is best looked upon from the point of view of reversing, or offsetting, your position. Let's look at an example in a vacuum, just to illustrate the point. If you sell a crude oil contract short at $59, and the price drops to $54, you have a $5 profit. At that point, if you decide that you've made enough of a profit, you then offset the position by buying back the contract to cover your short sale. In other words, what you are selling short is the contract, and by offsetting the position, you are now finished with the trade.

✔ **Locals,** which means the people in the trading pits. They're usually among the first to react to news and other events that affect the markets.

✔ **Front month,** which refers to the futures contract month nearest to expiration. This time frame may not always feature the most widely quoted futures contract. As one contract expires, the next contract in line becomes the front month.

✔ **Orders,** which are instructions that lead to the completion of a trade. They can be placed in a variety of ways, including

- A *stop-loss order,* which means that you want to limit your losses at or above a certain price.

  A stop-loss order becomes a market order (see next entry) to buy or sell at the prevailing market price after the market touches the stop price, or the price at which you've instructed the broker to sell. A buy stop is placed above the market. A sell stop is placed below the market. Stop orders can also be used to initiate a long or short position, not just close (offset) an open position.

- When you place a *market order,* you're not trying to get fresh fish. It means that you'll take the prevailing price that the market has to offer.

- A *trailing stop* is a self-adjusting stop order. When you place a trailing stop, it changes automatically depending on the price of the underlying asset.

✓ **Hedging,** which is a trading technique that's used to manage risk. It may mean that you're setting up a trade that can go either way, and you want to be prepared for whichever way the market breaks. In the context of large producers of commodities, *hedging* means that they put strategies in place in case the market does the opposite of what is expected, such as a major and sudden rise in oil prices caused by a hurricane.

Some terms that can help you understand hedging are

- *Putting on a hedge,* which means that you're setting up a trading situation that enables you to cover all the bases for whichever way the market decides to go. *Hedgers* often account for 20 percent to 40 percent of all the open, or active, futures contracts in a particular market. They're usually companies or large entities that are protecting their investments against the risk of price fluctuation in the future by buying or shorting futures contracts.

- A *cross hedge* isn't fancy shrubbery; it's the act of using a different contract to manage the risk of another contract in which you're primarily interested. For example, an oil company may use gasoline contracts to hedge the risk of their crude oil contracts.

✓ **The Pit,** which isn't Hell, although if you're on the wrong end of the trade, it can be. The pit is where all futures contracts are traded during a regular-hours trading session in the futures markets.

✓ **Speculators,** which are traders (usually small- to medium-sized) who are trying to make money only from the fluctuation of prices without intending to take delivery of the contract.

✓ **Floor brokers,** who are agents that receive a commission to buy and sell futures contracts for their clients, who generally are futures commission merchants. A floor broker may also trade for his own account, under certain restrictions. Floor traders rarely make agent trades. They use their exchange membership to buy and sell futures for their own accounts, taking advantage of very low commissions and immediate access to market information. Floor brokers, by exchange rules, cannot place their own orders ahead of yours. Your broker can trade for himself, but he cannot put his order in ahead of yours.

✓ **Bid,** which means the price at which you want to buy something.

✓ **Offer,** which means the price at which you are willing to sell something.

✓ **Taking delivery,** which means that you will take the product on which you were speculating.

✓ **Supply and demand equation,** which is trader talk referring to whether there are more buyers than sellers. When there are more sellers than buyers, the equation tilts toward supply, and vice versa.

✔ **Expiration,** which isn't referring to death or breathing out. When a contract expires, expiration means that it's no longer trading.

✔ **Delivery,** which is what futures contracts are all about — someone actually delivering or handing something to someone else in exchange for money.

Understanding the Individual Players

As I mention in "Who Trades Futures?" earlier in this chapter, the two major categories of traders are hedgers and speculators.

Hedgers ain't pruners

Farmers, producers, importers, and exporters are hedgers, because they trade not only in futures contracts but also in the commodity, equity, or product represented by the contract. They trade futures to secure the future price of the commodity of which they will take delivery and then sell later in the cash market. By buying or selling futures contracts, they protect themselves against future price risks.

People who buy commodities, or *holders,* are said to be long, because they're looking to buy at the lowest possible price and sell at the highest possible price.

Short sellers sell commodities in the hope that prices fall. If they are correct, they offset, or close, the position at a lower price than when they sold it.

Futures contracts are attractive to longs and shorts, because they provide price and time certainty, and reduce the risk associated with *volatility,* or the speed at which prices change up or down. At the same time, hedging can help lock in an acceptable *price margin,* or difference between the futures price and the cash price for the commodity, and improve the risk between the cost of the raw material and the retail cost of the final product by covering for any market-related losses. *Note:* Hedge positions don't always work, and in some cases, they can make losses worse.

The best current example of a hedger is an airline in the post September 11, 2001, world, and its fuel costs. Aside from labor, airplane fuel is by far the most expensive component of an airline's costs. A good airline also has expertise in the oil market.

Let's say that Duarte Air (I know, I know, it's self-serving promotion) is projecting a need for large amounts of jet fuel for the summer season, based on the trends in travel during the past decade. Because I'm the CEO, my airline also knows that demand for gasoline tends to rise in the summer; thus prices for the jet fuel I need are also likely to rise because of refinery usage issues — refineries switch a major portion of their summer production to gasoline.

Wanting to hedge my costs for crude oil in the summer, Duarte Air starts buying July crude oil and gasoline futures a few months ahead of time, hoping that as the prices rise, the profits from the trades can offset the costs of the expected rise in jet fuel.

Say for instance that Duarte Air bought July crude futures at $50 per barrel in December, and by June they were trading at $60 per barrel.

As the prices continued to rise, Duarte would start unloading the contracts, pocketing the $10-per-barrel profit and using it to offset the higher costs of its fuel in the spot market (during the summer travel season).

On the other hand, if Duarte's hedging was wrong, and the price of oil went down, the airline could always use options to hedge the futures contracts, or go short, by selling futures contracts high and making money by buying them back at lower prices if there was a sudden price drop. See *Being short* in "Talking the talk," earlier in this chapter.

Speculators don't wonder

Speculators, in contrast to hedgers, are betting on the price change potential for one reason only — profit. Speculators are doing the opposite of the hedgers; they're looking to increase risk and increase the chances of making money.

A hedger tries to take the speculator's money and vice versa. So a normal futures transaction is likely to include a member of each of these subgroups. A speculator, then, would likely be buying a contract from a hedger at a low price, while the hedger is expecting the price to decline further.

Think of this dance in terms of risk. Hedgers are transferring the risk of price variability to others in exchange for the cost of the hedge. Speculators assume price variability risk, thus making the transfer possible in exchange for the potential to gain. A hedger and a speculator can both be very happy from the outcome of price variability in the same market.

This interaction between speculators and hedgers is what makes the futures markets efficient. This efficiency and the accuracy of the supply-and-demand equation (see the earlier "Talking the talk" section) increase as the underlying contract gets closer to expiration and more information about what the marketplace requires at the time of delivery becomes available.

Margin Basics

Margin is what makes futures trading so attractive, because it adds leverage to futures contract trades. The downside is that if you don't understand how trading on a margin works, you can take on some big losses in a hurry.

You can reduce the risk of buying futures on margin by

✔ Trading contracts that are lower in volatility.

✔ Using advanced trading techniques such as *spreads,* or positions in which you simultaneously buy and sell contracts in two different commodities or the same commodity for two different months, to reduce the risk. An example of an *intramarket spread* is buying March crude oil and selling April crude. An example of an *intermarket spread* is buying crude oil and selling gasoline.

Trading on margin enables you to leverage your trading position. By that I mean that you can control a larger amount of assets with a smaller amount of money. Margins in the futures market generally are low; they tend to be near the 10 percent range, so you can control, or trade, $100,000 worth of commodities or financial indexes with only $10,000 or so in your account.

Trading on margin in the stock market is a different concept than trading on margin in the futures market.

In the stock market, the Federal Reserve sets the allowable margin at 50 percent, so to trade stocks on margin, you must put up 50 percent of the value of the trade. Futures margins are set by the futures exchanges and are different for each different futures contract. Margins in the futures market can be raised or lowered by the exchanges, depending on current market conditions and the volatility of the underlying contract.

Generally, when you deposit a margin on a stock purchase, you buy partial equity of the stock position and owe the balance as debt. In the futures market, a margin acts as a security deposit that protects the exchange from default by the customer or the brokerage house.

When you trade futures on margin, in most cases you buy the right to partici-pate in the price changes of the contract. Your margin is a sign of good faith, or a sign that you're willing to meet your contractual obligations with regard to the trade.

In the futures market, your daily trading activity is *marked to market,* which means that your net gain or net loss from changes in price of your outstand-ing futures contracts open in your account are calculated and applied to your account each day at the end of the trading day. Your gains are available for use the following day for additional trading or withdrawal from your account. Your net losses are removed from your account, reducing the amount you have to trade with or that you can withdraw from your account.

I provide more detail about margins in Chapters 4 and 5, which are about options.

Chapter 4

Understanding the Not-So-Hair-Raising Truth about Options

*I*f you're confused about options, you're not alone. You've probably heard many crazy stories, such the as one I heard from an old friend about how he lost his entire college loan portfolio on the advice of a fellow who had a brother who supposedly was an options wizard.

The two of them, my friend and his pal, gave all the money they received for college aid to the broker brother, who then quickly lost it in the markets making bad trades.

That kind of story is enough to put a chill on anyone's best intentions of exploring how options work. And although risk exists, the options market nevertheless is an area of the investment arena that truly goes hand in hand with the futures markets.

In fact, when used properly, options give you an opportunity to diversify your holdings beyond traditional investments and to hedge your portfolio against risk. That's what this chapter is about: discovering how to use options the right way.

Decisions, Decisions: Figuring Out Whether Options Are for You

Options probably are the most misunderstood members of the family tree of securities. First, they go by strange names like puts and calls, and trading strategies in the options markets sound even worse, with names like spreads, hedges, strangles, and straddles.

Other confusing terms like premiums and strike prices also make understanding options even more complex.

In a world where the stock market rules the publicity roost and mutual funds rarely use options as a main part of their strategies, the average investor thinks of these instruments as something better left alone.

The truth is, average investors probably are correct in avoiding options and futures until they've at least done their homework. However, futures traders, as you know, are not average investors. Futures traders, at least the ones who survive the initial stages of torment and can ride out the inevitable and discouraging down periods, are by nature risk takers. And options are an integral part of the trading game that futures traders play, although it is worth noting that options and futures are viable stand-alone vehicles for trading.

Here is a quick checklist that should give you a good idea whether to include options in your trading platform, although most of these points hold true in one form or another for most investments:

- ✔ **Options are a zero-sum game.** By *zero-sum game,* I mean that for every dollar someone makes, someone loses a dollar. In other words, options, like futures, have both a seller and a buyer. The exception is when you sell a covered call and the stock prices go up, you can exercise the call and no one loses.

  When you make a losing trade, someone else gets an amount equal to your losses transferred to his or her account, and you get charged commission. The exchanges also get a fee.

- ✔ **If you win, you will probably owe taxes.** The treatment of options in the tax code is complex, and much of it deals with whether you have short-term or long-term gains. The details are provided in the option disclosure statement, which is required reading before you ever trade options. You need to read that document carefully and discuss the tax-related details with your accountant before trading. The statement is part of the packet of information your broker gives you along with the account application.

- ✔ **When you trade options, you're up against ruthless, skilled, and veteran professionals.** Their main goal is to take your money away from you. Some options market opponents are individuals, but others are well-paid and well-informed traders for large corporations that trade options every day as part of their business strategies.

- ✔ **You need to know your trading opportunities well.** George Kleinman, in *Trading Commodities & Financial Futures* (Financial Times Prentice Hall), calls patience "the number one essential quality for trading success." A patient trader waits for the right opportunities. Being overanxious, he says, uses up your capital and kills your account over time. Patience works on both sides of the equation. If you find a good trade, then you must be able to wait until it plays itself out before you sell.

- ✔ **Forget on-the-job training.** Go into your trades with a well-thought-out and well-researched plan.

- ✔ **Lose the emotion, but keep the guts.** That means you must be able to cut your losses, admit that you were wrong, and wait for the next opportunity.

Can you win at the options-trading game? The answer: Yes, as long as you understand the game and develop your trading plan accordingly.

Before you trade though, visit the Commodities Futures Trading Commission (CFTC) Web site at www.cftc.gov/opa/brochures/opafutures.htm. There you can find a Web page entitled, "What You Should Know Before You Trade." It's an excellent resource that provides you with a summary of what you need to know before you open an options trading account and what to avoid after you open one.

Although some traders trade options (and do it well) purely as a primary vehicle of speculation, the primary function of a listed option (as it was intended) is risk management, not speculation. This, of course, like anything else, can be a controversial topic. For example, options, when applied properly, do offer limited risk and unlimited reward potential, and can be more compelling than straight futures, especially for those who want to speculate with less than $30,000.

Getting the Lay of the Land: Stocks Versus Options

Just like stocks and futures contracts, options are securities that are subject to binding agreements. The key is that *options* give you the right to buy or sell an underlying security or asset, without being obligated to do so, as long as you follow the rules of the options contract.

The key differences between options and stocks are

- **Options are derivatives.** A *derivative* is a financial instrument that gets its value not from its own intrinsic value but rather from the value of the underlying security and time. Options on the stock of IBM, for example, are directly influenced by the price of IBM stock.

- **Options, like futures contracts, have expiration dates, while stocks do not.** In other words, while you can hold the stock of an active company for years, an option will expire, worthless, at some point in the future. Options trade during the trading hours of the underlying asset.

- **Owning an option doesn't give the holder any share of the underlying security.** The right to buy or sell that security is what options are all about.

Options, Not Love, American Style

The two major categories of options are based on the way they can be exercised. When you exercise an option, you invoke the right to do what the options contract gives you the right to do with regard to ownership of the underlying asset. For example, if you own a *call option,* a bet that an underlying asset will rise in value, and you exercise that bet, it means that you pay for and now own the underlying asset.

- *American-style options* can be exercised, or acted upon, if your intent is to do what the option gives you the right to do on or before the expiration date. The person holding the option decides.

- *European-style options* can be exercised only on the date of expiration. European-style options are traded on many of the cash-based indexes that I detail in the next section. Most individual stock options and some index options are traded under American-style options exercise rules. All options can be exercised only once.

The advantage of American-style options is that you have more flexibility when and how to exercise them. The advantage of European-style options is that you are certain about the timeline you have until the option is exercised.

All stock options and some index options are American-style options. Some cash-based index options are European-style. In addition, index options are cash-based.

For example, options based on the S&P 500 and the Dow Jones Industrial indexes are European-style. This distinction was put in place because of pressure from institutional investors, large-scale traders who often have a difficult time in executing strategies without tipping off the market that something is going on.

If a large mutual fund has a complex option strategy in place that's based on American-style options, and a rival trader exercises the options involved in the strategy, the mutual fund stands to lose millions of dollars without expecting to do so.

By using European-style options, the fund may lose the same amount of money upon exercise by a rival, but it doesn't come as a surprise, because the fund manager knows when the option can be exercised. In other words, the mutual fund has the opportunity to put a strategy in place to counteract the effect of a potential exercise before it happens.

In other words, institutions prefer to write options on instruments that restrict exercising by the buyer to only one day so that they can maintain the hedge for the majority of the life of the trade and collect as much of the premium generated before buying back the position to close out. European style allows them to do this while American style does not.

It's also important to note that when institutions want to avoid tipping off the market of their identity, they use brokerage accounts with different brokers or have their orders worked offshore through the third market or Over The Counter.

Choosing an options broker

One of your most important decisions about options trading is whether you want to use a broker, which entails whether you want assistance with strategy development, research, monitoring open positions, working orders, and trade ideas or whether you want to do that yourself. Your futures broker usually can handle your options activity as it relates to futures and may be able to handle stock option transactions. If you want to do all that stuff yourself, then you just want to get access to the markets through the lowest cost medium, usually an online discount broker.

Con artists, and unscrupulous advisors, lurk around every corner and prey on the unsuspecting and uninformed options trader, so doing your options homework is prudent and highly advisable. A few extra days or weeks of caution are not going to hurt you in the long run.

Unscrupulous people prey on the innate human need to have more than what they start with and their generalized need to get something for nothing.

For example, just because someone recommends their brother-in-law to you as an options wizard, you don't necessarily want to give the guy your life's savings. Remember the example I described at the start of this chapter and follow this advice:

✔ Be careful of financial advisors that advertise instant riches based on small amounts of money and promise that they will return all of your money.

> ✔ Get to know who's doing the trading and what methods they're using before you give them any of your money. Radio and television show hosts who spend a lot of time on the air aren't very likely to even see your money, much less protect it. They're too busy promoting their shows and their management firms. They'll have someone who they employ do the trading. It may be someone who's qualified or someone who'll cost you a great deal of money fast.

If you are interested in trading options, but aren't sure about your own ability to trade them, you need to find out everything that you can about the markets and find a good options broker/advisor to help you out.

When selecting a broker/advisor, you need to ask him or her these important questions before deciding whether you'll go with an advisor/broker or just a broker who executes your trades. These questions are applicable to broker and advisor candidates for online and managed accounts:

> ✔ What kinds of services does the brokerage firm offer?

> ✔ What commissions and other costs are charged and under what circumstances?

> ✔ How experienced in options trading is the broker who was assigned to me?

> ✔ Is my broker registered with the Commodities Futures Trading Commission/National Futures Association (CFTC/NFA)? This is applicable to options on futures only. For stock options, the NASD and CBOE memberships are critical.
>
> If so, you can contact those organizations to find out whether the firm or the broker is in good standing or if public records of previous disciplinary actions exist.
>
> If disciplinary actions have been taken, ask for audited results, and check out the auditor because they've had their own problems.

> ✔ What kind of results can I expect from the broker assigned to me?

Compare fees and services between the different advisor/broker candidates, and match their results with their costs.

If you decide to establish a managed account, make sure early on that you're getting your money's worth. Aside from getting good results, you're paying for customer service. If an advisor won't talk to you and explain what he or she is doing and why, or won't meet with you on a regular basis to discuss the account, that advisor probably is the wrong choice, especially when you're losing money. Most advisors will meet with you at least on a yearly basis. Many meet with you on a quarterly basis.

Conversely, if your advisor is a little too friendly, you again may want to consider changing. Developing more than a professional relationship can be costly.

If you're an active trader and your advisor calls you with trades frequently, make sure that he's giving you winning trades. Otherwise, he's probably churning your account.

Make sure that you tell your advisor how much risk you are willing to take and how involved you want to be. If he or she does things that make you uncomfortable despite your wishes regarding the amount of risk you're willing to take, it's time to say goodbye to that advisor. A good advisor tells you whether (or not) you're a good customer-match for the methods he's accustomed to using. When I meet with clients whose risk tolerance is different from my own, I never take on their accounts. Avoiding discomfort before money changes hands is the best course.

Risk tolerance is best measured in the context of your overall personality. If you own a nice car and you have to go to the garage in the middle of the night to see whether there are scratches on it, you are not a good candidate for options trading.

What you want to know before trading

Not all options are created equal. In his book, *Starting Out In Futures Trading* (McGraw-Hill), author Mark Powers offers the following checklist of what you need to know before you start trading, which I'm paraphrasing:

- ✔ **Are you trading a U.S. or a foreign option? And is it an exchange-traded or dealer-traded option?** U.S. options are easily followed, and they're regulated by the CFTC and so are all the parties involved in issuing the contract. Exchange-traded options are standardized contracts that are more liquid and can be hedged better against risk. That isn't always the case with other, over-the-counter options.

- ✔ **Who is guaranteeing the transaction?** U.S. exchanges and firms are constantly monitored for liquidity and solvency. Foreign institutions are not necessarily as well monitored, so their futures and options contracts need to be checked individually, especially in the case of foreign options or options that are not exchange traded. You want to know what the markup is on the premium.

- ✔ **How much of the premium that you pay is actually the value of the option?** In some cases, the fees involved when you deal with independent options dealers can be very high and can hurt your transaction.

- ✔ **What is the break-even price for your option?** In other words, how much price appreciation will be needed before you make money?

- ✔ **How much in commissions are you paying, and what kind of service are you getting for what you're paying?**

✔ **Will your advisor/broker check several independent sources to find out what expectations are with respect to the future price of the underlying asset?** If there is a widespread expectation that price will change very little in the future, the premium that you pay should be low.

✔ **How will you and your advisor/broker exercise your option, and what will you receive when you do?** Always know how you and your broker will communicate. That means that you have to read and understand the terms of the management contract carefully before you put any money down.

✔ **How will your broker let you know when your options contract has been executed, and what the status of your account is?** Online brokers usually let you know this information automatically after your trade is executed. Some traditional brokers call you sometime after the order is executed. You have to do what is most comfortable for you. It's important to keep in mind, though, that options trading can be very short-term oriented, and that the more you know combined with the greatest speed, the better your chances are of keeping up with your account, and the better the set of decisions you can make.

Types of options

Two types of options are traded. One kind lets you speculate on prices of the underlying asset rising, and the other lets you bet on their fall. Options usually trade at a fraction of the price of the underlying asset, making them attractive to investors with small accounts.

Calls

I think of a call option as a bet that the underlying asset is going to rise in value. The more formal definition is that a *call option* gives you the right to buy a defined amount of the underlying asset at a certain price before a certain amount of time expires. You're buying that opportunity when you buy the call option. If you don't buy the asset by the time the option expires, you lose only the money that you spent on the call option. You can always sell your option prior to expiration to avoid exercising it, to avoid further loss, or to profit if it has risen in value.

Call options usually rise in price when the underlying asset rises in price.

When you buy a call option, you put up the option premium for the right to exercise an option to buy the underlying asset before the call option expires. Buying the call option gives you the right to exercise it. When you exercise a call, you're buying the underlying stock or asset at the *strike price,* the predetermined price at which an option will be delivered when it is exercised.

Puts

Put options are bets that the price of the underlying asset is going to fall. Puts are excellent trading instruments when you're trying to guard against losses in stock, futures contracts, or commodities that you already own.

Buying a put option gives you the right to sell a specific quantity of the underlying asset at a predetermined price, the strike price, during a certain amount of time. Like calls, if you don't exercise a put option, your risk is limited to the option premium, or the price you paid for it.

When you exercise a put option, you are exercising your right to sell the underlying asset at the strike price.

Puts are sometimes thought of as portfolio insurance, because they give you the option of selling a falling stock at a predetermined strike price.

You can also sell puts. For more details, check out the section "Being bullish with puts," later in this chapter.

Types of traders

Option buyers are also known as *holders,* and option sellers are known as *writers.*

Call option holders have the right to buy a stipulated quantity of the underlying asset specified in the contract. Put option holders have the right to sell a specified amount of the underlying asset in the contract. Call and put holders can exercise those rights at the strike price.

Call option writers have the potential obligation to sell. Put option buyers have the potential obligation to buy.

Understanding option quotes

When you trade options, you have to look at quote boards on your machine, even if you're using a broker. You need to be familiar with what the broker is looking at when he or she is providing you with an options quotation.

Figure 4-1 shows you a good generic example of a quote board provided by the Chicago Board of Options Exchange, www.cboe.com, in an excellent online tutorial at www.cboe.com/LearnCenter/Tutorials.aspx and www.cboe.com/LearnCenter/cboeeducation/Course_01_01/mod_01_01.aspx.

On the quote board, you find information about option classes, series, and pricing.

Call Quote	XYZ	Put Quote
* 6.50-7.00	* APR25	* 0.15-0.25 *
* 1.55-1.90	* APR30	* 0.15-0.25 *
* 0.15-0.25	* APR35	* 3.10-3.50 *
* 6.50-7.00	* MAY25	* 0.05-0.15 *
* 4.10-4.50	* MAY27$\frac{1}{2}$	* 0.15-0.25 *
* 1.75-2.00	* MAY30	* 0.20-0.45 *
* 0.45-0.70	* MAY32$\frac{1}{2}$	* 1.15-1.40 *
* 0.15-0.25	* MAY35	* 3.10-3.50 *
* 6.90-7.40	* AUG25	* 0.15-0.25 *
* 2.75-3.10	* AUG30	* 0.90-1.00 *
* 0.50-0.75	* AUG35	* 3.40-3.80 *

Figure 4-1: A sample options quote board, courtesy of CBOE. The circled price is the premium paid in the example described.

The strike price for the option in Figure 4-1 is $30, which means that upon exercise, if you own a call, you can buy 100 shares per contract at $30 per share, or if you own a put option and the strike price is $30 and you exercise it, you can sell 100 shares per contract at $30 per share.

The May 30 call option for XYZ is the example used in Figure 4-1. So XYZ is the option class, while May 30 is the option series, which is a grouping of puts or calls of the same underlying asset with the same strike price and expiration date. If you look above and below the May 30 series, you find other option series listed, such as the May 25 puts and calls, listed two sections above the circled series.

The *premium,* or the price, on the May 30 XYZ is two points. If this was a call to buy XYZ stock, you'd pay $200, because options for stocks give you the right to control 100-share lots of the stock.

Here's an example of how options can be used efficiently:

> Say you bought 100 shares of XYZ at $30. In that case, you'd pay $3,000 plus commission for the same number of shares that you can control with a May 30 call option of XYZ.
>
> If your XYZ shares went down $4 and you sold them at $26, you'd be out $400. In contrast, if you own the option, even if you were to allow it to expire worthless without exercising it, you'd lose only $200, your original option premium.

The attractiveness of buying call options is that the upside potential is huge, and the downside risk is limited to the original premium — the price you pay for the option.

Don't forget the expiration date

All stock options expire on the third Friday of the month. Options on futures expire on different days depending on the contract. Sometimes different classes of options expire on the same day.

These days are known as double-, triple-, and quadruple-witching days:

- **Double-witching days** are when any two of the different classes of options (stock, stock-index options, and stock index futures options) expire.
- **Triple-witching days** are when all three classes expire simultaneously, which happens on the third Friday at the end of a quarter.
- **Quadruple-witching days** are when all three classes of options expire along with single stock futures options.

A summary of a sample call option trade

The CBOE tutorial summarizes how an options trade works and provides a good overview of how the process works. See Figure 4-1 for an illustration.

Assume that you think XYZ stock is going to trade above $30 per share by the expiration date, the third Friday of the month. So you buy a $30 call option for $2, with a value of $200, plus commission, plus any other required fees.

If you're right, and XYZ is up to $35 per share by the expiration date, you can exercise your option, buy 100 shares of XYZ at $30, which costs you $3,000, and then sell it on the open market at $35, realizing a gain of $500 minus your initial $200 premium, commissions, and other fees.

In this case, your option is *in the money,* because the strike price is less than the market price of the underlying asset.

When you, the option holder, put in your order, the dealer searches for someone on the other side of the trade, in other words the option writer, with the same class and strike price of the option. The writer is then assigned the trade and must sell his shares to you, if you exercise the option.

So, a *call assignment* requires the writer, the trader who sold the call option to you, to sell his stock to you. A *put assignment,* on the other hand, requires the person who sold you the put on the other side of the trade (again, the put writer) to buy the stock from you, the put holder.

You have two other possibilities: You can hold the stock, knowing that you have a $5 cushion, because you bought it at a discount, or you can sell the option back to the market, hopefully at a profit.

According to the CBOE, most options never are exercised. Instead, most traders sell the option back to the market.

A summary of a sample put option trade

For this example, you need to check out Figure 4-2. It shows a typical CBOE options quote board, this time highlighting an August XYZ 30 put. If you buy this put option, you buy the right to sell 100 shares of XYZ at a strike price of $30 per share by or on the expiration date.

Here is a typical situation where buying a put option can be beneficial: Say, for example, that you bought XYZ at $31, but you start getting concerned, because the stock price is starting to drift down because the market is weakening.

Figure 4-2:
A sample options quote board, courtesy of CBOE, includes price information for both put and call option series.

Call Quote	XYZ	Put Quote
* 6.50-7.00 *	* APR25 *	* 0.15-0.25 *
* 1.55-1.90 *	* APR30 *	* 0.15-0.25 *
* 0.15-0.25 *	* APR35 *	* 3.10-3.50 *
* 6.50-7.00 *	* MAY25 *	* 0.05-0.15 *
* 4.10-4.50 *	* MAY27$\frac{1}{2}$ *	* 0.15-0.25 *
* 1.75-2.00 *	* MAY30 *	* 0.20-0.45 *
* 0.45-0.70 *	* MAY32$\frac{1}{2}$ *	* 1.15-1.40 *
* 0.15-0.25 *	* MAY35 *	* 3.10-3.50 *
* 6.90-7.40 *	* AUG25 *	* 0.15-0.25 *
* 2.75-3.10 *	* AUG30 *	* 0.90-1.00 *
* 0.50-0.75 *	* AUG35 *	* 3.40-3.80 *

A good way to protect yourself when you're in this situation is to buy a put option. So you decide to buy an August 30 put for a $1 premium, which costs you $100.

By buying the put, you're locking in the value of your stock at $30 per share until the expiration date on the third Friday in August. If the stock price falls to $20 per share, you still can sell it to someone at $30 per share, as long as the option has not expired. Indeed, the put option gives you the right to sell the stock at $30 no matter how low the price falls.

Using the put option as portfolio insurance fixes your worst risk at $200, which includes the $100 premium you paid for the put option and the $1 per share you can lose after originally paying $31 per share for the stock, if you exercise the put.

Your other alternative when the stock falls below $30 is to sell the put to the market and profit from the appreciation of the option while holding onto the stock.

Being bullish with puts

You can sell put options and become a put writer. In doing so, you're hoping that the price of the underlying stock rises in a bullish strategy that actually is more commonly used than the more highly publicized buying of puts.

When you write a put, you're buying the obligation to buy the stock at the striking price, and you receive the put option premium. If the underlying stock advances and the put expires worthless, your maximum profit is equal to the premium you received.

The catch to selling puts is the large downside risk. If the stock falls in price, the put option appreciates and you can face large losses.

Writing uncovered puts is a strategy that's similar to writing covered calls. The least aggressive application of this strategy is to write the put when the price of the stock is above the striking price.

For most beginning traders, it may be best to become familiar with covered-call writing first, and then research this technique thoroughly, trying it out on paper until you become comfortable with it.

Options on Futures

The major difference between trading stock options and options on futures — the real meat of this discussion of options, in general — is that aside from committing all the basic concepts of options to memory, you need to know the particulars of the futures contract underlying your option strategy.

A good example is an option that is based on the S&P 500 Index futures contract. The major characteristics of an S&P 500 Index futures contract are that the underlying value of the contract is $250 multiplied by the value of the S&P 500 Index. So if you have a single contract that settled when the value of the S&P 500 Index was 1,000, the value of the futures contract would be $250 × 1,000, or $250,000. If the contract rose three points in value for that day, you'd make $250 × 3, or $750.

The language barrier

You need to know several terms to be able to trade options. Most of this stuff is fairly simple after you get the hang of it. But, if you're like me, it isn't much fun when you start. Still, if you're going to trade options, you must dig in and continue to grapple with the lingo, including these terms:

- **In *the money*:** A call option is said to be *in the money* whenever the strike price is less than the market price of the underlying security. A put option is in the money whenever the strike price is greater than the market price of the underlying security.

  An example of an in-the-money call is when the XYZ stock was trading at $35 per share while the call option's strike price was $30 per share.

- **At the money:** Options are considered at the money when the strike price and the market price are the same.

- **Out of the money:** Calls are out of the money when the strike price is greater than the market price of the underlying security. Puts are out of the money if the strike price is less than the market price of the underlying security.

The Greek stuff

Options require you to pick up a bit of the Greek language, which is okay, because you need to learn only four words, but they all are important.

The Greeks, as they are commonly called, are measurements of risk that explain several variables that influence option prices. They are delta, gamma, theta, and vega.

John Summa, who operates a Web site called OptionsNerd.com (www. optionsnerd.com), summarizes the four terms nicely in an article he wrote for Investopedia.com, which you can find at www.investopedia.com/ articles/optioninvestor/02/120602.asp.

But before actually getting into the Greek, you need to know the factors that influence the change in the price of an option. After that, I tell you how it all fits into the mix with the Greek terminology.

The three major price influences are

- **Amount of volatility.** An increase in volatility usually is positive for put and call options, if you're long in the option. If you're the writer of the option, an increase in volatility is negative.

✔ **Changes in the time to expiration.** The closer you get to the time of expiration, the more negative the time factor becomes for a holder of the option, and the less your potential for profit. Time value shrinks as an option approaches expiration and is zero upon expiration of the option.

✔ **Changes in the price of the underlying asset.** An increase in the price of the underlying asset usually is a positive influence on the price of a call option. A decrease in the price of the underlying instrument usually is positive for put options and vice versa.

Interest rates, a fourth influence, are less important most of the time. Higher interest rates make call options more expensive and put options less expensive, in general. Now that you know the major and minor influences on price, I can describe the Greeks.

Delta

Delta measures the effect of a change in the price of the underlying asset on the option's premium. Delta is best understood as the amount of change in the price of an option for every one-point move in the underlying asset or the percentage of the change in price of the underlying asset that is reflected in the price of an option.

Delta values range from –100 to 0 for put options and from 0 to 100 for calls, or –1 to 0 and 0 to 1, if you use the more commonly used expression in decimals.

Puts have a negative delta number, because of their inverse or negative relationship to the underlying asset. Put premiums, or prices, fall when the underlying asset rises in price, and they rise when the underlying asset falls.

Call options have a positive relationship to the underlying asset and thus a positive delta number. As the price of the underlying asset goes up, so do call premiums, unless other variables are changed, such as implied volatility, time to expiration, and interest rates.

Call premiums generally go down as the price of the underlying asset falls, as long as no other influences are putting undue pressure on the option.

Here is how it works: An at-the-money call has a delta value of 0.5 or 50, which tells you that the option's premium will rise or fall by half a point with a one-point move in the underlying asset.

Say, for example, that an at-the-money call option for wheat has a delta of 0.5. If the wheat futures contract associated with the option goes up 10 cents, the premium on the option will rise approximately by 5 cents, or $0.5 \times 10 = 5$. The actual gain will be $250 because each cent in premium is worth $50 in the contract.

The further into the money the option premium advances, the closer the relationship between the price of the underlying asset and the price of the option becomes. When delta approaches 1 for calls, or –1 for puts, the price of the option and the underlying asset move the same, assuming all the other variables remain under control.

Key factors about delta to remember are that delta:

- ✔ Is about 0.5 when an option is at the money and moves toward 1.0 as the option moves deeper into the money.

- ✔ Tends to increase as you get closer to the expiration date for near or at-the-money options.

- ✔ Is not a constant, because the effect of *gamma* (see the next section) is a measure of the rate of change of delta in relation to the underlying asset.

- ✔ Is affected by changes in implied volatility. (See the section on "Understanding Volatility: The Las Vega Syndrome," later in this chapter, for a full discussion of implied volatility.)

Gamma

Gamma measures the rate of change of delta in relation to the change in the price of the underlying asset, and it enables you to predict how much you're going to make or lose based on the movement of the underlying position.

The best way to understand this concept is to look at an example like the one in Figure 4-3, which shows the changes in delta and gamma as the underlying asset changes in price. The example features a short position in the S&P 500 September $930 call option as it rises in price from $925 on the left to $934 on the right and is based on John Summa's explanation of the Greeks. The chart was prepared using OptionVue 5 Options Analytical Software, which is available from www.optionvue.com.

The further out of the money that a call option declines, the smaller the delta, because changes in the underlying asset cause only small changes in the option premium. The delta gets larger as the call option advances closer to the money, which is a result of an increase in the underlying asset's price. In this case, the more out-of-the-money the option is, the better it gets for the short seller of the option.

Line 1 of Figure 4-3 is a calculation of the profit or loss for the S&P 500 Index futures 930 call option — $930 is the strike price of the S&P 500 Index futures option that expires in September, as featured in Figure 4-3. The –200 line is the at-the-money strike of the 930 call option, and each column represents a one-point change in the underlying asset.

Figure 4-3:
Summary
of risk
measures
for the short
December
S&P 500 930
call option.

P/L	425	300	175	50	-75	-200	-325	-475	-600	-750
Delta	-48.36	-49.16	-49.96	-50.76	-51.55	-52.34	-53.13	-53.92	-54.70	-55.49
Gamma	-0.80	-0.80	-0.80	-0.80	-0.79	-0.79	-0.79	-0.79	-0.78	-0.78
Theta	45.01	45.11	45.20	45.28	45.35	45.40	45.44	45.47	45.48	45.48
Vega	-96.30	-96.49	-96.65	-96.78	-96.87	-96.94	-96.98	-96.99	-96.96	-96.91

The at-the-money gamma of the underlying asset for the 930 option is –0.79, and the delta is –52.34. What this tells you is that for every one-point move in the depicted futures contract, delta will increase by exactly 0.79.

The position depicts a short call position that is losing money. The P/L line is measuring Profit/Loss. The more negative the P/L numbers become, the more in the red the position is. Note also that delta is increasingly negative as the price of the option rises.

Finally, with delta being at –52.34, the position is expected to lose 0.5234 points in price with the next one-point rise in the underlying futures contract.

If you move one column to the right in Figure 4-3, you see the delta changes to –53.13, which is an increase of 0.79 from –52.34.

Other important aspects of gamma are that it:

✔ Is smallest for deep out-of-the-money and in-the-money options.

✔ Is highest when the option gets near the money.

✔ Is positive for long options and negative for short options.

Theta

Theta is not often used by traders, but it is important because it measures the effect of time on options. More specifically, theta measures the rate of decline of the *time premium* (the effect on the option's price of the time remaining until option expiration) with the passage of time. Understanding premium erosion due to the passage of time is critical to being successful at trading options. Often the effects of theta will offset the effects of delta, resulting in the trader being right about the direction of the move and still losing money.

As time passes, and option expiration grows near, the value of the time premium decreases, and the amount of decrease grows faster as option expiration nears.

The following mini-table shows the theta values for the featured example of the short S&P 500 Index futures 930 call option.

	T+0	T+6	T+13	T+19
Theta	45.4	51.85	65.2	93.3

The concept of how theta affects the price of an option can best be summarized by looking in the fourth column of table, where the figure for T + 19 measures theta six days before the option's expiration. The value 93.3 tells you that the option is losing $93.30 per day, a major increase in time-influenced loss of value compared with the figure for T + 0, where the option's loss of value attributed to time alone was only $45.40 per day.

Theta rises sharply during the last few weeks of trading and can do a considerable amount of damage to a long holder's position, which is made worse when the option's implied volatility is falling at the same time.

Understanding Volatility: The Las Vega Syndrome

Vega measures risk exposure to changes in implied volatility and tells traders how much an option's price will rise or fall as the volatility of the option varies.

Vega is expressed as a value and can be found in the fifth row of Figure 4-4, where the example cited in the figure shows that the short call option has a negative vega value — which tells you that the position will gain in price if the implied volatility falls. The value of vega tells you by how much the position will gain in this case.

For example, if the at-the-money value for vega is –96.94, you know that for each percentage-point drop in implied volatility, a short call position will gain by $96.94.

Volatility is a measure of how fast and how much prices of the underlying asset move and is key to understanding why option prices fluctuate and act the way they do. In fact, volatility is the most important concept in options trading, but it also can be difficult to grasp unless taken in small bites. Fortunately, trading software programs provide a great deal of the information needed to keep track of volatility. Nevertheless, you need to keep in mind these two kinds of volatility:

- *Implied volatility* **(IV),** which is the estimated volatility of a security's price in real time, or as the option trades. Values for IV come from formulas that measure the options market's expectations, offering a prediction of the volatility of the underlying asset over the life of the option. It usually rises when the markets are in downtrends, and falls when the markets are in uptrends. Mark Powers, in *Starting Out In Futures Trading* (McGraw-Hill), describes IV as an "up-to-date reading of how current market participants view what is likely to happen."

- *Historical volatility* **(HV),** which also is known as statistical volatility (SV), is a measurement of the movement of the price of a financial asset over time. It is calculated by figuring out the average deviation from the average price of the asset in the given time period. Standard deviation is the most common way to calculate historical volatility. HV measures how fast prices of the underlying asset have been changing. It is stated as a percentage and summarizes the recent movements in price.

HV is always changing and has to be calculated on a daily basis. Because it can be very erratic, traders smooth out the numbers by using a moving average of the daily numbers. Moving averages are explained in detail in Chapter 7, which is about technical analysis. In general, though, the bigger the HV, the more an option is worth. HV is used to calculate the probability of a price movement occurring.

Whereas HV measures the rate of movement in the price of the underlying asset, IV measures the price movement of the option itself.

Most of the time, IV is computed using a formula based on something called the Black-Scholes model, which was introduced in 1973 (see the next section). The goal of the Black-Sholes model, which is highly theoretical for actual trading, is to calculate a fair market value of an option by incorporating multiple variables such as historical volatility, time premium, and strike price. I'll let you in on a little secret here: The Black-Sholes formula alone isn't very practical as a trading tool, because trading software automatically calculates the necessary measurements; however, the number it produces, IV, is central to options trading.

HV and IV are often different numbers. That may sound simple, but there's more to it than meets the eye.

In a perfect world, HV and IV should be fairly close together, given the fact that they are supposed to be measures of two financial assets that are intrinsically related to one another, the underlying asset and its option. In fact, sometimes IV and HV actually are very close together. Yet the differences in these numbers at different stages of the market cycle can provide excellent trading opportunities. This concept is called *options mispricing,* and if you can understand how to use it, options mispricing can help you make better trading decisions.

When HV and IV are far apart, the price of the option is not reflecting the actual volatility of the underlying asset. For example, if IV rises dramatically and HV is very low, the underlying stock may be a possible candidate for a takeover. Under those circumstances, the stock probably has been stuck in a trading range as the market awaits news. At the same time, option premiums may remain high because of the potential for sudden changes with regard to the deal.

The bottom line is that HV and IV are useful tools in trading options. Most software programs will graph out these two variables. When they are charted, big spreads become easy to spot, and that enables you to look for trading opportunities.

An overview of the Black-Scholes formula

The Black-Scholes formula was discovered by economists Myron Scholes, Robert Merton, and the late Fischer Black. Scholes and Merton won the Nobel Prize in economics for this formula in 1997. The formula is viewed by some in the financial world as akin to the discovery of the DNA double helix. Figure 4-4 presents this formula in all it's glory.

The good news is that options software easily calculates values for HV and IV, so as long as you know that option prices and their behavior are based on the Black-Scholes formula and other models, all you have to do is worry about how to trade.

Option buyers want to see high volatility, but sellers want to see low volatility. Figure 4-5, summarizes a short S&P 500 option position that has a negative vega, which means that the position will gain when IV falls. The negative vega also indicates how much the position will gain.

$$C = SN(d_1) - Le^{-rT}N(d_1 - \sigma\sqrt{T})$$

C is the current call option value.

S is the current stock price.

N(d_1) is a fraction (whose value is between 0 and 1) determined by the price of the stock, the exercise price, the risk-free interest rate, the time to maturity of the call option, and the volatility of the underlying stock price.

d_1 is derived from the following formula:

$$d_1 = \frac{\ln(S/E) + (r + \sigma^2/2)T}{\sigma\sqrt{T}}$$

where *ln* = natural logarithm, *S* = price of the stock, *E* = exercise price, *r* = risk-free interest rate

σ = the volatility of the stock

T = time to maturity of the option in years

L is the exercise price, the price at which you have the right to buy the stock when the call option expires.

e^{-rT} is a term that adjusts the exercise price, L, by taking into account the time value of money.

$$N(d_1 - \sigma\sqrt{T})$$

is a fraction (whose value is between 0 and 1) determined by the price of the stock, the exercise price, the risk-free interest rate, the time to maturity of the option, and the volatility of the underlying stock price.

Figure 4-4:
The Black-Scholes formula.

Option buyers want to see high volatility *after* they buy an option. Option sellers want to see low volatility *after* they sell an option. For both scenarios, the word "volatility" refers to both statistical and implied volatility.

Other vega facts that keep you out of the poorhouse are that it

✔ Can rise or fall without the price changes of the underlying asset.

✔ Can increase if the price of the underlying asset moves quickly, especially when the stock market declines fast or a commodity makes a big move.

✔ Falls as expiration of the option nears.

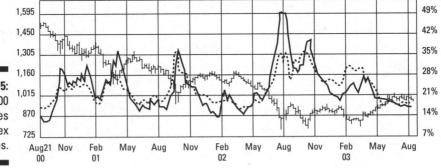

Figure 4-5:
S & P 500
Futures
Index
Volatilities.

Using volatility to make trading decisions

In *Options As A Strategic Investment* (Prentice-Hall Press), author Lawrence McMillan, one of the gurus of options trading, notes that some option traders ignore the price of the underlying asset, and trade the volatility chart. The volatility chart usually is in a trading range, unless something extraordinary happens, such as a takeover or a bad earnings report for a stock or a major disruption of supply and demand for commodities.

Think of decreasing volatility as a coiled spring that is about to explode. As a trader, you want to be able to predict when changes in volatility — and thus changes in prices — are coming. One way to do that is to keep tabs on HV. You can chart 10-, 20-, 50-, and 100-day volatility figures.

Watch the trends during each of the four periods. If the 100-day volatility was 60 percent and the 10-day volatility was 10 percent, the volatility in price of the underlying asset is slowing. When prices begin to congregate in narrower trading ranges, volatility begins to decrease, and it can be sign that a big move is coming. That's when you can

✔ Start paying closer attention to the option series and making potential trading plans.

✔ Decide whether IV is cheap or expensive, no matter what you may think the prospects of the underlying asset are.

✔ Play the momentum, which is also a good strategy with options, regard-less of volatility. A couple of simple but powerful algorithms are buying calls or selling puts in stocks currently trending higher, or buying puts and selling calls in markets currently trending lower. In other words, paying attention to strong price trends can outweigh all volatility considerations.

When the majority of traders expects the underlying asset to be nonvolatile, as indicated by low volatility measurements, or wide spreads between HV and IV appear (see the previous section), you need to be buying volatility. That means when everyone else is selling options, you need to analyze the situation and pick the options with the best potential to buy, always knowing that you can be wrong and making plans to get out of the positions before you lose a whole lot of money.

Selling expensive options and buying cheap ones

The key to trading options based on implied volatility and to buying and sell-ing them correctly at market extremes is to determine whether the option is at an extreme either because that's the way the market sees things or because someone with inside information is setting up to make some money when the news breaks.

Option premiums (prices) reach extremes for logical reasons. The two most common reasons are that the market has just reached an extreme — because the market is doing what it thinks is best — or that someone knows some-thing that the rest of the market does not and is setting up a trade to make some big money. That inside knowledge can be anything from a corporate takeover to obtaining grain or oil supply information in advance of its regu-larly scheduled release. Most of the time, these signs appear in near-term options, especially the at-the-money strike price and sometimes the next strike price out of the money.

The next step is recognizing that other option series are starting to gather momentum, because market makers smell that something is up and start buying options for their own accounts to cover their short positions. Market makers tend to be short more often than not to protect themselves, because with access to all the trading activity data, they have better information than the public in general.

When option volume and IV pick up, look at the underlying assets and at the action in other option series. If the underlying asset doesn't make a move and the action in other options doesn't start to pick up, then what's probably happening is that a hedge fund or other market mover is putting on a big hedge or establishing a large position to protect its portfolio.

Rising options prices combined with the propagation of high volume and/or implied volatility, with or without a rise in the price of the underlying asset, are signs that the options market makers are on the move. These smart guys usually can tell when someone is putting on a hedge or when something else is really up. Most of the time, market makers are in risky positions against the market trend. When the action starts to pick up, the first thing they do is try to figure out whether the spike in activity is something major or just a hedge. If market makers determine that something major is going on, they try to buy all the options they can find on the other side of their current positions. If they can't find options, they start buying the underlying assets — stocks or futures contracts.

When you see big rises in trading volume and implied volatility in an option, it's a fairly good sign that somebody knows something that few others know. Staying away from such trades, or at least not selling in volatility, is a good idea. These can be highly risky situations that can turn on a dime and can make you lose money very quickly.

I show you a real-time example of a series of options in Table 4-1 that I got using a shareware program. These options show high implied volatility and how to make sense of it. The program is called *Open Interest,* and you can download it for free from Rocky Point Software, www.rpsw.com/index.html. Shareware like *Open Interest* is a good way to get familiar with options data without spending a bunch of money.

The options series is for the volatile biotech stock Affymetrix, which has an options symbol that features the letters FIQ.

Table 4-1				Interpreting High Levels of Implied Volatility for May 2005 FIO Options								
Expiry	Strike	Bid	Ask	Last	Vol	OpInt	ImpV	Delta	Gamma	Theta	Vega	DTG
May05	20C	24.500	24.80	24.60	0	40	97	99.9	0.0	−0.003	0.000	27
May05	17.5P	0.000	0.050	0.025	0	45	141	−0.4	0.1	−0.004	0.002	27
May05	20P	0.000	0.050	0.02	0	105	122	−0.5	0.1	−0.004	0.002	27
May05	22.5P	0.000	0.050	0.025	0	143	105	−0.6	0.1	−0.004	0.002	27
May05	25P	0.000	0.050	0.025	0	130	90	−0.6	0.1	−0.004	0.002	27

As you can see in the table, implied volatility is high for the May series of calls and puts. The letters *C* and *P* next to the strike prices let you know whether the option is a *call* or a *put*. The software highlighted more put option series with high implied volatility than calls, however, which suggests that market makers feared something bad was going to happen.

I owned Affymetrix stock while writing this chapter, so I had a vested interest in knowing what was happening. I went to affymetrix.com, looked in its news link, and found that the company was going to be making several key scientific presentations at several meetings in May.

If you look at the open interest and volume columns in the table, you see that at least at the time I looked, no evidence that market makers were scrambling to cover their short positions could be found and nothing indicated that any negative news was about to hit the pipeline.

Screening for volatility with software

Options screening software helps you cut through the clutter. For more sophisticated analysis than the bare-bones provided by free software, you have to spend some money.

Many good options-trading programs are available. Among the most popular programs is OptionVue 5 Options Analysis Software. This program has been around since 1982, and it has just about everything anyone could want to analyze options and find trades. Many traders use OptionsVue and consider it the benchmark program.

Most programs on the market are good enough to generate decent data. You want to find the one that's easiest for you to use and in the right price range. *Technical Analysis of Stocks & Commodities* magazine, www.traders.com, has excellent software reviews, and it operates an annual readers' poll to determine which programs its readers think are the best. This magazine/Web site is a good place to do your homework.

Chapter 5

Yeah Baby! Basic Stock Option Strategies

In This Chapter

▶ Understanding the options agreement

▶ Applying margin principles to options

▶ Formulating basic option strategies and following up after you put them together

▶ Calculating the break-even point of your strategy

▶ Dealing with profits, losses, taxes, and dividends in your option positions

---

*T*his chapter covers the bare minimum of option strategies, so it isn't meant to cover every possible permutation of this complex style of investing. This chapter does, however, cover the more commonly used strategies and offers plenty of examples to get you going.

As a rule, *paper trading* — simulating or practicing real trades on paper — before you make real trades is *never* a bad idea. Another good rule for beginning traders who insist on trading real money is to trade only in small lots or small amounts of money, one contract at a time. Finding a good options advisor/broker, one with a conscience who can run your option strategies for you — at least until you get your feet wet — is another worthy consideration. If you find such a person, you need not balk if his or her fees are higher than the competition, because you probably are getting your money's worth.

The basic option techniques outlined in this chapter are complex but not complicated. You need to understand several important factors about the process, so you have to pay close attention not only to what you're doing but also to why you're doing it.

Before you decide to trade options, you need to know that some option positions have the potential for unlimited losses and that those losses can hit you hard and fast if you get caught on the wrong side of the trade.

The four mainstream groups of options available to trade are options on stocks, index options, options on futures, and long-term options on stocks. Each has its own particular quirks but still is dependent on the basic rules of volatility and the action of the underlying asset. This chapter deals mainly with options on stocks. Options on futures will be dealt with on an individual basis because they pertain to each area of futures and each individual strategy (see Chapters 13, 14, and 16).

Options on stocks are the most popular set of options, and, for the most part, they're widely listed and traded at several exchanges. The Chicago Board Options Exchange (CBOE), the American Stock Exchange (Amex), the Philadelphia Stock Exchange (PHLX), and the Pacific Stock Exchange (PCX) all trade in stock options. Your broker will route your trades to be executed at different exchanges at different times.

In this chapter, you dig into basic option strategies in the stock market. The goal is simple: Avoid losing your shirt.

Avoiding the Terrible Mistake

All traders, myself included, are prone to major screw-ups.

For some reason, even when you're good at following your trading rules, you have one of those periods where for years you ask yourself why you did what you did that one time that cost you a bunch of money. Trading in options is especially apt at bringing about these revealing moments about your lack of smarts. You're gonna do it anyway, so you may as well get it over with and move on.

One of my more regrettable trades occurred in 1994, as the Federal Reserve (the Fed) was ending a long line of interest-rate hikes.

I bought some Eurodollar futures. At that time, the interest-rate cycle had reached its inflection point, or the point where a market turns — which is totally unpredictable and becomes obvious only after the fact — and the price of the contract was experiencing some volatility. I bought a futures contract that had plenty of time left in it, just so I could be patient.

But when the volatility started, I just couldn't stand it. I started freaking out about getting a margin call. I didn't want to be stopped out or automatically taken out of my position because of volatility only to see my former position rally without me. So I was following the trade by making phone calls on a frequent basis to check how I was doing, because online trading was not as advanced then as it is now.

After three worrisome days of market watching, I was completely exhausted, and made one of those, "Oh my God," phone calls to Lind-Waldock, the broker where I had my account, and got out of the contract in the after-hours session on Globex.

Within a few days of my panic sale, the bond market began a huge rally as the Fed signaled that it was through raising rates. Eurodollar futures soared, and I could have made a nice tidy little sum, several hundred dollars, if I remember correctly, if I hadn't been so nervous.

The worst thing is that I knew I was right about interest rates, because all my indicators were flashing buy signals, and the economic data was showing good evidence that the Fed had done its job in slowing the economy, and the market was acting right.

Nevertheless, I truly got psyched out by the market's movements and the thought of getting a margin call.

The most important things to remember: Never trade against the trend, and you have to stick with your trading plan.

In this case, I was right about everything and totally blew it on the execution end, because I got totally freaked out about getting a margin call. The biggest mistake I made was that I didn't have a good trading plan to start with, and I didn't have a good way to monitor my trade, and that is a recipe for losing your shirt.

And you need to be keenly aware of how much money you're willing to risk. If you're writing (selling) calls, for example, and the stock continues to rise, momentum is against you. If you're buying puts, and the stock keeps rising, that also is a sign that you're in trouble, and you need to make a decision.

A Little Bookkeeping First, Please: The Options Agreement

You have to sign an options agreement with your options broker to be able to trade options. An options agreement, by the way, is separate from a margin agreement. You actually need to sign both before you can trade options, which trade mainly from margin accounts. Margin agreements are fully covered in Chapter 3, which is about the futures markets.

Option trading agreements came into being after brokers were sued because of major losses in options trading by their clients. These documents are pretty stout, spelling out the risks of options trading above your signature and not only holding you liable for knowing the stuff on the agreement but also expecting you to make good on the promises you make in the agreement.

You can trade options in cash or margin accounts. Some IRAs enable you to trade certain kinds of options. *Trading For Dummies* by Michael Griffis and Lita Epstein (Wiley) gives you an excellent overview of trading-account requirements and details.

Rules for the use of margin on options accounts are very complex, and they can vary from dealer to dealer. An excellent overview of margin rules for options can be found at www.cboe.com/Institutional/Margin.aspx.

The Securities and Exchange Commission (SEC), which governs the trading of stocks and options on stocks, changed margin requirements for options trading in 1999 and now allows brokers to lend up to 25 percent of the required margin to options traders, which means you must keep 75 percent of the value of your positions in your account to be able to continue trading options on margin.

That amount is important because the amount of money that the broker is allowed to lend you to trade options is less than the amount of money he can lend you for trading stocks. In other words, options already have a great deal of leverage and risk built into them, and the SEC is trying to keep traders from taking risks to levels that can lead to losing the entire value of their account.

When trading stocks on margin, you must keep only 50 percent of the amount of the portfolio in your account.

For futures, on the other hand, you are allowed to keep much smaller amounts of margin in the account. Remember, margin in futures is a good-faith deposit. The broker is not lending you any money. Futures markets margins by design are lower than other margins, because futures contracts are meant to be highly leveraged trading instruments, and their main attraction is the potential they have for yielding large profits with small cash requirements. The flip side of course is the risk involved.

Margin requirements for different options and strategies sometimes are difficult to calculate and may vary among different brokers. Before setting up an account, read the options and margin agreements from your broker carefully so that you fully understand margin requirements for each individual class of options that you're trading.

Avoid Getting Caught Naked: All About Covered Call Writing

When you write a call, you sell someone the right to buy an underlying stock from you at a strike price that's specified by the option series. As the writer, you are now *short* the option. The buyer of your call is *long* the option. You also are obligated to deliver the stock if the buyer decides to exercise the call option.

When you write a *naked call option,* you're selling someone else a chance to bet that the underlying stock is going to go higher in price. The catch is that you don't own the stock, so if the buyer exercises the option, you need to buy the stock at the market price to meet your obligation.

When you write a *covered call option,* you already own the shares. If you're exercised against, you just sell your shares at the strike price.

As a call writer, naked or covered, you are hoping that

- ✔ The stock goes nowhere
- ✔ You collect the premium
- ✔ The option expires worthless so you don't have to come up with a hundred shares of the stock to settle when the holder exercises the call, which is what can happen with naked call writing

Covered call writing is a perfect strategy if you're looking to smooth out your portfolio's performance and collect the extra income from the call premiums.

When you write a *covered call,* it means that you already own the underlying stock. When the call expires worthless, you get to keep the stock and collect all the dividends that accrued during the time the call was in play — not bad, eh? When you write naked calls, however, it means that you do not own the stock, but if the call expires worthless, you still keep the premium.

Writing covered calls is a safer strategy than writing naked calls. If the holder exercises a naked call option, you have to buy the stock before you can deliver it to him. If the stock price has risen in the interim, you could sustain a serious loss in meeting the exercise.

Suppose ABC stock is selling at $50 per share, and a July 45 call sells for $5. For a covered call strategy on ABC, your investment is $5,000 to buy 100 shares, minus the $500 premium that you receive for selling the July 45 call. The potential return for this transaction is $500 ÷ $5,000, or 10 percent, without including any dividends that the stock pays during the holding period or the commissions you must pay to make the transactions.

If you sell an ABC July 45 call without owning the stock, your profit is limited to 5 points, or $500. You make money if ABC is at or below $50 per share when the call expires. However, if ABC rises in price, you can lose big bucks. For example, if the price goes up to $100, the call would be priced around $50. If you bought the option back at $100, you'd lose 50 points, or $4,500.

You can get around losing that much money when writing naked calls by figuring out your break-even point and unwinding the position if the price reaches that point. In the ABC example, it's $55. Getting out of the trade at your break-even point enables you to decide what you're willing to lose before ever making a trade. You have $500 in your pocket, so that's not a bad place to stop the bleeding if the trade goes against you.

Here are some tips to keep in mind about writing calls:

 ✔ A low volatility stock is perfect for call option writing.

 ✔ Writing in-the-money options offers better risk protection than writing out-of-the-money options; however, the profit potential is greater when you write out-of-the-money call options.

Think of your stock and your option as two different parts of one single position. Each part

 ✔ Has its own role to play and is dependent on the other to perform a complete job for your portfolio.

 ✔ Has its own cost, so you need to know the price of the stock when you bought it and add in the price of the premium that you gain when you sell the call.

Figure out how much you get from the strike price and the premium if the call option is exercised against you. Always know your worst-case scenario before you hit the trade button.

For the covered-call strategy to work best, you need to try to execute the trades — buy the stock and write the call option — at the same time by establishing a *net position* in which your goal is to achieve your *net price,* or the price you set as your investment goal for the order. You can establish a net position by placing a *contingent order* with your broker, which stipulates how you want the order executed.

Contingent orders — also referred to as net orders — are not guaranteed by the broker, who sometimes may refer to them as not-held orders, because if the broker thinks the order is too difficult to fill, you'll receive a "nothing done" report, and the order won't be filled.

If you're unwilling to sell the stock against which you're writing the covered call, you shouldn't even consider writing the option. You'll probably get hurt if someone exercises a call against you.

Here's an example, loosely adapted from Lawrence McMillan's *Options As A Strategic Investment.* Buy 500 shares of ABC stock, at $38, in January, and sell five July $40 call options at 3, for a total of $1,500. With this strategy, you've established a covered-call position with a six-month duration. Selling the options gives you $1,500, or 3 points (a point, in options language, as it pertains to this example is worth $100) per share of downside protection on your 500 shares of ABC.

You lose money on your overall position if the price of your stock falls more than the amount of downside protection you gained by selling the call option. In other words, if ABC drops below $35, you've lost money on the overall position, so you really need to do the math before you ever write a call.

Think about it. If the price of ABC falls three points ($3 per share) and you still own the stock, you've lost $1,500 of the value of that portion of the position. However, because you wrote call options, you had $1,500 worth of downside protection, so at the $35 price level, you're essentially breaking even. In other words, by using the call-writing strategy, you're essentially back where you started on the overall position. The alternative would have been a $1,500 loss (in the value of the stock — at least on paper), had you not written the call option and held the stock without the protection of the option strategy.

If you change your mind after selling an option, you can buy it back in the marketplace. The buyer can also sell his options to the marketplace. This rule applies to both puts and calls.

Service after the Sale: Following Up after Writing a Call

Your job as an options trader starts when you make the transaction. The heavy lifting is what lies ahead — managing the position, which is more difficult in some ways than opening the position. You can do some pretty tricky things with options, and in this section, I keep the examples and the techniques as simple as possible, because there's simply no way I can cover all the subtleties of position management in one section of one chapter.

Two factors that are important to managing the position include

✔ What to do if a stock falls after you've written a covered call

✔ What to do as the covered call approaches expiration

Protecting your trade by diversification

A diversification strategy is pretty simple, and it works best when you own more than a couple of hundred shares of a stock.

You can sell more than one covered call at different strike prices and for different time frames. Again, the goal is to spread out your risk against volatility and your risk against the call you sold being exercised.

You can accomplish this strategy by writing in-the-money calls on some stocks and out-of-the-money calls on other stocks in your portfolio. However, setting up this strategy is difficult because writing out-of-the-money calls theoretically works better when you write them against stocks that do well.

In other words, to carry out this strategy, you are forced to decide which stocks you think are likely to do better than others, which is difficult to do in a simple stock picking strategy without the option strategy.

Conversely, writing in-the-money calls works better for stocks with low volatility.

One way to get around this problem is to write half of the position against in-the-money and half against out-of-the-money on the same stock.

In the ABC example featured in the previous two sections, you can accomplish this position by writing July 35 calls on one half of the position and July 45 calls at the same time on the other half; but to make the transaction simpler, you'd have to own 600 shares — as opposed to the 500 shares you owned in the previous example.

Knowing what to do when the stock rises

If your stock goes up, you can just let the buyer have it at the higher price. You made your premium, and you sold your stock at a price that you were comfortable with.

If you want to be aggressive, you can buy back your option, and *roll up,* or write another call at a higher strike price. When you do, though, you incur a debit in your trade, because you have to put up more money into the account.

Rolling up can be risky, because you can end up with a loss. Lawrence McMillan, author of *Options As A Strategic Investment* (Prentice-Hall Press), suggests that you shouldn't roll up whenever you can't withstand a 10-percent correction in the stock's price.

Rolling forward

Rolling forward is what you may want to do as your option's expiration time nears. You have to buy back your option and sell a new one with a longer term but the same strike price.

You can let the stock be called away, but if your stock has low volatility and your option strategy has been working for you, rolling forward usually is best.

How you make your decision is based on your projected costs of commissions, fees, and what your break-even point will be for the position.

If you're writing calls, make sure you're willing to let the underlying stock get called away. Otherwise, you're likely to become sorry at some point. If the position is going against you and you keep rolling up and forward, you're probably only making matters worse. At some point, you will hit the panic button and buy back your calls at a loss. You'll probably start selling put options to generate some credits, but you'll also end up placing yourself in a position that can wipe out your whole account.

Hoping to Make Big Bucks with Small Amounts of Money: Buying Calls

Call buying is different than call writing, because it isn't usually used by traders as a hedge against risk. Instead, call buying is used to make money on stocks that are likely to go up in price.

Call buying is the most common technique used by individual investors, but beware that success in this form of trading requires good stock-picking skills and a sense of timing.

The main attraction of buying call options is the potential for making large sums of money in short amounts of time, while limiting downside risk to only the original amount of money that you put up when you bought the option.

When you buy a call option, you pay for it in full. You have to post no margin.

Here's some advice to keep in mind when buying call options:

- Choose the right stock. Easier said than done, right? Buy call options on stocks that look ready to break out. That means that you need to become familiar with charting techniques and technical analysis (see Chapter 7).
- Use charts over fundamentals when you trade call options.
- Out-of-the-money calls have greater profit potential and greater risk.
- In-the-money calls may perform better when the stock does not move as you expected.
- Don't buy cheap call options just because they're cheap.
- Near-term calls are riskier than far-term calls.
- Intermediate-term calls may offer the best risk/reward ratio.

Calculating the break-even price for a call

Before you buy any call option, you must calculate the break-even price by using the following formula:

Strike price + Option premium cost + Commission and transaction costs = Break-even price

So if you're buying a December 50 call on ABC stock that sells for a $2.50 premium and the commission is $25, your break-even price would be

$50 + $2.50 + 0.25 = $52.75 per share

That means that to make a profit on this call option, the price per share of ABC has to rise above $52.75.

Calculating the break-even price for a put

To calculate the break-even price for a put option, you subtract the premium and the commission costs.

For a December 50 put on ABC stock that sells at a premium of $2.50, with a commission of $25, your break-even point would be

$50 − $2.50 − 0.25 = $47.25 per share

That means the price per share of ABC stock must fall below $47.25 for you to make a profit.

As a rule, make sure that you understand the fee structure used by your broker before making any option trades. Fees differ significantly from one broker to the next. Brokers frequently charge *round-trip fees,* which refer to the fees that you're charged on the way in and on the way out of an options trading position. To figure out round-trip commission fees in the break-even formula above, simply double the commission cost.

Two reasons for buying call options are

✔ **Because you expect the stock to rise.** ABC stock is selling at $50, and you buy a six-month call, the December 55, at $3. You pay $300 for the position. For the next six months you have a chance to make money if the stock rises in price. If the stock goes up 10 points, or 20 percent, your option also will rise, and because of leverage, the option will be worth much more. If the price drops below $55 by the expiration date, all you lose is your original $300 if you didn't sell back the option prior to that.

✔ **Because you expect to have money later and don't want to miss a move up in a stock.** Say for example, that you expect a nice sum of money in a couple of weeks, and a stock you like is starting to move. You can buy an option for a fraction of the price of the stock. When you get your money, if you're still interested, you can exercise your option and buy the stock. If you're wrong, you only lose a fraction of what you would have by owning the stock.

Using delta to time call-buying decisions

Delta measures the amount by which the price of the call option will change, up and down, every time the underlying stock moves 1 point.

Options are not good for day trading, but McMillan recommends trading the underlying stock in a day-trading situation. This strategy follows the key concept of using *delta:* The shorter the term of the strategy, the greater your delta should be. The delta of the underlying stock is 1.0. Thus, the stock is the most volatile instrument and therefore is best suited for day trading. Here are some general rules to follow when using delta to time your call buying:

✔ For trades that you expect to hold for a week or less, use the highest delta option you can find, because its moves will correlate the closest with the underlying asset. In this case, short-term, in-the-money options are the best bet.

✔ For intermediate-term trading, usually weeks in duration, use options with smaller deltas. McMillan recommends using at-the-money options for this time frame.

✔ For longer-term trading, choose low-delta options, either slightly out-of-the-money or longer-term at-the-money options.

✔ How long you expect to hold an option determines in part which option to buy.

Two good rules to keep in mind after you buy a call option:

✔ If the underlying stock tanks, you need to consider whether to sell your option or to let it expire unexercised, because selling the option will incur a commission cost.

✔ If the option rises in price, especially if it doubles in a short period of time, take some profits.

A third rule consists of implementing a spread strategy by selling your profitable option and buying a higher strike price option in the same stock. The problem with this move is that you can lose money fast if the stock turns around. If you sold your profitable initial position and stayed out of the options in that particular stock, you kept your profit.

If you decided to do nothing, you can lose everything at expiration. For my money, a good profit in my pocket is better than a great one that may never come — the one that got away.

Spread strategies are extremely risky and recommended only for experienced traders. They require margin, and each individual brokerage firm has different specifications regarding how much margin is required. At the beginning of an options trading strategy, keeping it simple is the best way to go. As you become more experienced, you can start making more sophisticated bets. McMillan offers extensive reading in the area of spreads in his book.

From the Top: Basic Put Option Strategies

When you buy a put option, you're hoping that the price of the underlying stock falls.

You make money with puts when the price of the option rises, or when you exercise the option to buy the stock at a price that's below the strike price and then sell the stock in the open market, pocketing the difference.

So, if you bought an ABC December 50 put, and ABC falls to $40 per share, you can make money either by selling a put option that rises in price or by buying the stock at $40 on the open market and then exercising the option, thus selling your $40 stock to the writer for $50 per share, which is what owning the put gave you the right to do.

Buying put options

Put options are either used as pure speculative vehicles or as protection against the potential for stock prices to fall.

When you buy a put option, you are accomplishing essentially the same concept without some of the more complicated details of short selling. Put options also give you leverage because you don't have to spend as much money as you would trying to short-sell a stock.

By buying a put option, you limit your risk of a loss to the premium that you paid for the put.

Making the most of your put option buys

Out-of-the-money puts are riskier but offer greater reward potential than in-the-money puts. The flip side is that if a stock falls a relatively small amount, you're likely to make more money from your put if you own an in-the-money option.

McMillan points out an important point: Call options tend to move more dramatically than puts. You can buy the right put option, and the underlying stock may have fallen significantly. Still, the market decided that the put option should rise only 1 or 2 points. In an ideal world, you'd expect to be greatly rewarded for buying a put option on a stock that collapses. But, in the world of options pricing, things are not always what you'd expect them to be because of the vagaries of trading, the time to expiration, and other major influences on option pricing (see Chapter 4 for more about the Greeks).

To avoid this disappointment, you're better off by buying in-the-money puts unless the probability that the underlying stock is going to fall by a significant amount is extremely high.

In contrast to call options, you may be able to buy a longer-term put option for a fairly good price. Doing so is a good idea, because it gives you more time for the stock to fall. Buying the longer-term put also protects you if the stock rises, because its premium will likely drop less in price.

What to do if you have a huge profit in a put option

If you're lucky enough to get a nice drop in a stock on which you own a put option, you can do several things:

- ✔ **Take profits.** Doing so guarantees that you lock in a gain if you execute the trade in a timely manner.
- ✔ **Do nothing.**
- ✔ **Sell your in-the-money put and buy an out-of-the money put.** By opting for this strategy, you're taking partial profits and then extending your risk and your profit potential if the stock continues to fall.
- ✔ **Create a spread strategy by selling an out-of-the-money put against the one you already own.**

The first three strategies are self-explanatory, but creating a spread adds an important new wrinkle to the possible strategies you can use.

One way to create the spread is to sell a different put option than the one you already own.

You can, for instance, sell a December 45 put to offset the already profitable December 50 put that you own, all so that you make some money off the sale and lock in some of the costs of having bought the original December 50 put.

If the stock goes above 50, you lose everything. But if the stock falls below 45 and stabilizes, you make the 5-point maximum profit from the spread, which is the best of all worlds in this strategy.

The second spread involves buying a call option. You can buy a December 45 call to limit your risk if the stock rises. See the previous sections about writing calls. Again your cost would be 5 points. Some of your costs of owning the put have already been covered. And this spread guarantees you 5 points no matter where the stock closes at expiration.

Spreads get the best results when the stock stabilizes in price after the spread is put on. But it is more important that the stock price stays in the profit range of the spread.

Buying put options — fully dressed

Buying a put option without owning the stock is called buying a naked put. Naked puts give you the potential for profit if the underlying stock falls. But if you own a stock and buy a put option on the same stock, you're protecting your position and limiting your downside risk for the life of the put option.

A good time to buy a put on a stock that you own is when you've made a significant gain, but you're not sure you want to cash out. You can also use puts to protect against short-term volatility in long-term holdings.

In the first instance in the previous paragraph, your put option acts as an insurance policy to protect your gains. In the second instance, if your put goes up in value, you can sell it and decrease the paper losses on your stock.

You decide which put option to buy by calculating how much profit potential you're willing to lose if the stock goes up.

Out-of-the-money puts are cheap, but they won't give you as much protection as in-the-money puts until the stock falls to the strike price. In-the-money puts are more expensive but can provide better insurance.

Creating straddles

You can create a *straddle* when you simultaneously buy a put and a call for the same stock at the same strike price and of the same duration.

With a straddle, if the underlying stock moves far enough, you can

- Make large potential profits
- Keep your losses to the amount of your initial investment

Say, for example, that you built a straddle based on ABC stock at $50 per share and you bought a July 50 put option at 5 and a July 50 call option at 2. You'd pay the difference between the two, which is 3 points.

If the stock rises to $55 at expiration, your call option would likely be worth more than what you paid for it, and you could make money even if your put expired worthless. If ABC was at $45 at expiration, then your put option should be worth more than you paid for it, and you could make money on it.

If the stock is somewhere between the break-even points of $45 and $55 per share at expiration, you'll lose money.

The chances of losing all of your money in a straddle are small, but the chances of making money in this strategy when you hold the position until the expiration date also are small.

You want to build straddles on stocks that are likely to be volatile.

Taking small profits in a straddle can cost you money in the long run. You may have to take a few small losses before you hit a big win. This particular gut-wrenching quality about straddle strategy is what makes it more suitable for experienced investors. If you're interested in straddles, using an experienced options broker/advisor who truly understands this strategy, at least during your early trading experiences, may be your best, well, option.

You build a *strangle* with a put and a call that usually have the same expiration date but different strike prices.

Strangles work best when the put and the call are out of the money. Strangles are a risky strategy because you can lose money anywhere along the spread, as opposed to straddles where you can only lose money at the strike price.

Getting naked with put sales

Selling naked put options is similar to buying a call option, because you make money when the underlying stock goes up in price; however, it is a strategy that is used more often than a covered-put sale, which is a totally different and very complex strategy that isn't worth discussing in this context.

Selling naked puts means you're selling a put option without being short the stock, and in the process, you're hoping that the stock goes nowhere or rises, which enables you to keep the premium without being assigned. If the stock falls in a big way, and you get assigned, you can face big losses from having to buy the stock in the open market to sell it to the party exercising the put you sold.

You need to put up collateral to write naked puts, usually in an amount that is equal to 20 percent of the current stock price plus the put premium minus any out-of-the-money amount.

Here is how it works.

ABC is selling at $40 per share, and a four-month put with a striking price of $40 is selling for 4 points. You have the potential to make $400 here or the potential for a huge loss if the stock falls. Your loss is limited only because the stock can't go below zero.

The amount of collateral you'd need to put up would be $400, plus 20 percent of the price of the stock, or $800. The minimum you'd have to put up, though, would be 10 percent of the strike price, plus the put premium, even if the amount is smaller than what you just calculated.

For beginning traders, it's best to cut losses short whenever the underlying stock drops in price.

Selling covered puts

Selling covered puts is a strategy that rarely is used, because it may be among the most complex strategies in the options market and is not particularly recommended for beginners.

A put sale is covered, not by owning the stock, but rather by having an open short position on the underlying stock. Your margin is covered if you're also short the stock.

This strategy has the same kind of potential as buying a naked call — unlimited upside risk and limited profit potential.

Taxing issues: How the IRS gets at your put options

The IRS taxes short-term and long-term profits on every sale of every trade you make, except in a retirement account for which it taxes you later on, when you withdraw the money. Some tax-specific details you need to know if you're trading put options include the following:

✔ Buying put options has no tax consequences if you're a long-term holder, usually greater than six months.

✔ Forfeiting any accrued time during the holding period, if you're a short-term holder of the stock and you buy a put option. Holding time won't begin to accrue again until you sell the put, or it expires.

Be sure to consult with your accountant before you trade any options.

Dividing issues: How dividends affect put options

Dividends make put options more valuable, and the larger the dividend, the more valuable the put becomes.

When stocks go ex-dividend, the day the dividend gets paid out, the amount of the dividend reduces the price of the stock. As the stock falls, the put increases in value.

The prices of puts and calls are not reduced by dividends. Instead, the price reflects the effect of the dividend on the stock. Call prices fall as the stocks pay out their dividends. Put prices rise as of the ex-dividend date.

Exercising your put option

Put and call options rarely are exercised in the stock market. Most option traders take the gains on the options if they have them or cut their losses short as early as possible if the market goes against them.

But if you're the holder of a put option and you decide to exercise it, you're selling the underlying stock at the striking price, and you can sell the stock at the strike price any time during the life of the option. If you write, or sell, the put, you're assigned the obligation of buying the stock at the strike price.

You can sell stock that you own at the strike price or buy stock in the open market if you don't own it, as in the case of a naked strategy, and then sell it at the strike price.

You notify your broker how you'll deliver or receive the stock. You must make sure that you can satisfy any margin or other requirement involved, and the exercise procedure and share transfer will be handled by the broker.

Part II
Analyzing the Markets

The 5th Wave   By Rich Tennant

"COOKED BOOKS? LET ME JUST SAY YOU COULD SERVE THIS PROFIT AND LOSS STATEMENT WITH A FRUITY ZINFANDEL AND NOT BE OUT OF PLACE."

In this part . . .

Have you ever been confused by trader jargon or wondered how to make sense out of economic reports that move the markets? Part II of this book gives you the tools you need to wade through trader talk and use economic reports effectively to make money. I also tell you about the world of technical analysis, showing you the basics of reading price charts and using key technical indicators. You also get effective tips on trading techniques, how to spot key market turning points by using market sentiment, and knowing when to trade against the grain.

Chapter 6

Understanding the Fundamentals of the Economy

*W*hen I started trading, I was overwhelmed by the amount of data that was available. I had a hard time correlating how that data was related to the movement of prices, and I thought that the whole thing was random.

My first reaction was to ignore the data and concentrate on the charts. Although chart-watching worked well for a while, it wasn't good enough to get me in and out of positions fast enough or to prevent getting taken out of positions only to see them turn around and go in the direction that I expected them to go in the first place. I knew that I needed something else, so I began watching how the market moved in response to economic data.

This is not the only approach to trading, as there are purists on both sides of the aisle: those that propose charting as the best method, and those who swear by the fundamentals. But rather than confuse you with a bunch of jargon and useless justifications on either side, I can tell you that you'll decide what works best for you, and that for me, the best method is to use charts as well as to keep my hands on the pulse of the economy.

It's also fair to say that my problem in my early trading career was one of a lack of experience, which could have been remedied by a much finer use of different charting methods, as well as a better use of charts with different time frames. See Chapter 7 for more on technical analysis.

Just remember that as you progress, you'll gain your own insights into what works best for you. Think of this book as a great place to get started.

Achieving a balance between what I want to know about the economy, what I need to know, and what I can use took time. So, after considerable trial and error, I've reached a comfortable middle ground: I am both an avid *chartist,* or someone who studies price charts and uses technical analysis of the financial markets to make trades, and also an avid follower of trends in the economy, although not as in depth as you'd expect from a Nobel Prize–winning economist.

The bottom line: Like many other successful traders, I understand how the markets and the monthly economic indicators can morph into a nice and reliable trading method. And so this chapter focuses on the effects of important economic indicators on the bond markets, stock indexes, and currency markets.

I purposely chose to illustrate examples of how economic reports can affect the market from April 2005 for two major reasons. First, I wanted to show you that the concepts that I describe in the chapter are relevant to what's going on now, in a global economy, during a controversial period in U.S. history, the post-September 11, 2001, era. And second, the period of time chosen had just about anything that a futures trader could ask for in the way of data that can move the markets, especially a significant amount of activity in the oil market, a booming housing market, and a Federal Reserve that was just hitting its stride in a major cycle of interest-rate hikes.

Examples used to illustrate concepts and key economic reports in this chapter and throughout most of the book are fairly current — mostly from 2005. I like to make my books as current as possible. By the same token, I also look for examples that are classical in nature. In other words, my goal is to make the examples current but universal so that you can use them for an extended period of time. Most markets behave similarly, but certainly not identically, over time, so you have to be flexible in your interpretation of real-time trading. When I provide examples, my goal is to give you as classic a set of parameters as possible.

Understanding the U.S. Economy

Market experts and those well-versed in economic theory, along with politicians and pundits, like to muddle things up when it comes to interpreting data and formulating working summaries of economic activity. That's how they keep their jobs . . . by confusing the public when it comes to what's really happening with the economy.

But understanding how the economy works and making it fit your trading approach doesn't have to be that complicated. Simply stated, the United States economy, the largest in the world, is dependent upon a series of delicately intertwined relationships, so keep these factors in mind:

- ✔ Consumers drive the U.S. economy.

- ✔ Consumers need jobs to be able to buy things and keep the economy going.

- ✔ The ebb and flow between the degree of joblessness and full employment, how easy or difficult it is to get credit, and how much the supply of goods and services is in demand drive economic activity up or down.

As a rule, steady job growth, easy-enough credit, and a balance between supply and demand are what the Board of Governors of the Federal Reserve (the Fed) like to see in the economy. When one or more of these factors is out of kilter (teeters off balance), the Fed has to act by raising or lowering interest rates to either

- ✔ Tighten or loosen the consumer's ability to obtain credit.

- ✔ Rein in a too high of a level of joblessness.

- ✔ Increase or decrease the supply side to bring it in line with demand, or vice versa.

Each variable is monitored by individual government and private agencies that produce a key series of monthly and quarterly reports. These reports, in turn, are released on a regularly scheduled basis throughout the year. They provide futures-and-options traders with a major portion of the road map they need to decide which way the general-direction prices in their respective markets are headed. It's all about the government and private-agency reports and how the markets respond. Businesses are just the pawns of the Fed and the markets.

The overall focus of the markets is on only one thing . . . what the Federal Reserve is going to do to interest rates in response to the report(s) of the day (see Chapter 1). Based on how traders (buyers and sellers) perceive their markets before the Fed makes its move and their reactions after the Fed's response to economic conditions is announced, prices move in one direction or the other.

As a futures and options trader, you need to understand how each of these important reports can make your particular markets move and how to prepare yourself for the possibilities of making money based on the relationship between all of the individual components of the market and economic equation. Now that you know these basic truths about the U.S. economy, I'm going to discuss the most important sets of data released by key reporting agencies and how to use the information to make trades.

Getting a General Handle on the Reports

Economic reports are important tools in all markets, but they're a way of life for futures-and-options traders.

Each individual market has its own set of reports to which traders pay special attention. But some key reports are among the prime catalysts for fluctuations in the prices not only of all markets, but especially in the bond, stock, and currency markets, which form the centerpiece of the trading universe and are linked to one another. Traders wait patiently for their release and act with lightning speed as the data hit the wires.

Even so, some reports are more important during certain market cycles than they are in others, and you have no way of predicting which of them will be the report of the month, the quarter, or the year.

Nevertheless, Gross Domestic Product, the consumer and producer price indexes, the monthly employment reports, and the Fed's Beige Book, which summarizes the economic activity as surveyed by the Fed's regional banks, are usually important and highly scrutinized.

The Institute for Supply Management (ISM) report, formerly the national purchasing manager's report, produced by the Institute for Supply Management, also is important, and so is the Chicago purchasing manager's report, which usually is released one or two days prior to the ISM report.

Consumer confidence numbers from the University of Michigan and the Conference Board usually are market movers, with bond, stock, and currency traders paying special attention to them.

Sometimes weekly employment claims data can move the market if they come in far above or below expectations. Retail sales numbers, especially from major retailers, such as Wal-Mart, can move the markets, and so can the budget deficit or surplus numbers. Consumer credit data can sometimes move the market as well.

I highlight key reports that affect each individual market in the chapters that deal specifically with those markets.

Cable news outlets, major financial Web sites, and business radio networks — CNBC and Bloomberg are two that I follow — broadcast every major report as it is released, and the wire services send out alerts regarding the reports to all major financial publishers not already covering the releases. The government agencies and companies that are responsible for the reports also post them on their respective Web sites immediately at the announced time.

Exploring how economic reports are used

From a public policy standpoint, economic reports find their way into political speeches in the House of Representatives and on the Senate floor. The president and his advisors, other politicians, bureaucrats, and spin doctors quote data from these reports widely and often, using them to suit their current purposes.

From a trader's point of view, you can best use them as

- **Sources of new information:** No one should ever have access to the data in economic reports prior to their release — other than the press, which receives it expressly under embargoed conditions, with instructions not to release the data prior to the proper time — and key members of the U.S. government, such as the Fed and the president. Anyone else who has the data before the release can be prosecuted if they leak it to anyone else.

- **Risk management tools:** You can place your money at risk if you ignore any of the reports. Each has the potential for providing important information that can create key turning points in the market.

- **Harbingers of more important information:** Individual headlines about economic reports are only part of the important data. The markets explore more data beyond what's contained in the initial release. Sometimes data hidden deep within a report become more important than the initial knee-jerk reaction characterized within the headlines and cause the market to reverses its course.

- **Trend-setters:** Current reports may not always be what matters. The trend of the data from reports during the last few months, quarters, or years, in addition to expectations for the future, also can be powerful information that moves the markets up or down.

- **Planning tools:** Trading solely on economic reports can be very risky and requires experience and thorough planning on your part.

Gaming the calendar

As a trader, your world is highly dependent on the *economic calendar,* the listing of when reports will be released for the current month.

Each month a steady flow of economic data is generated and released by the U.S. government and the private sector. These reports are

- A major influence on how the futures and the financial markets move in general.
- A source of the *cyclicality,* or repetitive nature, of market movements.

You can get access to the calendar in many places. Most futures brokers post the calendar on their Web sites and can mail you a copy along with key information on their margin and commission rates — pretty convenient, eh? Customer service in the futures market actually is quite awesome if you can handle the greasy guys that you sometimes have to talk to.

The Wall Street Journal, Marketwatch.com, and other major news outlets also publish the calendar, either fully posted for the month or for that particular day or week.

The reports follow a familiar pattern, usually following each other in similar sequence from one month to the next.

Exploring Specific Economic Reports

Some reports are more important than others, but at some point, they all have the potential to influence the market. The reports that consistently carry the most weight and result in the biggest shifts in the markets tend to be the employment report, the Producer Price Index (PPI), the Consumer Price Index (CPI), and two reports on consumer confidence. Other economic data that have an important bearing on the markets include the Purchasing Manager's report from the Institute for Supply Management (ISM), Beige Book reports produced eight times a year by the Federal Reserve, housing starts compiled by the U.S. Department of Commerce, and of course, the granddaddy of all, the Index of Leading Economic Indicators, which the Fed also produces.

In addition to these major economic releases, each individual market has its own set of key reports. For example, the cattle markets (Chapter 15) aren't likely to be moved by data in the Purchasing Manager's Report, but may be moved by grain storage prices.

Working the employment report

The U.S. Department of Labor's employment report is the first piece of major economic data released each month. It's released on the first Friday of every month and is formally known as the Employment Situation Report. Bond, stock index, and currency futures are keyed upon the release of the number at 8:30 a.m. eastern time.

The release of the employment data usually is followed by frenzied trading that can last from a few minutes to an entire day, depending on what the data shows and what the market was expecting. The report is so important that it can set the trend for overall trading in the entire arena of the financial markets for several weeks after its release.

When consecutive reports show that a dominant trend is in place, the trend of the overall market tends to remain in the same direction for extended periods of time. The reversal of such a dominant trend can often be interpreted as a signal that bonds, stock indexes, and currencies are going to change course.

The employment report is most important when the economy is shifting gears, similar to the way it did after the events of September 11, 2001, and during the 2004 presidential election. During the election, the markets not only bet on the economic consequences of the report, but they also bet on how the number of new jobs would affect the outcome of the election.

Traders use the employment report as one of several important clues to predict the future of interest rates.

For trading purposes, the major components of the employment report are

- ✔ **The number of new jobs created:** This number tends to predict which way the strength of the economy is headed. Large numbers of new jobs usually mean that the economy is growing. When the number of new jobs begins to fall, it's usually a sign that the economy is slowing.

- ✔ **The unemployment rate:** The rate of unemployment is more difficult to interpret, but the trend in the rate is more important than the actual monthly number. A workforce that is considered to be fully employed usually is a sign that interest rates are going to rise, so the markets begin to factor that into the equation.

Other subsections of the employment report have their moments in the sun. For example, the *household survey,* which uses interviews from people that work at home, was heavily scrutinized during the 2004 election season. The *numbers of self-employed people* became more important as the election neared, because the market began to price in an economic recovery based on adding together the data from both the traditional establishment survey, which measures the people who work for companies, with the household survey.

Be ready to make trades based on the reaction and not necessarily the report. As with all economic and financial reports, the report may not be as important as the market's reaction to the report in terms of a trader making or losing money.

Probing the Producer Price Index (PPI)

The PPI is an important report, but it doesn't usually cause as big of market moves as the CPI and the employment report.

The PPI measures prices at the producer level. In other words, it's a measurement of the cost of raw materials to companies that produce goods. The market is interested in two things contained in this report:

✓ **How fast these prices are rising:** If a rise in PPI is significantly large in comparison to previous months, the market checks to see where it's coming from.

For example, the May 2005 PPI report pegged prices at the producer level as rising 0.6 percent in April, following a 0.7-percent increase in March and a 0.4-percent hike in February. At first glance, the market viewed the April increase (compared to the previous two months) as a negative number. However, market makers discovered a note deeper in the report, indicating that if you didn't measure food and energy — in this case (especially) oil prices — producer prices at the so-called core level rose only 0.1 percent. The market looked at the core level, and bonds rallied. You and I know that food and energy are important expenses, and that if they are more expensive, we pay more. But futures traders live in a different world when they're in the trading pits and in front of their trading screens, meaning they trade on their perceptions of the data and not what you and I find intuitive.

✓ **Whether producers are passing along any price hikes to their consumers:** If prices at the core level are tame, as they seemed to be in the April 2005 report, traders will conduct business based on the information they have in hand at least until the CPI is released — usually one or two days after the PPI is released. In this case, based only on the PPI, inflation at the core producer level was tame, so traders wagered that producers were not passing any added costs onto the consumer.

Browsing in the Consumer Price Index (CPI)

The CPI is the main inflation report for the futures and financial markets. Unexpected rises in this indicator usually lead to falling bond prices, rising interest rates, and increased market volatility.

Consumer prices are important because consumer buying drives the U.S. economy. No consumer demand at the retail level means no demand for products along the other steps in the chain of manufacturers, wholesalers, and retailers.

Here are some key factors that govern consumer prices and the inflation that they measure:

- **Prices at the consumer level are not as sensitive to supply and demand as they are to the ability of retailers to pass their own costs on to consumers.** For example, clothing retailers can't always or immediately pass their wholesale costs for fabric components or labor to consumers, because they'll start buying discount clothing if premium apparel is too expensive. Much of this volatility has to do with the fact that a large amount of retail merchandise is made in Asia, where labor is cheap and competition is stiff.

- **Supply tends to be more important in many cases than demand.** When enough of something is available, prices tend to stay down. Scarcities, however, don't necessarily mean inflation (but they certainly can accompany it).

- **Inflation is not a price phenomenon but rather a monetary phenomenon.** When too much money is chasing too few goods, inflation appears.

- **Inflationary expectations and consumer prices are related.** This factor is true because inflationary expectations are built into the cost of borrowing money.

- **By the time prices begin to rise at the consumer level, the supply-and-demand equation, price discovery, and pressure on the system have been ongoing at other levels of the price chain for some time.**

The relationship between prices and interest rates is key to developing an intuitive feeling for futures trading.

The true return on an investment is the percentage of the investment that you gain after accounting for inflation. If your portfolio gains 20 percent for five years and inflation is running at 10 percent during that period, you actually gained only 10 percent per year.

The release of the CPI usually moves the markets for interest-rate, currency, and stock-index futures, and it's one of the best reports with which to trade option strategies, such as straddles. (For more about options strategies, see Chapter 4.)

As with the PPI, traders want to know what the core CPI number is — that is, prices at the consumer level without food and energy factored in.

The April 2005 CPI was another classic report. The initial line from the Labor Department quoted consumer prices as rising 0.7 percent, a number that, if it stood alone, would have caused a big sell-off in the bond market. However, as the report revealed, that core number was unchanged, bonds and stock futures had a big rally, which spilled over into the stock market that day.

Managing the ISM and purchasing manager's reports

The Institute for Supply Management's (ISM) Report on Business usually moves the markets, or is a *market mover,* however you want to say it. It measures the health of the manufacturing sector in the U.S. This report is based on the input of purchasing managers surveyed across the U.S. and is compiled by the ISM.

The Report on Business is different from the regional purchasing manager's reports, although some regional reports, such as the Chicago-area report, often serve as good predictors of the national data. You also need to know, however, that the regional reports are not used as a basis for the national report.

The report addresses 11 categories, including the widely watched headline, the PMI index.

Here is how to look at the ISM report:

- ✔ A number above 50 on the PMI means that the economy is growing.

- ✔ You want to find out whether the main index and the subsectors are above or below 50.

- ✔ Just as important is whether the pace of growth is slowing or picking up speed. The report, which is available at the ISM Web site at `www.ism.ws/ISMReport/ROB052005.cfm`, clearly states whether each individual sector is growing or not growing, and whether it is doing so because its pace is slowing or picking up speed.

- ✔ The data for the entire report is included with a summary of the economy's current state and pace near the headline of the report.

The April 2005 report concluded that the economy had been growing for 42 straight months and that the manufacturing sector had been growing for 23 straight months. The report concluded that although prices paid by manufacturers were on the rise and inventories were low, both the economy and the manufacturing sector were still growing, but the growth rate was slowing.

The bond market rallied. The dollar strengthened. And stocks had a moderate gain.

This particular ISM report had something for everybody, especially when you compare it to the economic trends around the world in which Europe had flat-to-lower growth rates, and China had a robust but also moderating growth rate. A U.S. economy that is growing is good. But one that is growing too fast can lead to inflation, so the bond markets also liked the report. Steady growth with low production costs is good for company earnings, so the stock markets liked it. Economic growth is likely to keep interest rates steady or slightly higher, so the currency markets — which like to see steady to higher interest rates — liked the report, too, particularly the dollar.

Considering consumer confidence

The report that measures consumer confidence is a big report that comes from two sources that publish separate reports, the Conference Board, a private research group, and the University of Michigan.

The Conference Board Survey

The Conference Board, Inc., publishes a monthly report based on survey interviews of 5,000 consumers.

Key components of the Conference Board survey are

- The monthly index
- Current conditions
- Consumers' outlook for the next six months

In April 2005, the monthly index fell, and so did the current condition and outlook portions of the survey. The result: Bonds rallied, stocks rallied, and the dollar remained steady. The report became another piece of the economic puzzle at a key time in the U.S. economy. The way the market looked at the data, following eight straight Federal Reserve interest-rate increases, showed that the economy was starting to slow. To a layman, a slowing economy would be bad news, but to a futures trader, the data meant that the Fed may be nearing the end of its rate hikes (or that interest rates may be leveling off).

The University of Michigan Survey

The University of Michigan conducts its own survey of consumer confidence, and it publishes several preliminary reports and one final report per month.

Key components of the University of Michigan Survey are

- The Index of Consumer Confidence
- The Index of Consumer Expectations
- The Index of Current Economic conditions

In April 2005, the University of Michigan reported that "Consumer confidence sank in April, marking the fourth consecutive monthly decline, with the Sentiment Index falling to its lowest level since September 2003."

The report cited "rising gas prices" and a poor job outlook as reasons for the sag in consumer confidence and the increasingly negative data for consumer expectations. The impact on the markets was predictable. Bonds rallied and so eventually did stocks . . . after an initial dip.

Again, the key to the report was that consumer confidence was falling. When consumers are less confident, the Fed is less likely to continue to raise interest rates.

Perusing the Beige Book

The *Beige Book* is a key report from the Federal Reserve that is released eight times per year. In each tome, the Fed produces a summary of current economic activity in each of its districts, based on anecdotal information from Fed bank presidents, key businesses, economists, and market experts, among other sources.

The 12 Federal Reserve District Banks are located in Boston, New York, Philadelphia, Cleveland, Richmond, Atlanta, Chicago, St. Louis, Minneapolis, Kansas City, Dallas, and San Francisco.

The Federal Reserve produces the Summary of Commentary on Current Economic Conditions, otherwise known as the Beige Book. In it, the Fed summarizes anecdotal reports on the economy by district and sector and packages it into a comprehensive summary of the 12 district reports. Each Beige Book is prepared by a designated Federal Reserve Bank on a rotating basis.

The Beige Book is released to the members of the Federal Open Market Committee (FOMC) before each of its meetings on interest rates, so it's an important source of information for the committee members when they're deciding in what direction they'll vote to take interest rates.

On April 20, 2005, the Federal Reserve district in Dallas had its turn to publish the Beige Book and summarized its findings as follows:

> Eleventh District economic activity expanded moderately in March and early April. The manufacturing sector continued to rebound, while activity in financial and business services continued to expand at the same pace reported in the last Beige Book (the one released March 9, 2005). Retailers said they were disappointed with recent sales growth. Residential construction continued to cool from last year's strong pace, amid signs that commercial real estate markets were slowly improving. The energy industry strengthened further, and contacts said exploration

activity was expanding on the belief that energy prices would remain high. Agricultural conditions remained generally positive. While activity was strong in some industries, in many sectors contacts reported slightly less optimism about the strength of activity for the rest of the year, largely because demand has not been picking up as quickly as they had hoped.

Traders look for any mention of labor shortages and wage pressures in the Beige Book. If any such trends are mentioned, bonds may sell off, as rising wage pressures are taken as a sign of building inflation in the pipeline. In this edition, the book noted that banking and accounting were seeing some price competition caused by a shortage of qualified workers but added that "most industries said there was little or no wage pressure."

Here's a good habit to get into so you can capitalize on knowledge from one area of the market as you apply it to another: After the initial headlines and market reactions, I like to read through the report on the Internet. You can find links to it on the Fed's Web site, www.federalreserve.gov, or you can do a Google or Yahoo! search for "Beige Book."

What I look for when I scan the full text on the Web is what the Beige Book says about individual sectors of the economy. Under manufacturing in April 2005, the Beige Book said that although little pickup was reported in the growth for electronics, slightly rising demand was noted for networking switches and other related products in telecommunications.

If you see something like that, you can start looking at the action of key stocks in that sector. Interestingly, the stock of Cisco Systems, the leader in switches and related products, made a good bottom in the month of April, and on April 21, a day after the Beige Book was released, it began to rally. By May 20, the stock was up 13.26 percent.

The Beige Book usually is released in the afternoon, one or two hours before the stock market closes. The overall trend of all markets can reverse late in the day when the data in the report surprise traders.

Homing in on housing starts

Bond and stock traders like housing starts, because housing is a central portion of the U.S. economy, given its dependence on credit and the fact that it uses raw materials and provides employment for a significant number of people in related industries, such as banking, the mortgage sector, construction, manufacturing, and real-estate brokerage.

Big moves often occur in the bond market after the numbers for housing starts are released.

Released every month, housing starts are compiled by the U.S. Commerce Department and reported in three parts:

- ✔ Building permits
- ✔ Housing starts
- ✔ Housing completions

The markets focus on the percentage of rise or fall in the numbers from the previous month for each component.

For example, the April 2005 report showed a 5.3 percent growth in the number of building permits, an 11 percent growth in housing starts (with a 6.3 percent growth in single-family homes), and a 3.4 percent growth rate in housing completions.

A volatile series of numbers, this data can be greatly affected by weather, so it is also seasonally adjusted and includes a significant amount of revised data within each of the internal components.

For example, when winter arrives, snow storms and cold weather tend to halt or slow new and ongoing construction projects, so housing permits and housing starts can start to decline. If you don't know that, you can make trading mistakes by betting that interest rates are going to fall. The problem comes when the weather clears, and the projects get underway, and the numbers swell. Markets look at the seasonally adjusted numbers, which are smoothed out by statistical formulas used by the U.S. Department of Commerce.

Even then, this set of numbers is tricky. The Commerce Department disclaimer notes that it can take up to four months of data to come up with a reliable set of indicators.

Staying Awake for the Index of Leading Economic Indicators

The Conference Board looks at ten key indicators in calculating its Index of Leading Economic Indicators. Included are the

- ✔ Index of consumer expectations
- ✔ Real money supply
- ✔ Interest-rate spread
- ✔ Stock prices

- Vendor performance
- Average weekly initial claims for unemployment insurance
- Building permits
- Average weekly manufacturing hours
- Manufacturers' new orders for nondefense capital goods
- Manufacturers' new orders for consumer goods and materials

In April 2005, the overall index dropped and so did much of the economic data for that month. At the same time, the trend of economic growth remained up, once again confirming the notion that interest rate increases ordered by the Federal Reserve were starting to slow down the economy, but they weren't dragging it into a recession.

The Index of Leading Economic Indicators is another lukewarm indicator that sometimes moves the markets and other times doesn't. It is more likely to move the markets whenever it clearly is divergent from data provided by other indicators. For example, if in April, the leading indicators were showing a drastic decline, the markets would start worrying about a recession looming on the horizon. That, in turn, may be a catalyst to knock down stock and commodity prices and the value of the dollar, but on the other hand, it may bring about a huge rally in the bond markets.

Grossing out with Gross Domestic Product (GDP)

The report on Gross Domestic Product (GDP) measures the sum of all the goods and services produced in the United States. Although GDP can yield confusing and mixed results on the trading floor, it sometimes is a big market mover whenever it's far above or below what the markets are expecting it to be. At other times, GDP is not much of a mover. Multiple revisions of previous GDP data accompany the monthly release of the GDP and tend to dampen the effect of the report. Although the GDP is not a report to ignore, by any means, it usually isn't as important as the PPI and CPI and the employment report.

GDP has a component called the *deflator,* which is a measure of inflation. The deflator can be the prime mover whenever it is above or below market expectations.

Getting slick with oil supply data

Oil supply data became a central report outside of the oil markets in 2004 and 2005 as the price of crude oil soared to record highs after the war in Iraq.

The Energy Information Agency (EIA), a part of the U.S. Department of Energy, and the American Petroleum Institute (API) release oil supply data for the previous week at 10:30 a.m. eastern time every Wednesday.

Traders want to know the following:

- ✔ Crude oil supply
- ✔ Gasoline supply
- ✔ Distillate supply

A *build* is when the stockpiles of crude oil in storage are increasing. Such increases are considered *bearish* or negative for the market, because large stockpiles generally mean lower prices at the pump. A *drawdown,* on the other hand, is when the supply shrinks. Traders like drawdown situations, because prices tend to rise after the news is released.

Every week, oil experts and commentators guess what the number will be. Although they almost never are right in their predictions, the fact that they're wrong sets the market up for more volatility when the number comes out and gives you a trading opportunity if you're set up to take advantage of it.

A good way to set up for the oil report, or any report, is to set up an options strategy called a straddle (see Chapter 5 for details).

A straddle gives you a chance to make money if the market rises or falls; it essentially sets you up for any surprises. For the oil markets, you can set up straddles on crude oil, natural gas, heating oil, or gasoline futures. You can also set up straddles on individual oil stocks such as Valero Energy (NYSE: VLO), which usually is a big mover on reports.

Although crude oil supply is self-explanatory as the basis for the oil markets and is important year-round, two other supply factors are affected by these seasonal tendencies:

- ✔ Distillate supply figures are more important in winter, because they essentially represent a measure of the supply of heating oil.
- ✔ Gasoline supplies are more important as the summer driving season approaches.

Other holidays sometimes can affect oil supply numbers. The market tends to factor their effect into the numbers, though, so for other holidays to have a big effect on trading, the surprises have to be very big.

The market has changed, however, because of problems with refinery capacity in the U.S. and the aftereffects of two major hurricanes (Katrina and Rita) in 2005 in the Gulf of Mexico region. Volatility in the markets and supply numbers will evolve over the next few years. See Chapter 13 for a full rundown of the energy markets.

CNBC covers the oil supply release number. Sometimes, the reporter gets the gist of the data wrong, and the market can be increasingly volatile because of it. Although this scenario is not frequent, I've seen it happen, and I have seen it have an effect on trading.

Enduring sales, income, production, and balance of trade reports

The hodgepodge of data that trickle out of the woodwork throughout the month about retail sales, personal income, industrial production, and the balance of trade sometimes causes a bit of commotion in the futures markets, but these individual reports mostly cause only a few daily ripples, unless, of course, the effect of the data is dramatic.

As a futures and options trader, you need to know that these reports are coming, but a good portion of the time, they come and go without fanfare or trouble, unless the economy is at a critical turning point and one of these reports happens to be the missing piece to the puzzle.

Of these four reports, the one most likely to get the most press is the balance of trade report. Because the Chinese economy is getting so much attention these days, the currency and bond markets may move dramatically whenever the balance of trade report shows a much greater than expected trade deficit or trade surplus. If several consecutive reports show that the United States is reversing its trend toward more imports than exports, you may see a major set of moves in the futures markets.

The prices for imports also are an important factor in the trade data that can be a sign of inflation and, again, can affect how the Federal Reserve moves on interest rates.

Trading the Big Reports

The greatest effect that each of the reports highlighted in this chapter can have is on the futures and related options markets associated with bonds, stock indexes, and currencies. Thus, the best strategies for trading based on these reports are found in those markets.

Any report can make the market move up or down if the market finds something in the report to justify the move, but some general tendencies to keep in mind include the following:

- Reports that show a strengthening economy are less friendly to the bond market and tend to be friendlier toward stock-index futures and the dollar. Although this isn't a hard and fast rule, as always, trade what's happening, not what you think ought to happen (see Chapters 10, 11, and 12).

- Signs of slowing growth or a weak economy tend to be *bullish,* or positive, for bonds and less friendly toward stock indexes and the dollar.

- Short-term interest-rate futures, such as in Eurodollars (see Chapter 10), may move in the opposite direction of the 10-year Treasury note (T-note) or long-term (30-year) bond futures.

- Gold, silver, and oil markets may respond aggressively to these reports. (To find out more about the markets in these commodities, see Chapters 13 and 14.)

- The Federal Reserve may make comments that accelerate or reverse the reactions and responses to economic reports.

Making It Easy on Yourself: Straddle

Futures and options traders can set up complicated strategies in advance of the release of a big economic report, but here is one that is simple to execute that can be very profitable, if you set it up correctly.

You can, for example, set up a *straddle,* which means that you buy both a *call,* which gives you an opportunity to profit if the market rises, and a *put,* which gives you an opportunity to profit if the market falls (see Chapter 5 for details on setting up straddles), on the *front contract,* which is the most active and frequently quoted futures contract at any given moment. After establishing the straddle, you then can sell the option (put or call) that's on the wrong side of the report.

The market will respond when it's surprised by a report. When the report is released and the market responds, you can participate in the move with a defined amount of risk, based on the way you set up your straddle — compared to what you can lose if you played the futures markets directly or you owned individual stocks that responded to the report.

For example, if the market decides that a higher-than-expected consumer price index was not necessarily inflationary, bond prices may actually rise and interest rates would fall.

Looking at two scenarios, you can compare what would happen if you owned a short position on T-note futures or a straddle on T-note futures.

If you had the short position in T-note futures, you are betting that T-note futures prices will fall in response to the economic report. In this case, however, the bond market actually goes up. That means that you will lose money because you own a short position.

If, on the other hand, you set up a straddle, you'd be in a better position, because a straddle has two components:

- ✔ A call that lets you profit when the underlying asset goes up in price
- ✔ A put that lets you profit when the underlying asset goes down in price

All you have to do is wait for the report and the market's response. In the example, the correct response would be to sell the put and hold onto the call.

Timing is also important. Note that waiting until the day before an important report is released will typically result in some pretty horrible pricing for the straddle. Option sellers are also aware of the report's scheduled release, and they raise the implied volatility on the options that they sell. The trick is to find options whose implied volatility does not reflect the buyer's anticipated statistical/price volatility that will result from the data/report's release.

Some of the factors to consider when setting up your strategy are that you can

- ✔ **Establish your straddle at least a day before the release of the data.** You can do it at the close of regular trading, or by using Globex in the overnight session. If you own a call option and a put option on the U.S. 10-year T-note futures, the call will likely rise in price as the put falls when the market responds to the CPI report. As the put falls, you can sell it (and take your loss) and review your choices of how to capitalize on the opportunity provided by the call.

- ✔ **Build multiple strategies simultaneously.** Because long- and short-term interest rates can move in opposite directions in response to news from economic reports, you can build other strategies (in addition to your T-note straddle) by using other options and contracts to build another straddle using Eurodollars, which are short-term interest-rate instruments. The T-note straddle is a long-term interest play. If you set up a straddle for T-bills or Eurodollars, you're setting up a play on short-term interest rates.

  You can also use the same kind of straddle strategy in the currency markets for the same trade, although doing so may be a bit more difficult than hedging your bets in the interest-rate and stock-index contracts.

Time works against you in the options market. Don't assume that you can sell the part of the options straddle that's going against you right away without first considering the possibility of managing the position. You can best accomplish that by working with the scenarios of options strategies that I provide in Chapter 5. For example, holding onto the put option, even if the market moves in a way that makes your call option more profitable, may be the right thing to do. After a short period of time, the market may reverse itself, and at that point, you can take profits on the call and see what happens with the put.

No hard-and-fast rules exist here other than keeping your head in the game, understanding what can happen before it does, and having a good road map to guide your decisions.

Chapter 7

Getting Technical Without Getting Tense

I'm a visual person, and my first experience with trading came from reading a chart in 1988, right before Memorial Day weekend, when I made my first stock trade: 100 shares of Quanex Corp. (NYSE:NX), a steel pipe and tube maker. I bought the stock somewhere around $12 and sold it at essentially the same price in a few days after it hadn't done much of anything. I was most unhappy with the commissions I had to pay and the fact that the stock didn't do what I had expected it to do — rise substantially in price.

I bought the stock based on a chart that exhibited a cup-and-handle pattern, a chart pattern made famous by *Investor's Business Daily* founder William O'Neil. This pattern isn't very useful in futures trading, but it can be helpful in trading stocks. It shows up when a stock forms a rounded base and then trades sideways in a narrow range, giving the appearance or impression of a cup and a handle.

In my first trade, I identified such a pattern, from an *Investor's Business Daily* chart. I was lucky. My first stock trade cost me only a hundred bucks, and I had enough money left to keep on trading. But that failure within my small account — breaking even and paying a $50 commission on the purchase and the sale — is what prompted me to find out more about charts and how they work together with the fundamentals of the markets.

What I didn't realize at the time was that Quanex had only recently come out of some major difficulties and was restructuring. A longer-term view of the chart would've revealed that trading was volatile and that the stock was, in fact, stuck in a trading range and not in a significant up or down or breakout trend.

I also discovered that I didn't know anything about the state of the steel industry at the time, the company's management, or its plans for the future. All are important when trading futures, options, and their underlying equities.

My mistake was that the cup-and-handle pattern, although genuine, was only a snapshot of the trading action over a few months. Had I known better — as I do now — I would've looked at a multiyear chart, and put the cup-and-handle pattern from the newspaper in its proper context.

The major lesson that I brought home during that relatively traumatic experience was that a chart pattern is nothing more than a chart pattern. In essence, it's only a beginning. Although you can't be a great futures trader without understanding and using technical analysis, aside from its key role in decision-making, it's also a tool that leads you toward exploring more information about why the pattern suggests that you need to buy, sell, or sell short the underlying instrument. See Chapters 8 and 12 for speculating strategies and using technical analysis for trading stock index futures.

In this chapter, I introduce you to the basics of recognizing interesting chart patterns that can lead you either to more study of the situation or to plug in what you already know about a market that is giving you a visual signal.

Picturing a Thousand Ticks: The Purpose of Technical Analysis

I like to think of stock or futures charts as summaries of the collective opinions of all the participants in a market. In essence, a *chart* is a tick-by-tick history of those opinions as they evolve over time, factoring in everything that market participants know, think they know, and expect to happen with regard to the asset for which the chart was compiled.

And although a picture is worth a thousand words to most people, to a trader, a chart is worth a chance to make some money. *Technical analysis,* or the use of price charts, moving averages, trend lines, volume relationships, and indicators for identifying trends and trading opportunities in underlying financial instruments, is the key to success in the futures and options markets. The more you know about reading charts, the better your trading results are likely to be.

After you become better acquainted with the basic drivers and influences of a particular market and how that information — key market moving reports, the major players involved, and the general fundamentals of supply and demand — fits into the big picture of the marketplace in general, the next logical step is to become acquainted with how the fundamentals are combined with the data that is compiled in price charts.

By becoming proficient at reading the charts of various security prices, you gain quick access to significant amounts of information, such as prices, general trends, and info about whether a market is sold out and ready to rally or *overbought,* meaning few buyers are left and prices can fall. By combining your knowledge of the markets and trading experiences with excellent charting skills, you vastly improve your market reaction time and your ability to make informed trades.

Technical analysis takes into account so much data and methodology that I can't possibly cover everything about it in only one chapter. So here are a few recommendations of excellent books in which you can find useful information as you progress with chart reading and trading. This list by no means is comprehensive, but these references serve as great supplements to this chapter. The books are not named in any particular order, because each has something good to offer and can serve you in different ways at different times:

- ✔ *Technical Analysis For Dummies* by Barbara Rockefeller (Wiley)
- ✔ *Trading For Dummies* by Michael Griffis and Lita Epstein (Wiley)
- ✔ *Technical Analysis of the Financial Markets* by John J. Murphy (New York Institute of Finance)
- ✔ *Candlestick Charting Explained: Timeless Techniques for Trading Stocks and Futures* by Gregory L. Morris (McGraw-Hill)

By reading the information in *Futures & Options For Dummies* and the books in the preceding list, you can build a foundation for technical analysis. However, as you gain trading experience, technical analysis will become more of an individualized endeavor for you, because you'll find that you gravitate to some areas more than others.

My own experience is that the simpler the analysis, the better, so my analytical style relies on moving averages, trend lines, and a few oscillators and indicators. Your style will develop as you learn more.

These guidelines can help organize your expectations about reading charts:

- ✔ Charting, in my opinion, isn't meant to replace fundamental analysis. In my trading, charts are meant to complement and enhance it, enabling you to make better decisions. That's not to say that there aren't those very talented people out there who make millions as pure chartists, because there are. Just keep an open mind on this.
- ✔ Understanding the fundamentals of supply and demand in your particular segment of the market is necessary for you to be able to trade futures and options based on charted technical signals. Knowing the fundamentals and the technical analysis makes investing your hard-earned money easier.
- ✔ Becoming familiar with more than one set of indicators and being able to combine them gives you more than one perspective from which to view

the markets. I use different combinations of indicators for different types of trading to find more ways of looking at the markets. Narrow-minded traders don't go too far.

✔ Learning the basics of following moving averages, identifying trend reversals, and drawing trend lines is important so you can add new layers of analysis, such as moving average crossover systems, Fibonacci retracements, and other more sophisticated techniques as you gain more experience. I discuss them all in this chapter.

✔ Continuing to expand your knowledge of technical analysis is important. You can do so by reading books and magazines like *Technical Analysis of Stocks & Commodities* and *Active Trader* magazine, which are excellent sources of interesting articles. *Investor's Business Daily,* either the print or the digital version of the paper on its Web site, is a chart reader's paradise for stock and futures traders.

✔ Exercising care so that you avoid clutter in your charts, even as you become more sophisticated in your approach to trading futures and options, is important. The simpler your charts, the better the picture you get and the better your decisions will be.

First Things First: Getting a Good Charting Service

You need a reliable *charting service* — a provider of quotes, charts, and market data — either one that your broker provides or an independent one such as Barchart.com, and you need a reliable set of software tools to be able to trade well. Many such services, programs, and combinations of the two are available. Some online trading houses offer a range of services, from bare-bones to sophisticated charting modules, on their respective Web sites.

Charting and quote services come in different packages. They start at bare minimum with basic charts and indicators and work their way up to very complex systems used by professionals.

Some brokers charge you extra for using their in-house, more sophisticated charting and software services, but others let you use them as part of a package deal, especially if you're an active trader placing trades through the sponsoring trading house. Extra charges vary, but a difference of $30 to $40 per month between the low end and the high end are not uncommon. You need to check with each individual service before deciding on a charting service.

No matter what, you're obligated to pay exchange fees to get real-time quotes from the exchanges, and those fees can add up to hundreds of dollars per month, depending on the number of exchanges from which you get quotes.

A good way to start is with a bare-bones charting system or the next step up. You can move up to progressively more elaborate systems as your trading skills become more sophisticated.

Software and charting services are available as downloads or as individually boxed packages that are Web ready.

Here are the characteristics that a charting service/online brokerage must have:

- **Reliability:** The service must be up and running when you want to place trades, and the data it provides must be accurate. If your service tells you to come back later because it's unavailable anytime when the markets are open — in other words, during peak trading times — you need to quit the unreliable service, demand a refund, and find another more reliable service. A good way to know whether a service is reliable is to find user's groups online or in your town and read their bulletin boards, or you can attend a meeting or two and listen to any complaints. You also need to sign up for a trial period so you can see how you like the system before you pay for it.

- **Accessibility:** The service needs to be available to you virtually anywhere, either online or by the use of a convenient online interface. You need to be able to check your quotes, open positions, and make your decisions from home, work, or elsewhere — even on your laptop at the airport.

- **Support:** Make sure that the service offers a toll-free telephone number to call for support and that it provides online support. Call the toll-free number before you purchase the software, just to test the availability of support. If your software malfunctions and you have to wait 30 minutes before talking to anyone, think about what effect that kind of a delay may have on your investments, especially if you're trying to place a trade when a big economic release is moving the markets.

- **Charting tools:** The charts provided by your charting service must be easy to read and user-friendly. You shouldn't have to punch five or ten keys or toggle your mouse for ten minutes while trying to make your chart look right. Sure, you can expect a learning curve with most programs, but if you can't make the software do what you want (and what the provider says it will do) after a few days, it isn't the right setup for you, and you need to consider getting a new program.

- **Real-time quotes:** Trading futures without real-time quotes is a sure path down the road to ruin. *Real-time quotes* are up-to-the-minute market prices, as they happen. They provide you with up-to-the-minute pricing for your particular security, futures contract, or option, thus enabling you to make timely decisions. Without them, the prices you get from your charting service may be subject to a standard 20-minute delay, during which markets can move to their limits (or even reverse course), leaving you faced with a margin call.

✔ **Live charts:** If you're going to trade, you need access to *live charts* that actually change with every tick (up or down movement) of the market. You can set them up to update the bars or candlesticks in your charts over a broad range of different time frames. The key: You want your chart to be updated to reflect the direction in which the market is trading.

✔ **Time-frame analysis:** Make sure that your charting service enables you to produce intraday charts. You want to be able to look at different time frames simultaneously. For example, if the long-term trend in the S&P futures is headed up on a six-month chart, but you see that a top is building on your intraday chart, your strategy for your S&P 500 Index fund may not be affected. But if you have two S&P 500 long contracts open and a few call options, you may need to adjust the strategies on your futures positions. For example, you may want to consider moving a sell stop closer to the current price if you're concerned about remaining in the position. Or you may want to sell the position outright.

✔ **Multiple indicators:** Make sure that the service to which you subscribe lets you plot price charts and multiple indicators at the same time. A standard page may include prices, a combination of moving averages, stochastics, and MACD and RSI oscillators. I go into more details on these indicators, and how to use them, in Chapter 8. Chapter 13 features a great example of how to use RSI in the energy markets. But for now, you need to concentrate on the charting information you need for technical analysis.

Some charting services offer access on hand-held electronic devices. This feature may be attractive to you if you're on the road and have open positions. Don't trade and drive, though.

You can get a pretty good preview of a good, basic, real-time charting program online at currency brokerage Xpresstrade.com: `www.xpresstrade.com/forex_charts.html`. This set of pages gives you free access to real-time quotes in the currency markets and provides a good overview of several levels of charting that are available. You can sample many free currency charts on this site, which also offers trading software. In general, this site is a good place to get your feet wet and to make use of some of the concepts in this chapter as they apply to the currency markets. The basic charting principles that you discover in one market are easily applicable to other markets.

Stockcharts.com (`www.stockcharts.com`) has an excellent free Java charting system on which you can practice drawing trend lines and analyzing charts.

Deciding What Types of Charts to Use

Security analysis relies on these four basic types of charts: line charts, bar charts, candlestick charts, and point-and-figure charts. Line charts almost never are used in trading. Bar and candlestick charts commonly are used in stocks and futures trading, and point-and-figure charts have a smaller but loyal following as trading tools.

I don't use point-and-figure charts, so I won't include them in this discussion. However, for a nice short overview of point-and-figure charting, check out *Technical Analysis For Dummies* (Wiley). If you like what you read there and want even more information about it, I also recommend John Murphy's *Technical Analysis of the Financial Markets* (New York Institute of Finance).

In general, I concentrate on bar and candlestick charting, but the bulk of my explanation in this chapter is based on candlestick charts, because they're the most commonly used charts in futures trading, and they offer the best information for shorter holding periods (like the ones common to day trading) or for longer trading periods where you have open positions that you may stay with for a few days.

Confused? Don't be. Both types of price charts are useful, and you'll develop your own style and preferences for the ones that work best for you. At this point, however, you merely need to be aware of what these charts are, how to recognize them, and how you can start thinking about putting them to use.

Bar charts are made up of thin single bars that define the movement of a price over a period of time. You can use one for analyzing a longer period of the market. I like them for this purpose because they're a bit less cluttered.

Candlestick charts, on the other hand, are made up of thin- and thick-bodied candles, such as in Figure 7-1, which explains why they basically look like candles with wicks at both ends. Figure 7-3, on the other hand, shows how you can incorporate candlestick patterns with key indicators, such as moving averages and oscillators. Both sets of charts offer the same basic kind of information — price, volume, and general direction of the market.

Stacking up bar charts

Bar charts used to be the most commonly displayed charts on most trading software programs. The bars displayed low and high prices for the specific time frame of the chart, with the body of the bar representing the range of trading action during that time frame. The time frame of a bar chart can be set according to whatever time period the user wants to use, regardless of whether it's for part of a day, a day, a week, a month, a year, or longer.

No hard-and-fast rules govern whether one type of chart is better than another. For example, bar charts and candlestick charts can be used for trading during any time span that you like, whether day trading or trading intermediate-term positions in which you stay with the underlying asset as long as the trend remains in your favor.

I prefer to use candlestick charts for intraday charts, because the color tells me what I want to know rapidly. For longer-term charts from which I just want to get the big picture about whether I want to buy or sell the underlying asset, I tend to use bar charts. The best thing to do is work with both kinds of charts when you are a beginner and develop your own tendencies.

Bar charts are useful when

- You're looking for a quick snapshot of a particular instrument, sector, or market, or when you're doing basic trend analysis.
- You're trading individual stocks or mutual funds, and you're looking at a long-term chart, such as a five-year time span.

Weighing the benefits of candlestick charts

Candlestick charts provide the same sort of information as bar charts, but they're better for making trading decisions, because they take the guesswork out of the overall trend in the underlying contract by the use of color coding. They're especially suited for the short-term trading that's common in the futures markets.

Candlestick charts can be broken down into several parts, including the following:

- **Real body:** The *real body* is the box between the opening and closing prices depicted by the candlestick. The body can be white or black. White bodies are bullish, meaning that the price depicted is rising. Black bodies are bearish, meaning that the price depicted by the candlestick is falling.
- **Lower and upper shadows:** The thin lines that extend above and below the real body (the candlewicks) are the *lower and upper shadows*. The shadows, or wicks, extend to the high and low prices for the time frame. Figure 7-1 summarizes the basic anatomy of candlestick charting.

Although bearish candlesticks traditionally are solid black, many software programs and charting services have replaced the black color with red to correspond with the standard method of displaying falling prices on quote systems. They've also replaced normally white bullish candlesticks with green ones, again to conform with the quote systems standards. In fact, many software programs will even let you decide which color you want to use for bullish or bearish charts. In this chapter, though, green and white refer to bullish conditions, and red and black mean bearish.

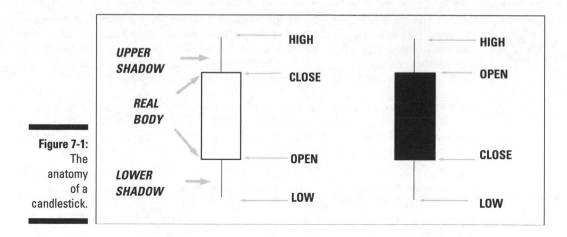

Figure 7-1:
The
anatomy
of a
candlestick.

When a candlestick has no body but only vertical and horizontal shadows, meaning that it is a line with no box, it forms what is known as a doji pattern. *Doji patterns* are a sign of indecision in the market. The three types of doji patterns (see Figure 7-2) are

- ✔ **Plain:** A *plain doji* looks like a cross and may just be a sign of a short-term pause. Other kinds of doji bars can be important signs of a trend reversal.

- ✔ **Dragonfly:** A *dragonfly doji* has a long lower shadow, or single-line body — the dragonfly appears to be flying upward. If you see this kind of pattern, it means that sellers were not successful in closing the contract at the lows of the day. When that happens as the price is bottoming out, it can mean that buyers are gaining an upper hand. If a dragonfly doji occurs after a big rally, it can mean that buyers are not able to take prices any higher.

- ✔ **Gravestone:** A *gravestone doji* looks like an upside-down dragonfly, with a longer upper shadow — the dragonfly appears to be flying downward. Gravestone dojis occur when buyers push prices higher but can't get prices to close at those higher levels. If a gravestone doji appears after a rally, it can signal that a reversal is coming.

On the other hand, a gravestone doji in a downtrend may mean that a bottom is forming.

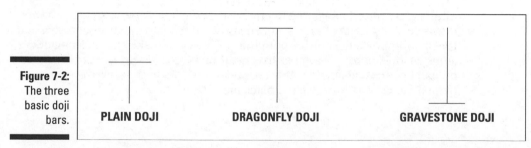

Figure 7-2:
The three
basic doji
bars.

Barbara Rockefeller points out in *Technical Analysis For Dummies* that a doji is best interpreted in the context of the pattern that you see in the preceding candlesticks.

Here is why candlesticks can be superior to bar charts:

- ✔ **Trends are easier to spot.** For example, a sea of rising green (or white), meaning a large grouping of bullish candles on a candlestick chart, is hard to mistake for anything other than a strong uptrend. Because candlesticks tend to have a body in most cases, the overall trend of the market often is easier to identify.

- ✔ **Trend changes are easier to spot.** Candlestick patterns can be dramatic and can help you identify trend changes before you can recognize them on bar charts. Some candlestick patterns are reliable at predicting future prices.

- ✔ **Shifts in momentum are as easy to spot.** Conditions in which a security is oversold and overbought, along with trends and other kinds of indicators, may be easier to spot on candlestick charts than on bar charts because of the presence of doji candles and color. For example, an engulfing pattern (see Figures 7-3 and 7-6 and the "Engulfing the trend" section, later in this chapter), which can be either negative or positive, is easier to spot in a candlestick chart.

Candlestick bars that are changing in size, especially at the end of a market run in a single direction, often are a sign that traders have reached an important point in how they're looking at the market and that an important end point may have been reached. For example, a long green (white) bar after a big rally often means that buyers are out of gas, and that's when you need to start paying attention to other signs of weakness. The same can be said after a long red (black) bar that follows a major bout of selling — you can start looking for signs of strength.

Getting the Hang of Basic Charting Patterns

Charting patterns can get out of control if you're not careful, so I like to keep it simple. That means that if you understand the basic tenets of charting and the most important, easy-to-spot patterns, you can make solid trading decisions as long as you remember that charting is most useful to you when you couple it with fundamental and situational analysis of the markets.

So before you start looking for patterns, follow this three-step rule:

1. **Get the feel for whether the basic trend is up or down.**

   Just look at the chart. If the price starts low and rises, it's an uptrend. If the opposite is true, it's a downtrend.

2. **Gauge how long that trend has been in place.**

   Using longer-term charts sometimes can help you spot just how long the trend has been in place.

3. **Consider the potential for a reversal.**

   The longer the trend has been in place, the higher the chance that it can turn the other way.

After you get comfortable with this process, you can advance to looking for the charting patterns that I describe in the sections that follow.

Analyzing textbook base patterns

Bases, whether tops or bottoms, are sideways patterns on price charts; they're pauses in the uptrends or downtrends in security prices. Bases are formed as some traders take profits and other traders establish new positions in the other direction.

In futures markets, someone always buys, and someone always sells. So a *base* is what happens when the number of buyers and sellers is in fairly good balance and prices remain steady.

Bases, in general, are points in the pricing of a security at which the market takes a break before deciding what to do next. A base can come before the market turns up or down, and it can last for a long time, even years. If after it forms a base, the market decides that more selling is called for, a new downturn, or falling prices, can start on a candlestick chart, despite the fact that the market has based after a decline. When the base forms after a rally, it can either resolve as a top, and the market can fall, or indicate only a pause in a continuing uptrend. You can't, however, predict with full certainty which way the markets will break after they pause (in either direction).

Figure 7-4 (later in this chapter) shows some key technical terms, including price tops and bottoms and basing patterns.

A base and a bottom accomplish the same thing, except that they can occur at different places. A base can be seen after the market climbs, after the market falls, or even during an uptrend or downtrend. A *bottom* usually is seen in retrospect, after the market rallies from the basing pattern. Similarly, a *top* usually is seen in retrospect, after the market declines from a basing pattern.

Although you can't predict tops and bottoms with 100-percent certainty, some reliable indicators can help you make better guesses than without them. Some reliable indicators are

- ✔ Specific patterns seen in price oscillators, such as when the RSI and MACD indicators move in different directions than the price of the security (see Chapters 8 and 13).

- ✔ Major turns in market sentiment (see Chapter 9).

- ✔ Key price movements above and below important price areas, such as resistance or support points (see Figure 7-4 and the section on "Using lines of resistance and support to place buy and sell orders," later in the chapter).

Downtrends

Here are some important factors to remember about a base at the bottom of a downtrend:

- ✔ A good trading bottom usually comes when everyone thinks that the market will never rise again.

- ✔ Downtrends can die in two ways: in a major selling frenzy or over a long period of time in which a base forms.

- ✔ At some point, all markets become oversold, and they bounce. Any such bounce can be the beginning of a new bullish uptrend in the market. After a long time of falling prices, you have to be ready to trade all turns in the market, even if you get taken out as the downtrend reasserts itself.

The most important area of a chart that is making a bottom is known as support. *Support* is a chart point, or series of points, that puts a floor under prices. That's where the buyers come in.

Uptrends

Here are some important factors to remember about a base at the top of an uptrend:

- ✔ Most participants at the top in the market are bullish, which is why three or four failures often occur before the market breaks toward the downside.

- ✔ Downturns that follow long-term rallies tend to spiral downward for a long time. That's exactly what happened with the multiyear chart of the dollar index shown Figure 7-5, later in the chapter.

> ✔ Tops are more likely to lead to reflex rallies, meaning that long-term downtrends are likely to be more volatile than are uptrends. For short sellers, it's a very rough ride, no matter which market you're trading.

The most important area of a chart that is making a top is known as resistance. *Resistance* is a chart point, or series of points, that puts a ceiling above prices. That's where sellers come in.

Using lines of resistance and support to place buy and sell orders

Drawing lines of resistance and support for a particular market or security (see Figure 7-4) can help you maintain your focus when placing your buy, sell, and short-sell orders. *Buy orders* usually are placed above resistance lines, and sell orders and sell-short orders are placed below support levels. One thing you can count on in the futures markets is the disciplined way by which traders respond to the signals, and that's what makes technical analysis ideal for futures trading.

Support and resistance lines define a *trading range*. In Figure 7-4 (later in the chapter), the trading range is called a basing pattern, because it precedes a breakout.

Support and resistance levels can be fluid, flowing up and down within the trading range. When combined with a moving average (see the next section), they provide a useful tool that indicates how market exit and entry points are progressing in relationship to the price of the security.

Moving your average

Moving averages are lines that are formed by a series of consecutive points that smooth out the general price trend. Moving averages are a form of a trend line.

In terms of a security's closing price, for example, a 50-day moving average is a line of points that represent the average of the closing prices of the security during each of the previous 50 days of trading.

Figure 7-3 shows two classic moving averages that are frequently used in technical analysis, the 50-day and 200-day moving averages. This particular figure shows a bullish long-term trend in which the bond fund is trading above the 200-day moving average and a crossover in which the price of the bond fund began trading above the 50-day moving average, a sign that prices were moving higher.

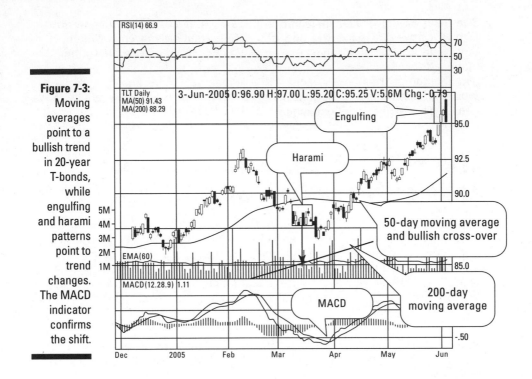

Figure 7-3: Moving averages point to a bullish trend in 20-year T-bonds, while engulfing and harami patterns point to trend changes. The MACD indicator confirms the shift.

Moving averages come in many different types, but for illustrative purposes, I use these three classics:

- ✔ **20 days:** The 20-day moving average traditionally is thought of as a short-term indicator.

- ✔ **50 days:** The 50-day moving average is considered a measure of the intermediate-term trend of the market.

- ✔ **200 days:** The 200-day moving average is considered the dividing line between long-term bull and bear markets.

As a general rule, when a market trades above its 200-day moving average, the path of least resistance is toward higher prices; however, no hard-and-fast rules exist. Some traders prefer to use a 21-day moving average instead of the 20-day average, while others think moving averages are useless altogether. I personally like using them to define dominant trends in the markets but not necessarily as guides to placing buy or sell stops.

Short-term charts, such as the charts used for day trading, where one price bar can equal as short a period of time as 15 minutes, have moving averages that measure minutes instead of days. The same decision rules apply, though.

The exception for me is when a market has been in a major uptrend or downtrend for an extended period, and it suddenly breaks below or above the 200-day average, which can signal that the long-term trend in that market has made a drastic change in the opposite direction.

Most trading software programs offer moving averages as part of their default charting systems. You may have to adjust these moving averages to your particular trading style or delete them if you decide that you don't like them.

The moving averages that you use in futures trading more than likely will be defined in terms of minutes or hours — rather than days or week — depending, of course, on the time frame you use to make your trades. Nevertheless, knowing the longer-term trends of the markets in which you're trading is essential for knowing when to make trades with the trend rather than against it. The basic rules are the same.

You can give your position more room to maneuver by using longer-term moving averages. In the futures markets, however, that strategy is not always the best, because some markets are more volatile than others. If you're using moving-average trading methods, your best bet is to back test several different combinations of moving averages for each specific market.

Back testing is a trading method by which you review or test your proposed strategy over a period of time using historic charts. For example, if you want to see how a market relates to its 20-day moving average, you can look at a five-year chart that includes the 20-day moving average and gauge what prices do when that market is priced above or below that average. When back testing, you're better off looking at many different indicators and combinations of them. You usually can find a combination that works best for any particular market.

When you back test your strategy, you improve your chances of finding the best combination of indicators to keep you on the right side of the trend.

Breaking out

A *breakout* happens when buyers overwhelm sellers and prices begin to rise. Breakouts usually follow some kind of basing pattern, or sideways movement in the market. A good rule is that the longer the base, the higher the likelihood of a good move after the underlying security breaks out of its trading range.

Figure 7-4 shows a great example of a chart breakout coming out of a head-and-shoulders pattern, a basic and easy-to-find pattern that can be found in all markets. Notice the almost perfect head-and-shoulders bottom in the crude oil contract marked *H* for the *head* and *S* for the left and right shoulders, as it forms the basing pattern that precedes the crude-oil price breakout in textbook fashion.

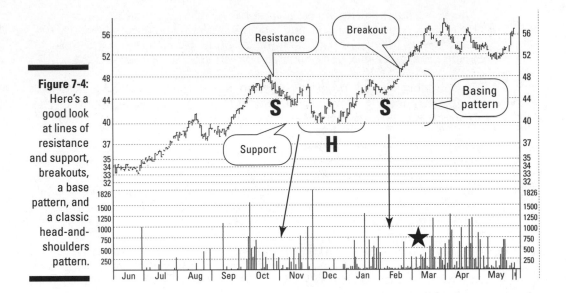

Figure 7-4:
Here's a good look at lines of resistance and support, breakouts, a base pattern, and a classic head-and-shoulders pattern.

Some of the characteristics of a head-and-shoulders base are that it

✔ Is a common but not always reliable technical pattern. It doesn't always point to a breakout the way it does in Figure 7-4.

✔ Always is shaped like a head and shoulders. Arrows in Figure 7-4 illustrate how the volume drops off as the shoulders are being formed, a textbook characteristic of the head-and-shoulders bottom. Head-and-shoulder tops are the same formation turned upside-down. When they happen, they can lead to a breakdown in the underlying asset.

✔ Indicates that any resulting breakout will take out the resistance at the neckline of the head-and-shoulders pattern.

✔ Results in an increase in share volume as the price breaks out above the head-and-shoulders bottom (see the five-pointed star in Figure 7-4). The volume increase is another important characteristic of a chart breakout, and it indicates that many buyers are interested in the security and that prices are likely to go higher.

Using trading ranges to establish entry and exit points

Markets often trade in channels. A *channel* is another name for a trading range. Figure 7-5 shows a rising or uptrending channel. The upper line defines the top of the channel, and the lower line defines the bottom of the channel.

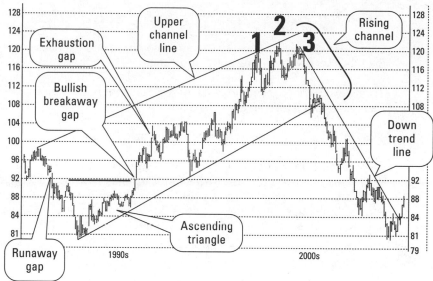

Figure 7-5:
Gaps, channels, trend lines, triangles, and other basic technical analysis patterns.

Regardless of whether the trend is up or down, channel lines can point to great places to set trading entry and exit points for these reasons:

✔ The longer the channel holds in place, the more important a break above or below it becomes for a particular market or security.

✔ They can indicate a multiyear bear market if the breakout occurs below the rising channel. (That's what happened to the dollar in the late 1990s in Figure 7-5.)

✔ They can indicate that a major bottom is in place and that a bear market has come to an end if a downtrend line is broken. (That's what happened to the dollar in 1985 and 2005 in Figure 7-5.)

Resistance is the opposite of support, because it's a price point on a chart above which prices cannot move higher. It's also the place where sellers are lurking and a place where breakdowns ultimately occur. A *breakdown* is a point in the market when sellers overwhelm buyers and prices begin to fall. A breakdown usually comes after a market forms a top. Figure 7-5 shows the U.S. Dollar Index making a multiyear top. In this case, the top actually is indicated by a triple top, because the dollar failed to move higher in three separate attempts. (The numbers *1, 2,* and *3* correspond to the three tops, or failures, before the breakdown began in Figure 7-5.)

As with most definitive bases at the top of an uptrend, the crucial signal is the failure to make a new high for the move. Note how the number *3* top is lower than the number *2* top and then is followed by fast and furious selling.

Seeing gaps and forming triangles

Gaps and triangles are two of the more common occurrences on price charts. Each has its own meaning and importance.

Triangle, or wedge formations, can predict future price actions more reliably than gaps, but gaps can also be useful.

The three basic triangle shapes found on price charts are

- **Ascending triangles:** These triangles point upward and can be good signs of a price pattern with an upward bias (see Figure 7-5). In that example, the Dollar Index uses the lower rising channel line as support to build an ascending triangle. A horizontal line (above the triangle) marks the resistance point that completes the triangle.

- **Descending triangles:** These triangles point downward and are the opposite of ascending triangles, usually coming before downtrends.

- **Symmetrical triangles:** These triangles are symmetrical in that they show neither an upward nor downward trend and thus are unpredictable price formations.

Gaps, on the other hand, are unfilled points on price charts. They are more frequently visible and therefore less important in the price charts of thinly traded instruments, such as obscure futures contracts and some small stocks. However, when they occur in more common contracts and more heavily traded stocks, they can be much more important and have the following effects (Figure 7-5 shows all three such gaps):

- **Breakaway gaps:** This gap happens when an underlying security gets out of the gate very strongly at the start of the trading day. Breakaway gaps often come after the release of economic indicators, such as the monthly employment report. They are signs of a strong market.

    Breakaway gaps are more meaningful when they are bigger than the usual trading range of a security. For example, if you know that a futures contract usually trades within a range of three point ticks and it opens ten ticks higher or lower, the result is a major breakaway gap.

> ✔ **Runaway gap:** This gap occurs when a second gap appears on a price chart in the same direction as a breakaway gap. Runaway gaps are signs of continuing and accelerating price trends.
>
> ✔ **Exhaustion gap:** This gap is a sign that a market has run out of buyers or sellers and indicates almost a last gasp in the market before the trend is reversed. Some exhaustion gaps may have telltale candlestick patterns associated with them, such as a hanging man (see the next section), doji, or cross.

Seeing through the Haze: Common Candlestick Patterns

Even though candlestick patterns are not 100 percent reliable, they certainly are worth paying attention to. As you gain more and more experience, you'll come to know many different patterns. In this section, I concentrate on the more common and meaningful patterns that can serve as signals that a market is starting to reverse course.

Engulfing the trend

An *engulfing pattern* is what you see when the second (or next) day's real body, or candlestick, completely covers the prior day's candlestick. An engulfing pattern signals a potential reversal. Figures 7-6 and 7-3 show first a schematic of bullish and bearish engulfing patterns (Figure 7-6) and a real-time (Figure 7-3) engulfing pattern. Note that the body of the second candle is larger than the first candle and that it predicts a change of the trend. The bullish engulfing pattern predicts a trading bottom, and the bearish engulfing pattern, a top. Action on the third day often is key to whether the pattern will hold.

Engulfing patterns are characterized by a second-day candlestick that is larger than, or engulfs, the first day's candlestick. The larger candlestick predicts a potential change in the trend of the underlying security's price. For example, a *bullish engulfing pattern* usually appears at or near a trading bottom and predicts an upturn in prices, while a *bearish engulfing pattern* appears at or near the trading top and predicts a downturn in prices.

Engulfing

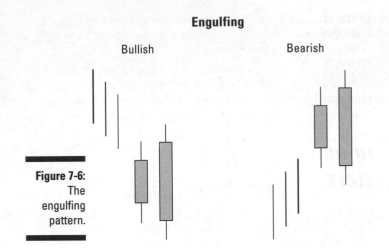

Bullish

Bearish

Figure 7-6:
The
engulfing
pattern.

In *Candlestick Charting Explained* (McGraw-Hill), Greg Morris, a mutual fund manager (PMFM funds), software designer, and an early proponent of candlestick charting, offers several important rules of recognition for engulfing patterns:

- ✔ **A definite trend must be under way.**

- ✔ **The second-day candlestick's body must completely engulf the prior day's candle.** In other words, the high and low prices of the second-day candlestick must be respectively higher and lower than the high and low for the previous day. Morris points out the subtleties of engulfing patterns by indicating that if the tops and bottoms of both candlesticks are identical, the pattern isn't engulfing, but if one or the other are equal and the second-day candle still engulfs the previous day's candle on the other end, the pattern is valid.

- ✔ **The color of the first day's candle must reflect the trend.** So if prices are trending upward, and the first candle is red, the pattern doesn't hold.

- ✔ **The second day's candle must be the opposite color of the prevailing trend.** This rule is the corollary to the previous rule. If the first day's candle is red or black, showing a downtrend in prices, the second day's candle must be green or white.

Figure 7-3 (earlier in the chapter) offers a great example of a real-life engulfing pattern that meets all criteria. Notice the following:

✔ The bar started out at a higher opening price, but clearly closed at a lower level, a sign of a clear reversal.

✔ The engulfing bar was huge compared to the prior day.

Hammering and hanging for traders, not carpenters

The hammer and the hanging man also are common patterns. A *hammer* is a small white candlestick with a long shadow, while a *hanging man* is a small black candlestick with a long shadow (see Figure 7-7).

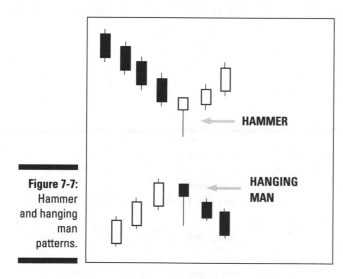

Figure 7-7:
Hammer
and hanging
man
patterns.

Making sense of these patterns is difficult, because they can appear virtually anywhere on just about any chart. They are best used after a long series of bars of the same color and are most reliable as indicators of a possible reversal.

A white-body hammer that follows a long series of black bars in a downtrend usually means that a reversal is coming. A black hanging man pattern that appears after several white bars in an uptrend usually means that some selling and a downturn is on the way.

Seeing the harami pattern

A *harami pattern* is an excellent example of a reversal pattern. It forms when a long candlestick of one color is followed by a smaller candlestick of another color. The color of the second candle indicates which way the market is likely to go. You can see it in a real-world example back in Figure 7-3.

The harami is an excellent pattern for indicating a trend change or pause. The stock needs to be in a strong trend, and for the harami to be a valid pattern, the second real body must form completely inside the first. The color of the second candle needs to be the opposite of the first. Confirmation of this pattern is recommended.

A harami pattern is most useful when a trend has been in place for some time, like the six-week downtrend in Figure 7-3, but you need to keep close tabs on the volume along with the candlesticks (the way I explain in the next few paragraphs).

Say, for example, that you've been selling bonds (I use the exchange traded fund TLT in this example, but it is equally applicable to bond futures) short for several days and suppose that you're starting to get comfortable with a downtrend when you spot a long red (black) candle on your chart. Your initial response, especially if you're using bar charts, is to think that the downtrend is extending and that you're going to make more money in the next few days.

However, on the next day, prices reverse and close higher after other short sellers have covered their short positions.

Although the bar for the second day is green (white), it's nevertheless smaller as new short sellers come into the market at the end of the day. They're thinking that the downtrending security is a good opportunity to initiate new short sales after missing out on the last move.

You gain a more accurate picture of the situation by looking at the volume on the two days, as shown by the down-pointing arrow in Figure 7-3. Average volume on the long black day followed by higher volume on the short white day suggests that the trend is about to change, and you indeed have a harami pattern.

Bears, bulls, and a bunch of crazy names

According to John Murphy's *Technical Analysis of the Financial Markets* (New York Institute of Finance), 68 different candlestick patterns are commonly used by futures traders. Murphy lists 8 bullish continuation patterns, 8 bearish continuation patterns, and 26 bullish and bearish reversal patterns. Some candlestick patterns are composed of two, three, four, and five candlesticks. Some of my favorite names for patterns are

- ✔ Abandoned baby
- ✔ Dark cloud cover
- ✔ Concealing swallow
- ✔ Three white soldiers
- ✔ Three black crows

The action on day three tells you whether the harami pattern will hold true and send prices higher.

Figure 7-3 shows real-time candlestick patterns that defined the trend in the bond market in 2005. The chart is of the Long-Term Bond Exchange-Traded fund (TLT). The TLT is closely related to the U.S. 10-year Treasury note and the U.S. Long Bond (30-year) futures contracts. The TLT can be traded both long and short, and offers a good trading vehicle for investors who want to participate in the overall trend of futures markets without actually opening an account with a futures broker. The commission and the effort spent trading the TLT is the same as with trading any stock.

Several important technical-analysis-related points to get out of the harami pattern in Figure 7-3 include

- ✔ The arrow shows the close correlation between the low-volume red or down day and the higher volume up day and clearly conforms to the rules laid out by Morris where a low-volume down day is followed by a higher volume up day.
- ✔ Day three is an up day, confirming the trend change.
- ✔ The harami was followed by more selling until the market hit a lower bottom.
- ✔ The MACD indicator also correctly correlated the bottom by crossing over a few days after the harami pattern occurred.

This is a perfect example of how you can use candlestick charts and standard indicators together to form accurate buy and sell signals.

Chapter 8

Speculating Strategies That Use Advanced Technical Analysis

In This Chapter
▶ Understanding one market's effects on other markets
▶ Using moving averages, oscillators, and trend lines to understand your market
▶ Aligning technical indicators to make a trade

*I*nexperienced investors tend to ignore the value of a good understanding of technical analysis. That ignorance, on the part of those who ignore charting, is, of course, bliss for traders like you (and me), because it gives you an advantage, albeit a small one, in light of the fact that the big guys with the big money are all chartists, and most of them are excellent at the craft. Bob Woodward, in his book about Alan Greenspan, aptly entitled *Maestro* (Simon & Schuster), describes how the chairman of the Federal Reserve has one of the best technical charting data arrays in the world and is an avid watcher of the financial markets using charts.

Good friends of mine in the business tell me about employees of the Federal Reserve they've taught as students at technical analysis seminars.

The truth is that any good speculator with an ounce of honesty will tell you that they rely as much on their charts as they do on information gathered by other means.

The true money-making trader uses both fundamental and technical analyses. To be sure, analyzing the futures and options markets is both an art and a science and just a little bit of cooking, like when you add that extra salt and pepper to a pot of chili.

The bottom line is that your trading will be enhanced when you apply what you know about the economy and the markets to your charts. And in this chapter, I put together several topics from the fundamental and technical worlds to help you do just that.

Using Indicators to Make Good Trading Decisions

Indicators are instruments that help you confirm what you see when you look at a chart. They are an intrinsic part of trading if you use technical analysis. Graphs produced by the indicators are displayed along with the prices of the underlying asset on the same chart. The indicators are derived from formulas whose components include the price of the underlying asset.

The more common ones are known as moving averages, oscillators, channels (of which there are several kinds), and trend lines. These indicators are part of most price charts in the futures markets (see Figure 8-1).

Making good use of moving averages

A *moving average* is a series of points that enable you to determine which way a major trend is moving within a market and whether your trade is with or against the trend (see Chapter 7). Long-term charts use days and weeks for moving averages. Short-term, intraday (within the same trading day) charts use minutes to create moving averages. Generally speaking, moving averages are useful tools because

✔ Markets trade higher when prices are consistently above the moving average.

✔ When markets cross over a moving average in one direction or the other (above or below), you need to be mindful of a potential change or shift in the existing trend.

✔ The longer the moving average, the more important the trend and trend reversals become. For example, when the dollar crosses above its 200-day moving average, the chance that the trend has changed from a falling market to one that's about to rise is greater than when it crosses a 50-day moving average.

✔ Trading by using only moving averages is risky business. Market prices can jump above and below them many times before actually starting a new trend or continuing an old one. Prices repeatedly jumping above or below a moving average during a short period of time are a great example of a *whipsaw*. Whipsaws can occur when you use extremely short-term moving averages or even when you use long-term moving averages (like the 200-day moving average).

Comparing multiple moving averages of varying lengths (20, 50, and 200 days) with the daily price for an instrument enables traders to find important breakout and crossover points that they use to formulate their trading plans. Figure 8-1 compares these key data from June 2004 to June 2005 with that of the euro currency. Note how in October 2004 the value of the euro rallied above its 20- and 50-day moving averages and how the 20-day moving average of the euro moved above its 50-day moving average, creating a bullish crossover. A *bullish crossover* is an episode in which a shorter-length moving average crosses above a longer-term moving average, which usually is good confirmation of a rising trend and a signal to buy the underlying asset. A *bearish crossover* is the opposite, when a shorter-length moving average falls below a longer-term moving average. It usually confirms a falling trend. Figure 8-3 also highlights a bearish crossover.

A good trading technique is to buy a small stake in a market when a bullish crossover occurs. That's what you see labeled as "buy point 1" in Figure 8-1. You can see that the euro moved sideways for a bit longer and then broke out; that's "buy point 2" in Figure 8-1.

The buy signal held true, and the euro's rally stayed alive until the bearish crossover occurred and the euro fell below both its 20-day and 50-day moving averages in January 2005.

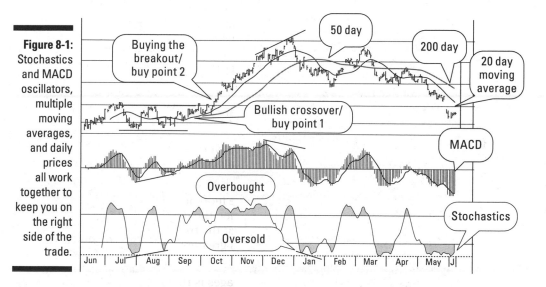

Figure 8-1: Stochastics and MACD oscillators, multiple moving averages, and daily prices all work together to keep you on the right side of the trade.

Figure 8-1 is important because the chart points to a significant amount of information about the value of the euro, including the following:

✔ **Downtrends:** When the euro traded below its 20-, 50-, and 200-day moving averages, it progressed through short-, intermediate-, and long-term downtrends.

✔ **A negative crossover:** When both the 20- and 50-day moving averages crossed below the 200-day moving average, the resulting *negative crossover* confirmed a long-term downtrend.

> ✔ **A positive crossover:** When the 20-day moving average crossed above the 50-day moving average, the resulting positive crossover confirmed an uptrend.
>
> ✔ **A sustained uptrend:** The rally in the euro that followed the positive crossover points to a sustained uptrend.

Understanding and using oscillators

Oscillators are mathematical equations that are graphed onto price charts so you can more easily decide whether the price action is a correction in an ongoing trend or a change in the overall trend. Oscillators usually are graphed above or below the price charts.

Several oscillators are commonly used by traders. In this section, I show you two of them, the MACD and stochastic oscillators, in detail. Discovering the basics of these two oscillators will enable you to easily understand the rest of them, because they all share the same characteristics.

Biting into a Big Mac without special sauce: MACD

The *Moving Average Convergence Divergence* (MACD) is the result of a formula that's based on three moving averages derived from the price of the underlying asset. When applied to the asset prices, the MACD formula smoothes out fluctuations of that asset. For example, in Figure 8-1, the MACD is smoothing out three moving averages based on the price of the euro. The software provided by your charting service will help you to display MACD oscillators based either on your own trading criteria or the software's default criteria.

The MACD data shown in Figure 8-1 are displayed as a histogram. An MACD oscillator that's moving up usually is considered a bullish development, confirming that an uptrend has been well established when it actually crosses above the zero line.

On the left side of the MACD oscillator chart, note how the line under the MACD slopes higher, while the line under the price of the euro on the index chart above it is flat. The sloping MACD means the oscillator established a higher low, even though the price remained flat, which is called *positive divergence.* Although prices did not rise, the positive divergence points to selling momentum that is less than it was during the previous low on the MACD oscillator, and that's a signal that prices may be getting ready to rise. In Figure 8-1, the MACD oscillator was right.

In November, however, a turnaround occurred as the MACD histogram rolled over. The price of the euro continued to rise, but the MACD provided a *nonconfirmation* signal, meaning that its overall direction was now lower. Note how the line above prices is on the rise from late November through early

January, but the second peak on the MACD is lower than the first. This divergence is a sign that buyers are getting tired and that prices may be getting ready to fall. And again, Figure 8-1 shows the MACD was right.

Taking stock with stochastics

Stochastic oscillators indicate classic overbought and oversold situations in the markets. An *overbought market* occurs when prices have been in a rising trend for a long time and buyers are starting to get tired. An *oversold market* is just the opposite; sellers are getting tired as prices are trending down. Whenever either of these situations occurs, as a trader, you need to know whether your position is in danger of getting caught in a trend change.

Markets can remain in overbought or oversold conditions for short or long periods of time before the trend changes. A four-month rally in the euro during the fall of 2004 was overbought for a long time based on stochastic oscillator analysis. So if you had sold based on this indicator alone, you would've missed out on making a lot of money. In fact, looking at Figure 8-1, you can see that the stochastic indicator showed the market was overbought when the breakout occurred at buy point 2. Without the crossover and MACD indicators for backup, you would've sold way too early.

Thus, like any indicator, stochastics need to be used in combination with other indicators. Figure 8-1 shows how you can combine MACD, stochastics, and moving-average crossovers to execute your trading plan most efficiently.

I use stochastic indicators as an early warning system. When stochastics signal overbought or oversold markets, I take it to mean that I should start paying close attention to my other indicators, such as MACD and moving averages.

Note in Figure 8-1 that before the rally, the second low on the stochastic indicator was higher than the first, just like the pair of lows on the MACD, thus providing *confirmation* of the MACD data by the stochastics, which also ultimately turned out to be correct.

The trend became clear in January when the stochastic oscillator indicated the market was oversold. The second low was lower than the first, correctly indicating a negative situation in which the euro fell to a lower low soon after the lower low was reached on the stochastic oscillator.

By using moving averages and two simple oscillators, you could've easily traded those profitable moves in the euro on the long and the short sides.

 When watching moving averages and oscillators together, use minute-based moving averages for shorter-term trading. The method is the same except that you're reading the pricing data in a different, shorter, time frame. You may want to give yourself another layer of information to confirm the shorter-term data by looking for key reversal patterns on candlestick charts.

Getting relative (not jiggy) with RSI

The RSI (Relative Strength Indicator) was developed by Welles Wilder and was introduced in 1978. I once got a letter from Wilder about an indicator that I developed in my early days in the business. I still have the letter and look at it once in a while. It was a nice thing for a well-known person in the business to do for someone who was just getting started. But more than stroke my ego, the letter got me interested in RSI.

RSI is a very useful tool, by itself or in combination with other oscillators.

RSI uses a mathematical formula to measure price momentum and calculate the relative strength of current prices compared to previous prices.

Like stochastic indicators, RSI's strength is that it's good at telling when the market is overbought or oversold (see the previous section).

I like to use RSI in markets that tend to stay in a particular trend for an extended period. Energy markets are an example. See Chapter 13 for a classic example of how to use RSI.

Seeing how trading bands stretch

As your use of technical analysis grows more sophisticated, you'll want to know the potential price limits of certain trades. This information helps you ponder when to enter and exit trades and when markets may stall and reverse trend. A good tool for those purposes is a trading band.

Trading bands also are known as trading envelopes, because they surround prices, thus providing visual cues about where price support and resistance levels are at any given time. I like to think of trading bands as variable channels. Chapter 7 shows you trading channels that are defined by trend lines that you draw. Trading bands are similar to trend channels in that they provide you a visual framework of a trading range. The only difference is that trading bands are more dynamic, because they change with every tick in the price of the underlying asset.

Don't get confused here. Trading bands are, in fact, trading channels that change with every tick. In other words, trend channels, which are drawn either by hand or with software, are straight lines, pointed either up or down, connecting the high or low points of the top or the bottom of the price range. When you look at trading channels, you're getting a visual representation of the trading range.

Trading bands go further by giving you both the parameters of the trading range along with clues as to where the trading range may be heading in the future.

The most commonly used trading bands are Bollinger bands, which were introduced and made famous by John Bollinger, a pioneering technical analyst and television commentator.

Introducing Bollinger bands

Bollinger bands essentially mark flexible trading channels that fluctuate by two standard deviations above and below a moving average. The bands are helpful in defining trading ranges and telling you when a change in the trend is coming. Bollinger introduced the bands with the 20-day moving average, but you can set them up for use with any moving average, and they'll work the same way.

In terms of the market, a *standard deviation* is a statistical expression of the potential variability of prices, or the potential trading range. The two-standard deviation method is a default used by most software programs because it catches most intermediate term trends. That means when you punch up Bollinger bands on your trading software, you'll see bands defining the trading range that are two standard deviations above and two standard deviations below the market price.

As you progress and become more experienced, you may want to use smaller or larger standard deviations. If you want more frequent signals, you shorten or use less standard deviation. For longer-term trading, you use larger or more standard deviation.

Don't get too hung up in the statistical language. The important concept to remember is that the market tends to follow some semblance of order, nonlinear order, which is predictably unpredictable.

The Bollinger bands are good at displaying the order for you. And here's how. Figure 8-2 shows you how to apply Bollinger bands to a trading situation that involves the price of the euro during the same period of time highlighted in Figure 8-1.

When using Bollinger bands to analyze the markets, you need to

- **Watch their general direction.** If the bands are rising, then the market is in an uptrend. If they're falling, the market is in a downtrend.

- **Watch the width between the upper and lower bands.** Shrinking Bollinger bands — where the distance between the upper and lower bands is narrowing — signal a decrease in volatility and indicate that a big move is on the way. I like to call this a *squeeze*. Arrows in Figure 8-2 point to a nice squeeze in the bands that preceded a false breakout and a clear downturn, or *breakdown*. Here's another good squeeze: Notice how the bands tightened around prices before the euro broke out and headed higher. Decreasing price volatility is usually a prelude to a big move. Widening bands usually are a signal that the trend has changed

and that the general tendency of prices is likely to continue in the direction of the new trend.

Futures traders work in a time frame of a gnat, and a breakdown can be two hours of falling prices if you're using charts featuring five-minute bars (see Chapter 7 for more about charting).

The direction is not always certain, though, so you need to wait until the market moves, and catch the move as early as possible.

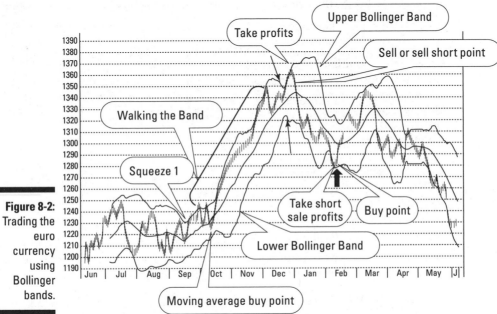

Figure 8-2:
Trading the euro currency using Bollinger bands.

Bollinger bands also are excellent for staying with the trend. Watch for prices to be

✔ **Walking the bands.** Markets that move along either of the (upper or lower) bands for an extended time are interpreted as a signal that the current trend is going to continue for some time. The bracket from September to November shows a nice example of how the euro walked the band for a good while during its late 2004 rally.

I realize that reference to "some time" can be frustrating and may be confusing to readers who require certainty in their trading and more precise time frames. But when you're trading, all you can do is understand the possibilities and monitor your trades accordingly until the market tells you that the trend has changed. That's one of the reasons that you should never rely on a single indicator without using others as backups. In Figure 8-2, the "some time" turned out to be three months. By monitoring your trade closely, you could've followed this market movement for the entire period.

✔ **Breaking outside the bands.** When a market's price breaks outside the bands around a moving average, it usually means you can expect reversal in the market — a trip to the opposite band. Breakouts don't always indicate a shift in the market, but if the market goes outside the bands enough times, the price eventually makes a trip in the opposite direction.

When the market touches either of the bands, it's only a matter of time before it eventually touches the other band; however, the specific amount of time it takes for this kind of reversal to occur is not as predictable.

The block arrow in February in Figure 8-2 points to a great example of how the lower band can serve as a launching pad for a bounce back up to the upper band. The euro not only touched the band, but spent several days just outside of it.

An easy way to remember how Bollinger bands work is to think of them as tight rubber bands and the moving average as a magnet. When the rubber bands get stretched too far, the magnet pulls the market back into a more normal state, inside the bands.

Trading with Bollinger bands

Bollinger bands can be used alone, but they work much better when used in combination with oscillators and other moving averages.

As with any indicator, Bollinger bands are not perfect. Sometimes, the price of the underlying asset rises above the upper band, and you think that a trip to the lower band is possible, thus prompting you to sell. Sometimes, you'll be right. At other times, however, prices fall back inside the band, stay there a couple of days, and rally right back up, continuing to walk along the upper band.

That's when other indicators, such as MACD and stochastic oscillators and moving-average crossovers, come in handy as checks and balances.

You can visualize a good example of Bollinger bands being used in conjunction with other indicators by viewing Figures 8-1 and 8-2 together. The squeezing Bollinger bands in Figure 8-2 occurred at the same time that the MACD oscillator failed to confirm the higher high in the euro currency. The combination of the two — the bands signaling that a big move was in the offing and the negative divergence in the MACD — was confirmed when the euro began a downtrend.

I use Bollinger bands on all my trades, regardless of whether I'm looking at intraday 15-minute candlestick charts or longer-term daily or weekly bar charts. And I always use a 20-period chart marked with candlesticks at 15-minute intervals for my intraday charting. Using short-term charts, I can tell what the market is doing much better than I can when using longer-term charts. You'll figure out what works best for you when you gain more trading experience. The only rule when it comes to charting: Use the parameters that you're comfortable with and that make you money.

You can use Bollinger bands, oscillators, and moving averages as guidelines when placing your trades. Here's how:

- ✔ **When looking to go long (see Chapters 7 and 20),** you can set your buy points just above the lower Bollinger band so that you catch the bounce when prices bounce back into the band, and a new uptrend starts.

- ✔ **When looking to go short,** you're selling high; thus you put your sell-short entry point as the market breaks, and it comes back inside the upper band. In this case, you're looking for prices to break and to profit from the break, which is why you're selling short.

- ✔ **When taking profits,** you can use the moving average to set your sell points to take profits based, of course, on where other indicators show the market is headed when market prices reach those points.

- ✔ **When adding to your position (buying),** you can use the moving average to establish new buy points to bolster your position. When prices fall back to the moving average and hold, you can add to positions there.

- ✔ **When the market breaks outside the upper band,** on the way up, you can sell your position there if you're long. See the "Take profits" arrow in Figure 8-2. As the market breaks back into the band, you can then sell the market short.

- ✔ **When the market drops below the lower band,** you can take profits on short positions and go long at the lower band.

Trading with trend lines

Trend lines are much like Bollinger bands but without so much flexibility. Trend lines directly reflect the overall trend of the market, but they're static because you draw them on your charts with the drawing tool in your software package. This tool is best used for spotting a key change in the overall direction of the underlying market.

Trend lines are just lines on charts, such as the ones shown in Figure 8-5 (numbered 1 through 4). The correct way to draw a trend line is to connect at least two points in the price chart without crossing through any other price areas. If you can draw the trend through more than two points, it can become more accurate; however, trend lines are another tool that needs to be used with other indicators.

You can use trend lines for both short- and long-term trading, and in both cases they tell you the same thing, the overall trend of the market. The important trend-line concept to remember is that rising prices remain in a rising trend as long as they're above the trend line. Likewise, falling prices remain in a downtrend as long as they're below the falling trend line. Breaks above or below the trend lines signal that the trend has changed. Correctly drawn trend lines (see previous paragraph) help you stay on the right side of the market as follows:

✔ **In uptrends,** trend lines connect the lowest low to the next low that precedes a new high without passing through any other points. Two uptrend lines, numbered 2 and number 3, are shown in Figure 8-3, a long-term chart covering five years of trading in the U.S. Dollar Index. The price break above Trend line 1 shows you when to buy right after a downtrend line is broken. Trend line 3 shows you how to add to your position as the price holds above the trend line.

✔ **In downtrends,** trend lines connect the highest high to the next high that precedes a new low without passing through any other points. Two downtrend lines in Figure 8-3 include an intermediate-term trend line that lasts for month, Trend line 1, and a long-term trend line, Trend line 4. Trend line 1 shows you how to remain in a short position as long as the price remains below the falling trend. Trend line 4 shows you that you need to be buying the dollar when the price of the dollar breaks above the multiyear trend. Needless to say, as long as prices stayed below Trend line 4, the primary trading direction was to be short the dollar.

Short-term trend-line trading

When trading futures, at times you can easily get caught up in the jargon. Short-term trading should never be confused with short selling. Short selling means that you're betting that prices will fall. Short-term trading means that you're not interested in holding a position for longer than a few hours or days at most.

To trade the long side (or buy by using trend lines), you can

✔ Buy a portion of your position when a downtrend that you've been following, or shorting, is broken (see Figure 8-3).

✔ Draw your trend line as the market is developing an uptrend and then buy when the market touches the uptrending line for the third time without breaking below it.

✔ Supplement trend lines with oscillators and moving averages to make sure that the odds of a winning trade are increased. You should never rely on only one indicator to make your trades.

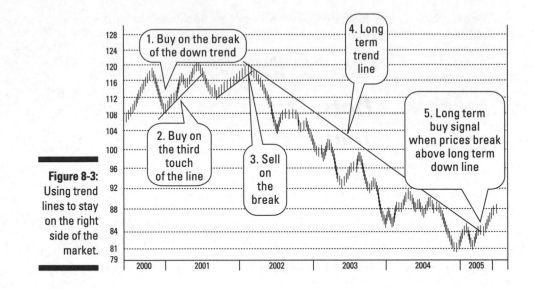

Figure 8-3:
Using trend lines to stay on the right side of the market.

I find it easier to trade after a trend line is initially broken. Sometimes I use *successful tests,* or price moves back to the trend line without breaking the line, to add to my position (see next section). This strategy works well in the oil markets and with the dollar.

Long-term trend-line trading

Say you've been short selling a downtrend in the value of the U.S. dollar for several weeks, but you're not sure how much longer the position will do well. Aside from using moving averages, Bollinger bands, and a few oscillators, a good trend line can be the best indicator for the job.

Figure 8-3, a five-year chart of the value of the U.S. dollar, provides a great example of how drawing trend lines on long-term charts can help you spot a meaningful change in a long-term trend.

A meaningful break in a long-standing trend often means that the trend is changing directions. You can see in Figure 8-3 that at least a meaningful inter-mediate-term advance in the dollar began in 2005 and lasted for several months following a break in a long-term downtrend.

If you're drawing trend lines, then it's a good bet that big-money players are drawing them, too. As Barbara Rockefeller points out in *Technical Analysis For Dummies* (Wiley), big traders sometimes sell their positions long enough to find out what happens when market prices touch the trend line. In essence, that means trend lines can encounter points of high volatility, and you can get shaken out of a position more than once if you're not careful, especially when you base your trades only on trend lines. Instead of relying on only one indicator, don't hesitate to use trend lines in conjunction with other indicators, just to make sure that the odds of success are as much on your side as possible.

Lining Up the Dots: Trading with the Technicals

Technical analysis is like solving puzzles — kind of like connecting the dots. You start with a price chart, and you start adding lines, bands, oscillators, and indicators.

As you go along, things can grow cluttered, and you can lose your way. The good thing is that trading software has "Clear" buttons, which means you can wipe out all the lines and squiggles on your charts and start over anytime things get out of control. Save your work first, though, in case you need to refer back to it.

In the next section, I deal with chart clutter by focusing on staying with the trend.

Identifying trends

Trading is not only about swimming with the tide; it's also about knowing when the tide is going to turn against you. Good traders figure out which way the trend is moving before they risk their money. It really is as simple as that. However, you also need to remember that several time frames are involved in price activity, and that knowing which ways the short-, intermediate-, and long-term trends are headed in your markets is equally as important.

Finding the trends is easy; you simply look at price charts for multiple time frames every day. Daily, weekly, and monthly charts, spanning months, weeks, and even years are the best way to go. Checking them all before you look at your intraday price charts will enable you to be on the right side of the market for the time frame in which you plan your trades.

If, for example, you're day trading in wheat, you at least want to know where the market has been during the last few weeks or months, because intraday prices of wheat are likely to be guided by that overall trend.

You can also use long-term price charts as the basis for spotting key long-term support and resistance points and for identifying those same points on your shorter-term charts.

Thereafter, you can use the trend lines in conjunction with moving averages and oscillators to help identify the dominant trend before you trade.

Think of short-term charts like the zoom lens on your camera; they help you zoom in for a closer look at the long-term action.

Before making a trade, make sure that you know the dominant trends. Keep a trading log so you can write them down on a daily basis before hitting the daily action.

Getting to know setups

As a trader, you're a hunter, and good hunters appreciate high levels of activity and the quiet periods in between. Remember, only three things can happen in a market. Prices can rise, fall, or move sideways for an extended period of time.

As a trader/hunter, your job is to look through all of your charts for *setups,* or chart formations that signal when a change is about to occur in the market you're studying and want to trade in.

As you look for trading opportunities, watch for the following:

- **Constricting Bollinger bands,** which point to the potential for a big move getting closer
- **Sideways price movements following advances and declines,** which indicate volatility is easing as traders try to decide what to do next
- **Breakouts** that occur when prices break above or cross over key support or resistance levels, trend lines, oscillators, moving averages, or other market indicators

After you find them, setups call for careful observation in which you apply the principles of the indicators explained earlier in this chapter.

A good rule to follow is to place your entry and exit points right above or below the setup in the direction of the dominant trend.

Buying the breakout

Breakouts are exciting. Prices suddenly burst out of a basing pattern. Volume can swell, and suddenly your trading screens are flashing my favorite trading color, green, as buyers come into the market.

A breakout is a signal for you to go to work. Because it can come at virtually any time, you need to be prepared to react.

Figure 8-1 (earlier in this chapter) shows you a classic example of a nice setup, a breakout, and the right outcome.

The euro formed a 4½-month base and then delivered a nice breakout in mid-October, after testing resistance levels in July, August, and twice in September. Important features to notice about this classic basing pattern are that the euro found support twice during the basing period, and its value did not retreat to the bottom of the trading range after September.

These two factors together indicated that buyers slowly were starting to take the upper hand. In addition, higher lows indicated by the MACD oscillator and positive basing action (see Chapter 7) predicted the breakout.

The ideal entry point (labeled in the figure) for buying the breakout is after the price clears all of the previous resistance and begins moving higher — in a hurry.

Don't be too concrete here. Setups are setups. They look the same on long-term charts as they do on short-term charts. For example, if you're using a chart to cover one day's trading, say around six hours, your bars or candle-sticks may be anywhere from 5 to 15 minutes, meaning that by the end of a few hours, your chart will be full. You can use the same indicators on these charts. Bollinger bands shrink just the same. Prices will rise and fall above nine-minute moving averages. And MACD and stochastic oscillators will be just as applicable. The key is that the principles stay the same, no matter the time frame.

Swinging for dollars

Swing trading enables you to take advantage of markets that are stuck in narrow trading ranges or prices that are moving sideways or within trading channels, up or down between levels of support and resistance. The euro in Figure 8-1 was in a narrow trading range before it broke out in October.

To be able to make profitable trades in markets with narrow trading ranges, swing traders rely on trend lines, Fibonacci levels, and moving averages to identify the levels of support and resistance that they use to establish price points at which they buy, sell, and sell short their investments. When prices reach support and resistance levels, swing traders take action, in general buying on weakness at the bottom of the trading range and selling on weakness at the top of the trading range. In other words, swing traders set targets for their trades and anticipate trend changes when the market reaches those targets based on their analysis of their respective markets.

The bible of swing trading is Alan Farley's *The Master Swing Trader* (McGraw Hill).

You can combine support and resistance lines with Bollinger bands and stochastic oscillators to become a pretty decent swing trader. The euro provided plenty of opportunities for swing trades in the 4½ months before its October breakout — shown in Figures 8-1 and 8-2. Note how the support and resistance lines, the market action close to the Bollinger bands, and overbought and oversold readings on the stochastic oscillator all work together as the euro reached the tops and bottoms of its multimonth trading range.

Swing trading, however, is risky business, the same as any other form of trading. In the Figure 8-1 example, you could've lost significant amounts of money if you happened to use the 200-day moving average to set up a swing trade in late April and May. The key: The MACD oscillator failed to confirm the attempted bottom above the moving average.

Selling and shorting the breakout in a downtrend

Regardless of whether you're a momentum trader buying on breakouts or a swing trader setting up and knocking down targets, changing trends are the trader's bread and butter. And one of the hardest things for a trader to do is getting up the guts to sell an instrument short. Fortunately, the complexities of the market, the popular psychology that shorting is immoral, and the high risk of losing large sums of money serve as three major deterrents against the practice.

And yet, if you keep close tabs on trend lines, oscillators, and moving averages to spot changes in a market's price trends, and watch Bollinger bands and Fibonacci retracement levels to predict when important shifts in the markets are likely, you can manage your risk and make some money selling short. You also need to use protective stops, just in case you're wrong.

Selling short is a different animal. It's essentially the practice of turning the world upside down and making money from someone else's miscues, whether political, corporate, or otherwise.

The two basic strategies for short selling are swing trading (see the previous section) and selling into the breakdown of prices.

When you're *selling into the breakdown,* you have to wait for bad things to happen. A good rule of thumb is to consider that a market is worthy of short-selling consideration when it has been going up for an extended period of time. It can be weeks, months, or years.

When selling short, or shorting, you can do the following:

✔ Anticipate the breakdown by looking at the Bollinger bands and

- Watching for the bands to constrict and the market to stop walking the band. If trend lines are broken toward the downside, you can short an instrument. Be sure to place a stop just above the trend line.

- Watching for the market action near the moving average inside the bands, which can signal support.

✔ Monitor your short sales positions carefully at all times but especially in markets that respond to news and at times of high political tension. Bonds and currencies are especially susceptible to news and political tensions.

✔ Give your short sales positions room to move. Setting your exit stops too tightly can get you whipsawed. Different markets have different inherent ranges. Before you sell an instrument short, you need to become aware of its normal price movements and adjust your position accordingly.

You can count several trading periods and get an idea of the average number of days that a particular market moves along rising or falling Bollinger bands. This time frame won't be exact, but you want to have a good idea nevertheless. Shares of Starbucks, for example, usually hug the lower Bollinger band anywhere from four to ten days before they bounce up. Although knowing that time frame doesn't guarantee that the bounce will last, you still can be on the lookout for increased activity that can affect your trades during that period of time in the market you're trading and in other markets. *Technical Analysis For Dummies* (Wiley) offers a fairly detailed introduction to these topics.

Setting your entry and exit points

Where you set entry and exit points — whether mentally or automatically on your trading platform — can make a big difference in your trading performance. Although no hard-and-fast rules determine where to set these points, some fairly reliable guidelines are available. Here's a quick lineup:

✔ **Tailoring the strategy to the market.** Get to know how fast your market moves and how volatile trading can be before you ever start trading. It's a good idea to do this through *paper trading,* a way to practice trading without assuming the financial risk. Most online futures brokers will have practice trading available on their Web sites. Use this technique to become familiar with each market you trade.

✔ **Knowing your risk tolerance.** If you know wheat moves too fast for your liking, try the U.S. Dollar Index, which moves more slowly.

✔ **Giving a fast-moving market more room to maneuver than a slower one.** As a general rule, you need to give fast-moving markets a bit more room to maneuver (bears repeating). I usually give myself a few ticks above or below the support or resistance area that I'm using as my line in the sand so I avoid getting whipsawed.

✔ **Setting sell stops.** Where you set your sell stops depends not only on your experience, but also on the market's volatility and your risk tolerance.

✔ **Using trailing stops.** You can reset these manually; use prices as a guide or percentages. Again, much depends on the inherent volatility and general tendencies of each individual market, which is why you need to exercise care and be aware of how all contracts that you trade fluctuate before committing any money to a trade.

✔ **Hurrying gets you nowhere.** Never be in a hurry when trading. Some traders like to give markets an extra day before selling or buying. For example, if you spot a trend change on the S&P 500 futures chart on Tuesday, you may want to wait until Wednesday before you make your decision.

✔ **Using technical analysis to establish market entry and exit points.** Fibonacci levels, moving averages, trend lines, and support and resistance points provide you with plenty of references for where to place entry and exit points. The figures in this chapter offer a good foundation for beginning strategies.

✔ **Expanding your strategies.** As you gain more trading experience, you can find out more about the Fibonacci theory, Eliott waves, and Gann strategies by reading more about them and other approaches to trading. *Technical Analysis For Dummies* (Wiley) offers a fairly detailed introduction to those topics.

Chapter 9

Trading with Feeling Now!

· ·

· ·

*A*s a contrarian thinker, my first memory of a real-life experience with contrarian market analysis was in 1990. Sure, I'd read the books and articles that tell stories about how stocks need to be sold when the shoeshine boy starts recommending stocks to you as he polishes your shoes at the airport. But, for me, 1990 was the literal proof in the pudding.

At some point in August 1990, stocks were failing in the United States markets, and the price of crude oil was testing the $40-per-barrel resistance level. At the time, $40-per-barrel oil was an extremely high price, but cheap compared to the $60 prices to which it eventually soared in 2005.

Both times the rise in the price of oil to what was then a record high was caused by a war in Iraq.

During the latter stages of the oil rally in 1990, a picture of an Arab holding a gun was on the cover of *BusinessWeek* magazine with the headline of headlines above it: "Hostage To Oil."

That caught my eye. And sure as shootin' that cover story appeared only a few weeks before the price of oil topped out and actually collapsed when the United States invaded Iraq a few months later.

My contrarian stance was reinforced once again by the markets in 1991; that's when the first U.S. invasion of Iraq touched off a decade-long bull market in the stock market.

In this chapter, I take you through the major aspects of contrarian thinking and explain how to know when to use it and how to make it part of your trading arsenal.

Understanding Contrarian Thinking

Contrarians trade against the grain at key turning points when shifts in market sentiment become noticeable.

For example, a contrarian may

- Start looking for reasons to sell when everyone else is bullish.
- Think a good time to buy is when pessimism about the markets is so thick that you can cut it with a knife.

More can be made of contrarian trading than just using the prevailing sentiment in the market, because sentiment trading is inexact and can lead to losses whenever you pull the trigger too early during the cycle.

The bullish extremes reached during the buildup of the Internet bubble were unprecedented. Although traders who sold early were vindicated, they nevertheless lost a great deal of money by getting out too early. Another extreme is when the bear market in stocks ended in 2002. Traders who got into stocks during the seven-month period from June 2002 to March 2003 were *whipsawed,* or shaken out of positions with losses and tortured by the extremes in volatility that can happen as the final bottom of the mega bear market finally formed.

Throughout the three-year period during which the bear market in stocks unfolded, plenty of opportunities opened up to trade on the long side, meaning to buy stocks based on sentiment, but most of them proved false until the final bottom was reached.

Unfortunately, sentiment analysis, although an inexact science, is only part of the picture, a part that works better when combined with technical analysis.

This chapter helps you combine sentiment and technical analyses within your trading arsenal to lead you to better decision-making.

Survey Says: Trust Your Feelings

Two popular sentiment surveys affect the futures markets: Market Vane and Consensus, Inc.

Consensus, Inc., `www.consensus-inc.com`, is based in Kansas City, and is published weekly as a newspaper that you get in the mail or as an Internet publication.

Consensus offers sentiment data on the following:

- **Precious metals:** Silver, gold, copper, and platinum
- **Financial instruments:** Eurodollars, U.S. dollar, Treasury bills (T-bills), and Treasury bonds (T-bonds)
- **Currencies:** The U.S. dollar, Euro FX, British pound, Deutschemark, Swiss franc, Canadian dollar, and the Japanese yen
- **Soybean complex:** Soybeans, soybean oil, and soybean meal
- **Meats:** Pork bellies, hogs, cattle, and feeder cattle
- **Grains:** Wheat and corn
- **Stock indexes:** The S&P 500 and NASDAQ 100 stock indexes
- **Foods:** Citrus fruits, sugar, cocoa, and coffee
- **Fibers:** Cotton and lumber
- **Energy complex:** Crude oil, natural gas, gasoline, and heating oil

Market Vane, `www.marketvane.net`, offers a similar set of measures under the name Bullish Consensus. Snapshots of both surveys for stocks, bonds, Eurodollar, and Euro currency are available weekly in *Barron's* magazine, under the Market Laboratory section or at Barron's Online, `www.barrons.com`.

What you'll find when reading Barron's or another of these publications are percentages of market sentiment, such as oil being 75 percent bulls, or bullish, which simply means that 75 percent of the opinions surveyed by the editors of *Market Vane* or *Consensus* are bullish on oil. Usually such sentiment is interpreted as a sign of caution, but not necessarily as a sign of an impending top.

After you find out the market sentiment, technical analysis kicks in. A high bullish reading in terms of sentiment should alert you to start looking for technical signs that a top is in place, checking whether key support levels or trend lines have been breached, or checking whether the market is struggling to make new highs. See Chapters 7 and 8 for more details on technical analysis.

Sentiment surveys are popular tools used mostly by professional traders to gauge when a particular market is at an extreme point with either too much bullishness or too much bearishness. Their major weakness is that they're now so popular that their ability to truly mark major turning points is not as good as it was even in the late 1980s or early 1990s. Still, when used within the context of good technical and fundamental analysis, they can be useful.

Of the two sentiment surveys, Market Vane is better known, and according to its Web site, Market Vane's *Bullish Consensus* has been published on a weekly basis since 1964 and on a daily basis since 1988. Other particulars that describe the sentiment surveys are that they are

- ✔ Based on advisor polls that are conducted either by reading the latest publications sent to the survey editors or by telephone polling of a group of advisors.
- ✔ Indirect measures of public opinion about the individual markets.
- ✔ Interpreted as a measure of public opinion because they're based on advisory opinions usually subscribed to by the public. However, market professionals traditionally considered the public to be wrong, especially at market turning points.

Sentiment survey readings must be at extreme levels to be useful. In other words, sentiments below 35 to 40 percent for any given category usually are considered bullish, because few advisors are left to recommend selling.

You can use sentiment surveys as trend-following systems. A market that hits a new high as sentiment is rising along with it — without hitting any cautionary points on the charts — can be taken as a sign that more upside potential exists. Even so, when using sentiment to help guide your decision-making, always

- ✔ Check your charts and other indicators to confirm what the surveys are saying.
- ✔ Avoid trading on sentiment data alone, because doing so is too risky.
- ✔ Check sentiment tendencies against technical and fundamental analyses, even though it may make you a little late in executing your entry or exit trades. Making sure is better than missing a significant part of an advance if you're long or a decline if you're short.

Even though the sentiment surveys are not giving you textbook numbers, they nevertheless can be useful. Figure 9-1 highlights a set of key market turning points in the 2004–2005 time period.

Keep tabs on Consensus and Market Vane. One or the other is likely to give you a fairly timely and useful signal at most market turning points.

Figure 9-1:
Key tops
and bottoms
in the S&P
500 from
July 2004 to
June 2005
were
correctly
called by
sentiment
surveys.

Understanding Volume (And How the Market Feels about It)

Trading volume is a direct, real-time sentiment indicator. As a general rule, high trading volume is a sign that the current trend is likely to continue. But consider that advice as only a guideline. Good volume analysis takes other market indicators into account.

Figure 9-2, which shows the S&P 500 e-mini futures contract for September 2005, portrays an interesting relationship between volume, sentiment, and other indicators.

In April, the market made a textbook bottom. Notice how the volume bars at the bottom of the chart rose as the market was reaching a selling climax, as signified by the three large candlesticks, or trading bars. This combination of signals — large price moves and large volumes when the market is falling — is often the prelude to a classic market bottom, because traders were panicking and selling at any price just to get out of their positions.

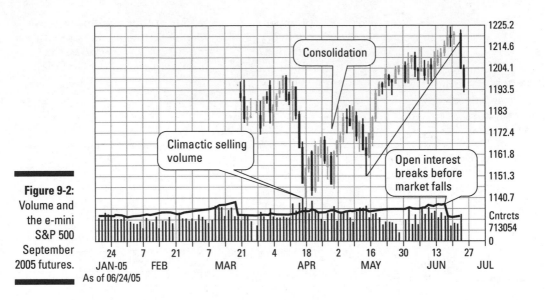

Figure 9-2:
Volume and
the e-mini
S&P 500
September
2005 futures.

Notice how the volume trailed off as the market consolidated, or started moving sideways, making a complex bottom that took almost two weeks to form. *Consolidation* is what happens when buyers and sellers are in balance. When markets consolidate, they're catching their breath and getting set up for their next move. Consolidation phases are unpredictable and can last for short periods of time, such as hours or days, or longer periods, even months to years.

A third important volume signal occurred in late May and early June as the market rallied. Notice how volume faded as the market continued to rise. Eventually, the market fell and moved significantly lower as it broke below key trend-line support.

Finally, note in Figure 9-2 that open interest (see the "Out in the Open with Open Interest" section, later in this chapter) fell during the last stage of the rally in late June, which usually is a sign that more weakness is likely, because fewer contracts remain open, suggesting that traders are getting exhausted and are less willing to hold on to open positions.

Using volume indicators in the futures markets has limitations. The example in Figure 9-2 needs to be viewed within the context of these limitations:

- ✔ The release of volume figures in the futures market is delayed by one day.

- ✔ Higher volume levels steadily migrate toward the closest *delivery month,* or the month in which the contract is settled and delivery of the underlying asset takes place. That migration is important for traders, because the chance of getting a better price for your trade is higher when volume is better. In June, for example, the trading volume is higher in the S&P

500 futures for the September contract than for other months, because September is the next delivery month. Volume for the delivery-month contract increases for a while as traders move their positions to the *front month*, or the commonly quoted (price) contract at the time. Say, for example, that the volume data for June 24, 2005, shows 36,717 contracts traded in the September 2005 contract, 170 in the December 2005 contract, and 21 in the March 2006 contract. None of the other listed contracts had any volume on that day.

✔ *Limit days* (especially limit up days), or days in which a particular contract makes a big move in a short period of time, can have very high volume, thus skewing your analysis. A *limit up day,* when the market rises to the limit in a short period of time, usually is a signal of strength in the market. Limit up or limit down days tend to happen in response to a single or related series of events, external or internal, such as a very surprising report. When markets crash, you can see limit down moves that then trigger *trading collars* (periods when the market trades but prices don't change) or complete stoppages of trading.

The opposite is true when you have a big move on low volume, such as the first of the last two bars pictured in Figure 9-2. On the day of the first break of the rising trend line, volume was lower than in the prior few days. On the second day of selling, volume rose, suggesting that more trouble was coming.

When analyzing volume, be sure that you

✔ Put the current volume trends in the proper context with relationship to the market in which you're trading, rather than thinking about hard-and-fast rules. It's important to note that trends tend to either start or end with a volume spike climax (typically twice the 20- or 50-day moving average of daily volume).

✔ Remember the differences in the way that volume is reported and interpreted in the futures market — compared with the stock market.

✔ Check other indicators to confirm what volume is telling you.

✔ Ask yourself whether the market is vulnerable to a trend change.

✔ Consider key support and resistance levels.

✔ Protect your portfolio by being prepared to make necessary changes.

Out in the Open with Open Interest

Open interest is the number of active contracts for any given security during any trading period. It is the most useful tool for analyzing potential trend reversals in futures markets.

A more formal definition is this: Open interest is the total number of contracts entered into during a specified period of time that have not been liquidated either by offsetting transactions or by actual delivery. Open interest applies to futures and options but not to stocks.

Open interest

- ✔ Measures the total number of short and long positions (shorts and longs).
- ✔ Varies based on the number of new traders entering the market and the number of traders leaving the market.
- ✔ Rises by one whenever one new buyer and one new seller enter the market, thus marking the creation of one new contract.
- ✔ Falls by one when a long trader closes out a position with a trader who already has an open short position.

In the futures markets, the number of longs always equals the number of shorts. So when a new buyer buys from an old buyer who is cashing in, no change occurs in open interest.

The exchanges publish open-interest figures daily, but the numbers are delayed by one day, so the volume and open interest figures on today's quotes, therefore, are only estimates.

Charting open interest on a daily basis in conjunction with a price chart helps you keep track of the trends in open interest and how they relate to market prices. Barchart.com (www.barchart.com) offers excellent free futures charts that give you a good look at open interest.

Open interest is one of the most useful tools you can have when trading futures. Even though the figures are released with a one-day delay, they still are useful when you evaluate the longer trend of the market.

Rising markets

In a rising trend, open interest is fairly straightforward:

- ✔ **Bullish open interest:** When open interest rises along with prices, it signals that an uptrend is in place and can be sustained. This bullish sign also means that new money is moving into the market.

  Extremely high open interest in a bull market usually is a danger signal.

- ✔ **Bearish open interest:** Rising prices combined with falling open interest signal a short-covering rally in which short sellers are reversing their positions so that their buying actually is pushing prices higher. In this case, higher prices are not likely to last, because no new buyers are entering the market.

✓ **Bearish leveling or decline:** A leveling off or decrease in open interest in a rising market often is an early warning sign that a top may be nearing.

Sideways markets

In a sideways market, open interest gets trickier, so you need to watch for the following:

✓ Rising open interest during periods when the market is moving sideways (or in a narrow trading range; see Chapter 8), because they usually lead to an intense move after prices break out of the trading range — up or down.

When dealing with sideways markets, be sure to confirm open-interest signals by checking them against other market indicators.

✓ Down-trending price breakouts (breakdowns). Some futures traders use breakouts on the downside to set up short positions, just like commercial and professional traders, thus leaving the public wide open for a major sell-off.

✓ Falling open interest in a trader's market. When it happens, traders with weak positions are throwing in the towel, and the pros are covering their short positions and setting up for a market rally.

Falling markets

In falling markets, open-interest signals also are a bit more complicated to decipher:

✓ **Bearish open interest:** Falling prices combined with a rise in open interest indicate that a downtrend is in place and that it's being fueled by new money coming in from short sellers.

✓ **Bullish open interest:** Falling prices combined with falling open interest is a sign that traders who had not sold their positions as the market broke — hoping the market would bounce back — are giving up. In this case, you need to start anticipating, or even expecting, a trend reversal toward higher prices after this give-up phase ends.

✔ **Neutral:** If prices rise or fall, but open interest remains flat, it means that a trend reversal is possible. You can think of these periods as preludes to an eventual change in the existing trend. Neutral open-interest situations are good times to be especially alert.

✔ **Trending down:** A market trend that has shifted downward at the same time open interest is reaching high levels can be a sign that more selling is coming. Traders who bought into the market right before it topped out are now liquidating losing positions to cut their losses.

Flat open interest when prices are rising or falling means that a trend reversal is possible.

Putting the Put/Call Ratios to Good Use

The *put/call ratio* is the most commonly used sentiment indicator for trading stocks, but it can also be useful in trading stock index futures, because with it you can pinpoint major inflection points in trader sentiment. Put/call ratios, when at extremes, can be signs of excessive fear (a high level of put buying relative to call buying) and excessive greed (a high level of call buying relative to put buying).

These indicators are not as useful as they once were because of more sophisticated hedging strategies that are now often used in the markets.

As a futures trader, put/call ratios can help you make several important decisions about

✔ Tightening your stops on open positions

✔ Setting new entry points if you've been out of the market

✔ Setting up hedges with options and futures

✔ Taking profits

Put/call ratios are best used in conjunction with technical analysis, so you need to look at your charts and take inventory of your own positions during the time frame in which you're trading futures contracts. In other words, a good time to check the put/call ratio is when you have a long position in S&P 500 Index futures and the stock market has been rising for several weeks, but it's running up against a tough long-term resistance level that it's failed to penetrate a few times during the last few weeks. From your read of the put/call ratio, you can consider which of the four strategies in the previous list you need to use. You can turn this scenario around for a falling market in which you have either a short position or hold put options.

The Chicago Board Options Exchange (CBOE) updates the ratio throughout the day at its Web site, `www.cboe.com/data/IntraDayVol.aspx`, and provides final figures for the day after the market closes.

The sections that follow describe two important ratios with which you need to become familiar when trading stock index futures.

Total put/call ratio

The total put/call ratio is the original indicator introduced by Martin Zweig, a prominent money manager and author who was one of the few traders who sidestepped the market crash of October 1987 and made money by buying put options. The put/call ratio is calculated using the following equation:

total put options purchased ÷ total call options purchased

The total ratio includes options on stocks, indexes, and long-term options bought by traders on the CBOE. Although you can make sense of this ratio in multiple ways, I've found it useful when the ratio rises above 1.0 and when it falls below 0.5. When the ratio rises above 1.0, it usually means too much fear is in the air and that the market is trying to make a bottom. Readings below 0.5, however, usually mean that too much bullishness is in the air and that the market may fall.

Index put/call ratio

The index put/call ratio is a good measure of what futures and options players, institutions, and hedge-fund managers are up to. When this indicator is above 2.0, it traditionally is a bullish sign, but when it falls below 0.90, it becomes bearish and traditionally signals that some kind of correction is coming. Because these numbers are not as reliable in the traditional sense as they used to be, please consider them only as reference points, and never base any trades on them alone. Don't forget that put/call ratios need to be correlated with chart patterns.

In June 2005, the CBOE index put/call ratio was high during the period from June 17 through 23, which included an options expiration week. During those five trading sessions, three readings of the index put/option ratio were above 2.00; the highest reading of 2.75 occurred on June 21. If you took these numbers at face value, you probably went aggressively long, expecting a likely rise in stock index futures. Unfortunately, you would have been wrong!

On June 23 and 24, the Dow Jones Industrial Average lost more than 290 points, and the rest of the market got clobbered, too. Hindsight obviously tells you that in this case, the rising put/call ratio was a signal that somebody, or a group of people somewhere, was aware of information that something interesting might happen that could shake the markets.

Common knowledge tells you that many people with lots of money have access to information to which you and I would never be privy and that we'd never be able to gather. The job of the trader is to look for signs that something may be brewing.

And there it was . . . on Thursday, June 23, China's third largest oil company, CNOOC, bid $18 billion to purchase American oil company Unocal. The political firestorm kicked off by this event certainly gave players a reason to sell stocks.

Put/call ratios are best used as alert mechanisms for potential trend changes. Traditionally, high ratios tend to signal that a great deal of pessimism exists in the markets and that the markets should move higher. However, the truth is that in current markets, where hedge funds and large institutions always are running complex derivative strategies, high put/call ratios can be misleading.

Don't ignore abnormal put/call ratio readings. Doing so can cost you significant amounts of money in a hurry. As a result, take the following actions apart from your daily routine:

- ✔ **Check the put/call ratios after the market closes.** The CBOE usually updates the numbers by 5 p.m. central time.

- ✔ **Favor thoughts of dramatic market reactions over thoughts of where the market is headed when you see abnormally high or low put/call ratios.** Be ready to handle dramatic changes.

- ✔ **Immediately look for weak spots in your portfolio whenever abnormal activity occurs in the options market.** Abnormal activity should trigger ideas about hedging.

When you see abnormal put/call ratio numbers, consider the following:

- ✔ Tightening stops on your open stock index futures positions.

- ✔ Exploring options strategies, such as straddles, and strangles. See Chapters 4 and 5 for an overview of the options market and option strategies.

✔ Reversing positions. If you have a short position in the market, make sure you're ready to reverse and go long or vice versa if you have a long position.

✔ Looking to the bond, currency, and oil markets for other trading opportunities with a goal of both hedging any problems in your stock index futures and options and possibly expanding your profits in those areas.

Combining Open Interest, Volume, and Options

Table 9-1 summarizes the relationship between volume and open interest. Figure 9-2 shows a great example of how to combine open interest and volume to predict a trend change.

Generally, volume and open interest need to be heading in the same direction as the market. When the market starts rising, for example, you want to see volume and open interest expanding. A rising market with shrinking volume and falling open interest usually is one that is heading for a correction.

Table 9-1	The Relationship Between Volume and Open Interest		
Price	*Volume*	*Open Interest*	*Market*
Rising	Up	Up	Strong
Rising	Down	Down	Weak
Declining	Up	Up	Weak
Declining	Down	Down	Strong

Note in Figure 9-2 how the market started to rally in early June. Both volume and open interest (the line coursing above the volume bars) moved up. This chart confirmed the rising trend in the E-mini S&P futures.

After June 13, however, the market started going sideways. Volume began to fade, and open interest began to flatten out. Three days before the June 24 break, open interest fell precipitously, signaling that the rally was running out of gas. Fading volume provided a great example of how smart money was taking profits and being replaced by new, weaker buyers. Likewise, falling open interest not only confirmed an impending downturn, but it also revealed to you that traders with weak short positions were bailing out. The market thus was losing buyers and sellers and its liquidity, which, in turn, made it vulnerable to external events, such as the CNOOC/Unocal news.

When you plugged in rising put/call ratios with falling open interest in stock futures, the result was a sign that the smart money sensed a rising risk in the market and was preparing itself by buying portfolio insurance in the form of put options, which rise in price during falling markets.

Smart money refers to large institutions, hedge funds, or individuals. They have better access to information than the market at times, and they tend to act ahead of the crowd. Sometimes they're correct, and other times they're wrong. In this example, they were correct.

Using Soft Sentiment Signs

Soft sentiment signs usually are out of the mainstream and are subtle, non-quantitative factors that most people tend to ignore. They can be anything from the shoeshine boy giving stock tips or a wild magazine cover (classic signs of a top) to people jumping out of windows during a market crash (a classic sign of the other extreme). These signs can be anywhere from dramatic to humorous, and they can be quite useful. By no means should you make them a mainstay of your trading strategy. But they can at times be helpful.

Scanning magazine covers and Web site headlines

Based on my 1990 experience with *BusinessWeek* and the top in oil prices, every time crude oil rallies, I start looking for crazy headlines.

When crude oil reached an all-time high on June 17, 2005, I scanned the covers of *Time, Newsweek,* and *BusinessWeek. Time's* cover featured the late Mao TseTung, *BusinessWeek* had senior citizens, and *Newsweek* had dinosaurs. None of them even mentioned oil — a good soft sentiment sign that the oil market still had some room to rise.

Monitoring congressional investigations and activist protests

Another soft sign that a top may be near is what politicians and activists say or do in relation to how the markets move.

So, as oil made a new high, I scanned the news for signs of senators and other members of Congress or of activists who were calling for investigations or alleging that the oil companies were price gouging.

It took a while, but by the end of June, with Congress in full swing, the attempted takeover of Unocal mobilized both sides of the aisle. Letters to President Bush were written. Hearings were held at which Fed Chairman Alan Greenspan and Treasury Secretary John Snow argued about China's newly found role as a world power and what the circumstances would likely be.

The markets worried about protectionism, as well they should . . . the last depression in the United States came as a result of Congress and President Herbert Hoover concocting the Smoot-Hawley tariff.

As a contrarian, you must understand that the public going wild over an issue can be a sign that a major turning point is on the way in the market.

Politicians and activists are no different these days, except that their lives usually are not touched by reality the same way yours and mine are. They start talking about something that you and I have experienced for months only after they've read a new poll or received lots of letters and phone calls from their constituents about the subject.

Political activity and outrage are no accident. It usually means that the public is interested in the current set of developments. The thing is, when politicians and activists finally pick up the chant, they do so because they see some kind of advantage for their cause or their chances of being re-elected. And that's usually a sign that things are at a fever pitch, and the trend can change, possibly in a hurry.

Don't be in a hurry. Just because your initial scan of the news fails to reveal important findings doesn't mean that those events are not on the way. People in Washington sometimes take several days to catch on to what's happening in the real world. Keep looking, especially when the market keeps moving in the same direction.

Watching the Drudge Report

Along with Congress, all good traders need to keep an eye on the Drudge Report. The Drudge Report almost replaced *BusinessWeek, Newsweek,* and *Time* as a barometer for when life has gone over the top. Aside from learning what former President Clinton, Mrs. Clinton, and anybody with a thirst for power is doing, the daily news report compiled by Matt Drudge also is a barometer for public opinion, or at least Drudge's current attempts to influence public opinion. As a contrary sign for the markets, the Drudge Report is a useful tool.

The Drudge Report headline on oil, after it closed at an all-time high of $59.18 per barrel on Friday, June 17, 2005, was benign. However, by Sunday night, Drudge had the following in huge letters at the top of the page:

> OIL $59

Still, because the revolving light that Drudge uses for his more dramatic Web headlines was not flashing, the report was something worth watching but not necessarily getting too worked up about.

If Drudge had known what he was doing, he would have used the flashing light next to a headline reading, "December Crude at $60," which truly was alarming and more telling of what the market was pricing in for the future.

By June 21, Drudge was in full swing, along with CNBC, CNN, and most local news outlets and newspapers. After the market closed that day, Drudge ran the following headline:

> Oil hits new high amid Norway strike fears . . .
> 'COULD TEST $70' . . .
> Pickens predicts $3 gasoline. . . . "

By the time the CNOOC/Chevron story hit the wires, Drudge was having a field day. During the weekend, on June 25, he ran this headline regarding the attempted takeover of Unocal by the Chinese:

> WHAT TO DO?

In comments at an oil conference, according to Reuters, famed Texas oil investor T. Boone Pickens told an audience that $70 oil was on its way within five years. But the wire services and the news hypers took the news out of context, and created the panic-type feeling that preceded the top.

Pickens became one of the loudest bull voices for the rising price of oil. Like Warren Buffet and George Soros before him, Pickens (and his billion-dollar fund) was out in front of the bull run, coaxing every tick higher. Whether he was selling into the frenzy, no one will know for sure. But the fact is that on June 27, 2005, oil topped out at $60.54 per barrel for the August contract. In December, the top was above $62.

What few of the mainstream news outlets carried was the fact that other analysts and experts who didn't manage billion-dollar investments in oil were scratching their heads, because oil supply figures were 8 percent ahead of what was available the year before.

That meant that at some point, oil prices had to crack because of all the misdirected hype.

By June 30, August crude had closed at $56.50, a 6.7-percent drop in three trading sessions and a potentially major hit to your oil contracts if you happened to get caught on the wrong side of the trade.

Figure 9-3 highlights the period during the month of June when many wild headlines were written about rising oil prices.

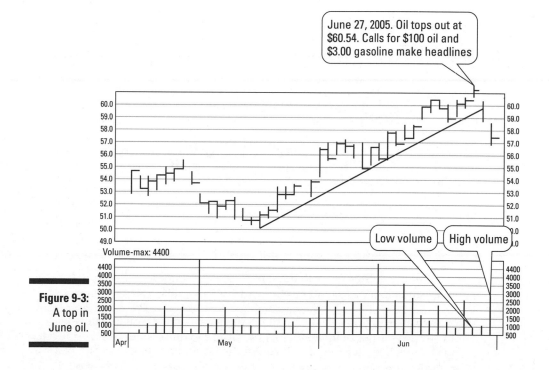

Figure 9-3:
A top in
June oil.

Despite all the soft media sentiment, some important technical signs also were worth noting during the crude oil rally:

- ✔ Low volume when the all-time high for that period of time was reached. The high volume on the second day of selling meant that the market was ripe for a correction.

- ✔ Low volume on a breakout, especially one that leads to all-time highs, is a sign of weakness.

- ✔ High volume as the market sells off is a sign that more selling is likely.

- ✔ A clean breakdown in the market, like the way oil prices cleanly sliced through the rising trend line, is notable because it means that little demand is in the market at the time and signals that more selling is coming.

As with put/call ratios, wild headlines, Congressional hearings, and plenty of attention on cable and local news channels are an alert that something dramatic is going to happen.

Developing Your Own Sentiment Indicators

A hot market eventually changes trends. It gets cold. No one knows when that market is going to change trends. By using sentiment indicators and confirming one with another, you can get early warnings of pending changes.

When any market makes a new high, I usually go to the Drudge Report and look for the headline. If it's sensational enough, I start being careful about that particular area of the market.

Here are two of my favorite personal indicators:

- ✔ If I start bragging to my wife about how much money I'm making in the markets, I look for reasons to sell.

- ✔ When my mother tells me that I need to start watching the NASDAQ the way she did in the summer of 1999, I start to shake in my boots.

When everybody starts giving me tips, I run for the door. You can develop your own private set of indicators by monitoring your own excitement level. If you start feeling invincible, as if you're the best trader in the world, being a little more careful is a good idea.

Make a mental checklist. I always check my gut when I trade. If I'm all tied up in knots, I'm less concerned than if I'm happy as a lark, because if I'm worried, I'm awake. Mind you, don't make yourself sick over it. If you can't stand what you're doing, then it isn't for you.

The key is to search for some kind of balance within yourself by keeping your eyes open, doing your homework, and comparing what's going on in the charts with what you're reading and hearing from others.

Part III
Financial Futures

The 5th Wave   By Rich Tennant

"My portfolio's gonna take a hit for this."

In this part . . .

This part is where you get into the big money, starting with interest-rate futures, going international with the currency markets, and taking stock of stock-index futures. These three markets often set the tone for the trading day in all markets, because they form a focal point or hub for the global financial system. What's good about these markets is that they're great places for you to get started in futures trading, so I provide you with tips for doing just that.

Chapter 10

Wagging the Dog: Interest-Rate Futures

The bond market rules the world. Everything that anyone does in the financial markets anymore is built upon interest-rate analysis. When interest rates are on the rise, at some point, doing business becomes difficult, and when interest rates fall, eventually economic growth is energized.

That relationship between rising and falling interest rates makes the markets in interest-rate futures, Eurodollars, and Treasuries (bills, notes, and bonds) important for all consumers, speculators, economists, bureaucrats, and politicians.

This chapter provides you with a detailed and useful introduction to a snapshot of how you can structure your analysis and trading in these major instruments, but it isn't meant to be an all-inclusive treatise on interest rates and trading techniques.

Bonding with the Universe

At the center of the world's financial universe is the bond market. And at the center of the bond market is its relationship with the United States Federal Reserve (the Fed) and the way the Fed conducts interest-rate policies.

By law, the Fed's two main functions are

- ✔ Creating and maintaining conditions that keep inflation in check
- ✔ Maintaining full employment

Full employment is viewed by some as being potentially inflationary, because it creates a scenario of too much money chasing too few goods and services — a primal definition of *inflation* that's not far from also defining capitalism.

Inflation decreases the return on bondholders' investments, acting the way sunlight does to a vampire. When you buy a bond, you get a fixed return, as long as you hold that bond until it matures or, in the case of some corporate or municipal bonds, until it's called in. If you're getting a 5 percent return on your bond investment and inflation is growing at a 6-percent clip, you're already 1 percent in the hole, which is why bond traders hate inflation.

The connection between the bond market, the Federal Reserve, and the rest of the financial markets is fundamental to understanding how to trade futures and options and how to invest in general. In the next section, I discuss the most important aspects of how it all works together.

Understanding the Fed and bond-market roles

The Fed cannot directly control the long-term bond rates that determine how easy (or difficult) it is to borrow money to buy a new home or to finance long-term business projects. What the Fed can and does do is adjust short-term interest rates, such as the interest rate on *Fed funds,* the overnight lending rate used by banks to square their books, and the *discount rate,* or the rate at which the Fed loans money to banks to which no one else will lend money.

As the Fed senses that inflationary pressures are rising through analyzing key economic reports, such as consumer prices, producer prices, the employment report, and its own Beige Book (see Chapter 6), it starts to raise interest rates.

The Fed usually raises the Fed funds target rate, which focuses on overnight deposits between banks. Occasionally, when the Fed wants to make a point that it's in a hurry to make rates rise, it raises the *discount rate,* the rate that the Fed charges banks to borrow at its discount window, which usually is a loan of last resort for banks and a signal to the Fed that the individual bank is in trouble.

When the Fed raises the Fed funds and/or the discount rates, banks usually raise the *prime rate,* the rate that targets their best customers. At the same time, credit-card companies raise their rates.

As the bond market senses inflationary pressures are rising, bond traders sell bonds and market interest rates rise. Rising market interest rates usually trigger rate increases for mortgages and car loans, which usually are tied to a bond market benchmark rate. For example, most 30-year mortgages are tied to the interest rate for the U.S. one-year Treasury note. I know that sounds confusing, but that's the way these things are structured.

When it comes down to recognizing when inflation is lurking, sometimes the bond market takes action ahead of the Fed, but other times the Fed is ahead of the market. Sometimes the bond market senses inflation before the Fed does. When that happens, bond prices fall, market rates rise (such as the yield on the U.S. ten-year T-note), and the Fed raises rates if its indicators agree with the bond market's analysis. Whenever the Fed disagrees with the markets, it signals those disagreements usually through speeches from Fed governors or even the chairman of the Fed. Interest rates are a two-way street: The bond market sometimes disagrees with the Fed, and the Fed sometimes disagrees with the markets.

Disagreements between the Fed and the bond market usually occur at the beginning or at the end of a trend in interest rates. Say, for example, that the Fed continually raises interest rates for an extended period of time. At some point, long-term rates, which are controlled by the bond market, begin to drop, even though short-term rates are on the rise. Falling long-term bond rates usually are a sign — from the bond market to the Fed — that the Fed needs to consider pausing its interest-rate increases. The opposite also is true: When the Fed goes too far in lowering short-term rates, bond yields begin to creep up and signal the need for the Fed to consider a pause in its lowering of the rates.

Hedging in general terms

In general, *hedging* is taking a position in the market that's in the opposite direction of a trading position you've already established; it's a form of insurance against a reversal of trends. You need to know what the opposition is doing anyway so that you're better able to make your market move. In the world of short-term interest rates, aside from speculators, the big money comes from money-market funds and corporations.

Generally, they (money–market fund managers and corporate traders) go long or short in the direction that's opposite their borrowing or lending. Borrowers generally want to hedge against rising interest rates, so they tend to short the market. That way, if interest rates rise, they either reduce their future interest-rate costs or actually profit from the situation.

Money-market funds and corporations borrow and lend millions of dollars on a daily basis, so the short-term interest-rate market, especially in Eurodollars and related contracts, is the way they hedge their exposure. Here's how hedging works for the various participants:

- ✓ **Lenders:** Banks and other lending institutions want to hedge against falling interest rates, so they tend to be long on the market. They know that they'll be lending money to someone in the future, and if interest rates continue to fall, their profits will be reduced accordingly. By using futures strategies, they lessen the impact of having to charge less interest and thus help curtail potential future losses.

   Institutions decrease their risk when they sense that rates are going to fall by establishing long positions in bonds, T-bills, or Eurodollar futures contracts and wanting to protect their future earnings. The money that they make when they sell their contracts goes to the bank's bottom line, balancing revenue lost from lending to customers at lower interest rates. This strategy is by no means perfect, but if it's done correctly by the institution, it at least cushions the blow.

- ✓ **Corporate treasurers:** These big-money institutions use sophisticated formulas based on the need to protect their cash flow and future expenses. They also hedge against the risk of adverse international and geopolitical events and against nonpayment by high-risk customers by using the short- and long-term interest-rate futures markets.

   For example, say you're the chief financial officer at an international paper products company that has multiple risks, such as the price of lumber and pulp to make paper and related products and a large customer base in Latin America, meaning that political instability is a major factor you must consider when running your business. By using lumber futures and currency hedges and by varying your strategies based on market conditions and analysis, you can decrease the risk of material shortages and political instability to your company's earnings.

- ✓ **Speculators:** Traders just like you and I always want to trade with the trend, which is why technical analysis (see Chapter 7) is so helpful in futures trading. By the time a tick is printed on a chart, it's as good of a snapshot as there is for all hedging and speculating that's taken place up to that instant in time.

Speculators generally trade on the long side when a particular market is rising and then go short when the market is falling. Speculative hedging techniques involve setting up option strategies that are the opposite of established trading positions, such as buying stock index put options on the S&P 500 to hedge a long S&P position.

The same is true when you have a short position. In that case, speculators buy call options on the S&P 500.

In a flat market, a speculator can write S&P 500 calls to hedge the same long position. And you can use intermarket trades. For example, if you have a long dollar position and you're not sure that the market is topping out, but you're not quite ready to sell your position, you can consider buying a gold call option, because gold tends to rise when the dollar falls. (For more about speculating strategies, see Chapter 8.)

Globalizing the markets

Globalization, or essentially the spread of capitalism around the world, has increased the number of short-term interest-rate contracts that trade at the Chicago Mercantile Exchange (CME) and around the world. Although details of market globalization are not the focus of this chapter, you nevertheless need to know that these contracts exist and that the volume of trades at times is just as heavy in Eurodollars as it is in T-bills.

In fact, just about every country in the world with a convertible currency has some kind of bond or bond futures contract that trades on an exchange somewhere around the world. The following are not complete lists, but they offer snapshots of some of the more liquid contracts.

Short-term global plays include the following:

- **Fed funds futures:** Fed funds futures trade on the CME and are an almost pure bet on what the Federal Reserve is expected to do with future interest rates. Fed funds measure interest rates that private banks charge each other for overnight loans of excess reserves. These interbank loans usually are intended to square or balance the books of the banks involved. The rates often are quoted in the media as a means of pricing the probability of the Federal Reserve raising or lowering interest rates at an upcoming meeting into the market, and they usually are accurate at doing so.

  Each Fed funds contract lets you control $5 million and is cash settled. The tick size as described by the Chicago Board of Trade (CBOT) is "$20.835 per ½ of one basis point (½ of $\frac{1}{100}$ of 1 percent of $5 million on a 30-day basis rounded up to the nearest cent)." Margins are variable, depending on the tier in which you trade, and they range from $104 to $675. A tier is just a time frame. The longer the time frame before expiration, the higher the margin. For full information, you can visit the CBOT's margin page at `www.cbot.com/cbot/pub/page/0,3181,2142,00.html#1b`. Fed funds contracts are quoted in terms of the rate that the market is speculating on by the time the contract expires, and they're based on the formula found at the CBOT: "100 minus the average daily Fed funds overnight rate for the delivery month (for example, a 7.25 percent rate equals 92.75)."

- **LIBOR futures:** These futures are one-month, interest-rate contracts based on the London Interbank-Offered Rate (LIBOR), the interest rate charged between commercial banks. LIBOR futures have 12 monthly listings. Each contract is worth $3 million. The role of LIBOR futures is to offer professionals a way to hedge their interest portfolio in a similar fashion to that offered by Eurodollars. The minimum increment of price movement is "0.0025 (¼ tick = $6.25) for the front month expiring contract and 0.005 (½ tick = $12.50) for all other expirations." The major difference: Margin requirements are less for LIBOR, at $473 for initial and $350 for margin maintenance, compared with margins of $945 and $700 for respective Eurodollar contracts. A good way for a new trader to decide between the highly liquid and popular Eurodollar and LIBOR contracts — which offer essentially the same type of trading opportunities — is to paper trade both contracts after doing some homework on how each contract trades.

It's easy to be put off by the large amounts of money that are held in futures contracts, such as the $3 million in a LIBOR contract. No matter what contract you trade, though, you need to think in terms of short holding periods, especially if the position is moving against you. Consider how much you may actually have to pay up (if you're long) if you don't sell before the contract rolls over (the amount specified by the contract — $3 million). Small traders usually trade Eurodollars, while pros with large sums and more experience tend to trade LIBOR. See the section on "Playing the Short End of the Curve: Eurodollars & T-Bills," later in this chapter.

- **Euroyen contracts:** These contracts represent Japanese yen deposits held outside of Japan. Open positions in these contracts can be held at CME or at the SIMEX exchange in Singapore. Euroyen contracts are listed quarterly, trade monthly, and offer expiration dates as far out as three years. That long-term time frame can be useful to professional hedgers with specific expectations about the future.

- **CETES futures:** These 28-day and 91-day futures contracts are based on Mexican Treasury bills. These instruments are denominated and paid in Mexican pesos, and they reflect the corresponding benchmark rates of interest rates in Mexico.

Longer-term global plays include Eurobond futures. The Eurobond market is composed of bonds issued by the Federal Republic of Germany and the Swiss Confederation that usually are the second most traded bond futures contracts in volume after the U.S. Treasury bonds. On some days, however, they can trade larger volumes than U.S. Treasuries.

Eurobonds come in four different categories: Euro Shatz, Euro Bobl, Euro Bund, and Euro Buxl. The duration on each respective category is 1.75 years, 4.5 to 5.5 years, 8.5 to 10.5 years, and 24 to 35 years. The contract size is for 100,000 euros or 100,000 Swiss francs, depending on the issuer. Eurobonds can be traded in the United States. The basic strategies are similar to U.S. bonds, because they trade on economic fundamentals and inflationary expectations, and they respond to European economic reports similar to the way U.S. bonds respond to U.S. reports.

Some particulars about Eurobond futures:

- ✔ Foreigners hold half of all Euro Bunds.

- ✔ Euro Bunds are the most active Eurobond contract traded at the totally electronic Eurex Exchange in Frankfurt.

- ✔ Both Euro-Schatz and Euro-Bobl contracts rank in the top ten of all futures contracts in global trading volume.

Yielding to the Curve

The *yield curve* is a representation on a graph that compares the entire spectrum of interest rates available to investors. Figures 10-1 and 10-2, respectively, are excellent illustrations of the U.S. Treasury yield curve and rate structure at a time when inflationary expectations are under control and the economy is growing steadily. The curve and the table are from July 1, 2005, just two days after the Federal Reserve raised interest rates for the ninth consecutive time in a 12-month period.

Figure 10-2 depicts a standard, table-style snapshot of all market maturities for the U.S. Treasury. You can view an up-to-date version at `bonds.yahoo.com/rates.html`.

As you review Figures 10-1 and 10-2, notice the following:

- ✔ **The longer the maturity, the higher the yield:** That relationship is normal for interest-paying securities, because you're lending your money to someone for an extended period of time, and you want them to pay you a premium for the extra risk.

- ✔ **The yield on all securities rose:** Starting with the 3-month Treasury bill (T-bill) and ending with the 30-year bond, all yields rose, compared with the previous week and month, after the Fed raised interest rates. That's because the Federal Open Market Committee (FOMC), in remarks made after announcing the most recent rate increase in the Fed funds rate, told the market that inflation was controlled, but economic growth still warranted a "measured" pace of continuing interest-rate increases. To a bond trader, that meant that the Fed would continue raising interest rates until it otherwise saw fit, and it meant that the economic perceptions of the bond market and the Fed were in agreement.

Had the bond market disagreed with the Fed, yields for longer-term maturities would have fallen, because the bond market would be signaling to the Fed that the economy was starting to slow and that it (the Fed) needed to consider taking a pause or even ending its rate hikes.

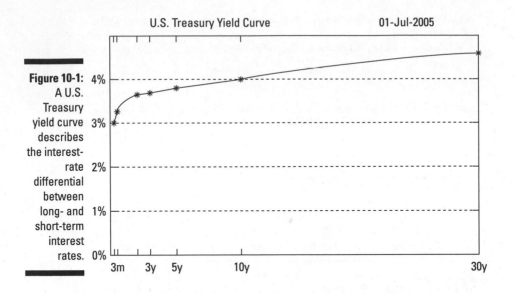

Figure 10-1:
A U.S.
Treasury
yield curve
describes
the interest-
rate
differential
between
long- and
short-term
interest
rates.

Figure 10-2:
A U.S.
Treasury
summary
shows all
the common
maturity
listings and
the price
changes.

U.S. Treasury Bonds				
Maturity	Yield	Yesturday	Last week	Last month
3 Month	3.00	2.96	2.93	2.81
6 Month	3.21	3.18	3.12	2.98
2 Year	3.73	3.62	3.56	3.46
3 Year	3.76	3.64	3.60	3.50
5 Year	3.82	3.69	3.68	3.61
10 Year	4.04	3.91	3.91	3.88
30 Year	4.29	4.18	4.21	4.23

Deciding Your Time Frame

From a trader's standpoint, you want to consider trading the short term, the intermediate term, or the long term.

Each position has its own time, place, and reasoning, ranging from how much money you have to trade, your individual risk tolerance, and whether your analysis leads you to think that the particular area of the curve can move during any particular period of time.

A quick and dirty rule of thumb is that the longer the maturity, the greater the potential reaction to good or bad news on inflation. In other words, the further out you go on the curve, the greater the chance for volatility.

Eurodollars are the best instrument for trading the short term, because they are liquid investments, meaning that they're easy to buy and sell because the market has a large number of participants. The opposite of a liquid market is a thin market, in which the number of participants tends to be smaller, the spread between bid and offer prices tends to be farther apart, and the potential for volatility is larger. Grain markets can be thin markets (see Chapter 16). For long- and intermediate-term trading, you can use the 10-year T-note and 30-year T-bond futures.

Eurodollars are well suited for small traders, because margin requirements tend to be smaller, and the movements can be less volatile; however, don't consider those attractive factors a guarantee of success by any means. Any futures contract can be a quick road to ruin if you become careless.

Ten-year T-note and T-bond futures can be quite volatile, because large traders and institutions usually use them for direct trading and for complicated hedging strategies.

You can use options for trading all of these interest-rate products by applying the basic options rules and strategies described in Chapters 4 and 5.

Shaping the curve

Several informative shapes can be seen on the yield curve. Three important ones are

- **Normal curves:** The *normal curve* rises to the right, and short-term interest rates are lower than long-term interest rates. Pretty simple, eh? Economists usually look at this kind of movement as a sign of normal economic activity, where growth is ongoing and investors are being rewarded for taking more risks by being given extra yield in longer-term maturities.

- **Flat curves:** A *flat curve* is when short-term yields are equal or close to long-term yields. This type of graph can be a sign that the economy is slowing down, or that the Federal Reserve has been raising short-term rates.

- **Inverted curves:** An *inverted curve* shows long-term rates falling below short-term rates, which can happen when the market is betting on a slowing of the economy or during a financial crisis when traders are flocking to the safety of long-term U.S. Treasury bonds.

Checking out the yield curve

By keeping track of the yield curve, you're achieving several goals that Mark Powers describes in *Starting Out In Futures Trading* (Probus Publishing). By checking out the yield curve, you can

✔ Focus on the cash markets. Doing so enables you to put activity in the futures markets in perspective and provides clues to the relationship between prices in the futures markets.

✔ Watch for prices rising or falling below the yield curve, indications that can be good opportunities to buy or sell a security.

✔ Know that prices above the yield curve point to a relatively underpriced market.

✔ Know that prices below the curve point to a relatively overpriced market.

Sound Interest-Rate Trading Rules

Interest-rate futures serve one major function. They enable large institutions to neutralize or manage their price risks.

As an investor or speculator who trades interest-rate futures, you look at the markets differently than banks and other commercial borrowers. The interest-rate market is a way for them to hedge their risk, but for you, it's a way to make money based on the system's inefficiencies, which often are created by the current relationship between large hedgers, the Fed, and other major players, such as foreign governments.

A perfect example of an inefficient market is when a large corporation wants to sell a big bundle of bonds but can't seem to find buyers. As market bids raise the yields on the bond offering, treasury prices may fall as some players sell treasury bonds to raise money to buy the corporate bonds.

That kind of situation arises occasionally and can create volatility. Sometimes, short-term gyrations can offer entry points into the bond market on the long and the short sides, depending, of course, on the prevailing market and the price trends at the time.

Generally, you want watch for the following:

✔ Opportunities to trade the long-term issues when interest rates are falling

✔ Opportunities to stay on the shorter-term side of the curve when interest rates are rising

Nevertheless, regardless of rules or general tendencies of markets, focusing on what's happening at the moment and trading what you see are important guidelines to follow.

When trading international interest-rate contracts, you must consider the effects of currency conversion. If you just made a 10-percent profit trading Eurobunds, but the Euro fell 10 percent, your purchasing power has not grown.

When getting ready to trade, make sure that you do the following:

- ✔ Calculate your margin requirements. Doing so enables you to know how much of a cushion for potential losses you have available before you get a margin call and are required to put up more money to keep a position open. Never put yourself in a position to receive a margin call.

- ✔ Price in how much of your account's equity you plan to risk before you make your trade.

- ✔ Canvass your charts so that you know support and resistance levels on each of the markets that you plan to trade, and then you can set your entry points above or below those levels, depending, of course, on which way the market breaks.

- ✔ Be ready for trend reversals. Although you need to trade with the trend, you also must be ready for reversals, especially when the market appears to be comfortable with its current trend.

- ✔ Understand what the economic calendar has in store on any given day. Knowing the potential for economic indicators of the day to move the market in either direction prepares you for the major volatility that can occur on the day they're released.

- ✔ Pick your entry and exit points, including your worst-loss scenario — the possibility of taking a margin call.

- ✔ Decide what your options are if your trade goes well and you have a significant profit to deal with.

Playing the Short End of the Curve: Eurodollars & T-Bills

When you trade the short end of the curve, you're using Eurodollars, T-bills, LIBOR, or short-term Eurobond futures as your trading vehicle.

Treasury bills and Eurodollars are not the same thing, although they are expressions of short-term interest rates and trade in the same direction. You can lose money trading T-bill futures, just as you can when you trade Eurodollar futures.

Eurodollar basics

A *Eurodollar* is a dollar-denominated deposit held in a non-U.S. bank. A Eurodollar contract gives you control of $1 million Eurodollars and is a reflection of the LIBOR rate for a three-month, $1-million offshore deposit. Eurodollars are popular trading instruments that have been around since 1981. Following are some facts about Eurodollars that you need to know:

- ✔ A *tick* is the unit of movement for all futures contracts, but in the case of Eurodollars, a point = one tick = 0.1 = $25. If you own a Eurodollar contract, and it falls or rises four ticks, or 0.4, you either lose or gain $100, respectively. Eurodollars can trade in ¼ or ½ points, which are worth $6.25 and $12.50, respectively.

- ✔ Eurodollar prices are a central rate in global business and are quoted in terms of an index. For example, if the price on the futures contract is $9,200, the yield is 8 percent.

- ✔ Eurodollars trade on the CME with contract listings in March, June, September, and December. Different Eurodollar futures contracts suit different time frames. Some enable you to trade more than two years from the current date. This kind of long-term betting on short-term interest rates is rare, but sometimes large corporations use it. For full details, it's always good to check with your broker about which contracts are available, or go to the CME Web site.

- ✔ Trading hours for Eurodollars are from 7:20 a.m. to 2 p.m. central time on the trading floor, but they can be traded almost 24/7 on *Globex,* the electronic trading home of a large variety of futures contracts. For Eurodollars, Globex is a shut down only between 4 and 5 p.m. nightly.

- ✔ The *initial margin,* or the minimum you'd need in your account as of June 20, 2005, to trade a single Eurodollar contract at CME was $945 for nonexchange members. The *maintenance margin,* or the minimum you need in your account to keep the trade going, was $700.

Trading Eurodollars

Eurodollars are the most popular futures trading contract in the world, because they offer reasonably low margins and the potential for fairly good return in a short period of time.

You want to trade Eurodollars when events are occurring that are likely to influence interest rates. If you grasp the concept of trading Eurodollars, you're also set to trade other types of interest-rate futures, as long as you understand that each individual contract is going to have its own special quirks and idio-syncrasies. The CME provides a good overview of all of its interest-rate con-tracts online in a PDF file called *How to Get Started Trading CME Interest Rate Products* at www.cme.com/files/I19_How_to_Interest.pdf.

If you trade interest-rate futures, here are some basic factors to keep in mind:

- ✔ Check the overall trend of the market.
- ✔ Consider whether the market is oversold or overbought.
- ✔ Decide how much you're willing to risk before you enter the trade.
- ✔ Look at the overall background for the trade you're going to execute before doing so.

Picking your spot to trade

A good opportunity for trading Eurodollars futures was the week ending July 1, 2005, when the economic calendar was heavy in terms of the number of releases and their importance regarding what the Fed was likely to do next with interest rates. Included on the calendar, the Fed had a two-day meeting scheduled at which it was widely expected to raise interest rates.

Aside from the Fed's announcement on interest rates the afternoon of June 30, the economic calendar featured two particularly tradable reports on July 1: the University of Michigan Consumer Sentiment Index and the Institute for Supply Management (ISM — purchasing manager's) report. Each is a key barometer of activity for a major cog in the economic food chain.

The Fed raised interest rates on June 30 and told the markets that they could expect them to be raising rates again in the future. Economic reports all showed signs of a strengthening economy. And the markets were poised for such a set of developments.

Figure 10-3 shows three months' worth of trading in the July 2005 Eurodollar contract. Note that the price break below the moving average, the thin line between the price bars, correctly predicted a fall in prices. Also note the over-all downtrend in the Eurodollar during the three-month period, which is a sign of rising interest rates. The implied (interest) rate for this contract at the close on July 1 was 3.6175 percent, up from 3.40 in May. You can calculate the implied rate by subtracting the contract price from 100, as described in the earlier "Globalizing the markets" section.

You want to trade with the trend, so the path of least resistance in this trade was to go short. (See Chapters 7, 8, and 20 for more information about going short.)

Figure 10-3:
A chart
of the
Eurodollar's
July 2005
contract
illustrates
a good
opportunity
to sell short
and how to
calculate
implied
contract
interest
rates based
on prices.

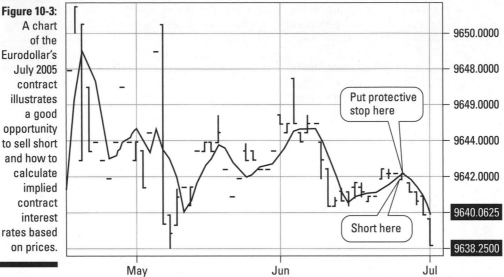

Eurodollars trade almost around the clock, so great gains from a good intra-day session can be wiped out or significantly reduced if a major event happens overnight. All futures that trade on Globex or other electronic round-the-clock systems are affected in the same way.

Managing your trade

Assume for a moment that you shorted one contract when the price slipped below the four-day moving average on June 27 so that your order was filled at the close of the regular session at 9,642. To protect yourself and cover your short position, you put a buy stop five ticks above the moving average, thus limiting your loss to $125 above the crossover price. Thereafter, you adjust the stop on a daily basis to protect your gains based on your risk tolerance. In this example, I use broad numbers, but you need to set your stop in a way that you don't risk a margin call if the trade goes against you. In other words, in this trade, your losses need to be limited to no more than $245 (roughly a ten-tick loss), because a $245 loss will get you a margin call if all you had to start with was the minimum margin of $945.

Setting your stop a good distance from the margin call is a good idea, though, to allow some leeway in case the market moves fast against you. The more room between your stop and the margin call, the better you are. The more you trade, the more you'll develop a sense of what your risk tolerance is.

A stop is not a guarantee that you'll get out of a position at the point specified by your stop-loss order. Sometimes you get the closest price to the stop, depending on market conditions. See Chapter 3 for a review of different types of orders.

The trade that I describe in this section is a high-risk and purely hypothetical trade that's intended only to illustrate how to manage your margin and how the Eurodollar market works. You should never trade any futures contract unless you have enough equity in your account to do so, which in this case you don't.

As a general rule, you should never risk any more than 5 percent of your equity on any one trade with a small account. The bare minimum requirement for trading futures as an individual small speculator is widely accepted to be no less than $20,000. See Chapters 17, 18, and 19 to review trading plans and strategies.

By the close of trading July 1, after a five-day holding period, the gain on the hypothetical trade was $937. If you had $945 in your account as your only margin, you essentially would have doubled your money.

During this trade, your margin never fell to $700, because you set your stop to get you out before you got a margin call.

A 1-point move in the July Eurodollar contract (Figure 10-3) is worth $2,500 per contract. This move is huge, so I'm only using it to illustrate the big picture.

If you happened to be short, or betting on falling Eurodollar prices, like in the example, a fall of this size would make you a good profit. If you were long, or betting on higher prices, you'd lose $2,500. In reality, if you used good risk-management techniques, such as a trailing stop like the one described in the example that accompanies Figure 10-3, you wouldn't let a Eurodollar contract move against you that far. See Chapter 17 for more about trading plans.

At this point, the example trade has earned a nice profit of 3.75 ticks, or $93.75 per contract over five days. So right before a three-day July 4th holiday weekend, when the Group of Eight was meeting in London with large numbers of demonstrators present, and a nine-country rock concert was planned to raise awareness for the famine in Africa, you could have

- ✔ Closed the position and taken your profits, less commissions.

- ✔ Tightened your short covering stop by setting it at 9641.05, just above the closing price (9,640.0625) on Figure 10-3.

✔ Sold a portion of your position if you had more than one contract, taking a part of your profits and adjusting the remaining position by tightening your stop.

✔ Considered establishing option strategies. In this case, because you're short, a call option would be the correct move. A put option would be the correct choice if you were long, because a put option generally rises in price when the market falls. (See Chapter 3 to find out how to select options.)

By now, you're probably wondering what to do if you're the subject of a margin call. For starters, you need to follow a good rule of thumb used by professionals: *Never risk more than 50 percent of your total account equity when trading.* For example, if you had followed that rule, you never would have bought the one Eurodollar contract in the example above, because you had only $945 in your account. Assuming that you had more money, and you made a good trade, in the future, you'd still buy one Eurodollar contract and keep 50 percent of your equity in your account.

If you do get a margin call, you can

✔ Liquidate your position to meet the call and then take a break for a few days until you get your wits back together.

✔ Sell some of your position to meet the call.

✔ Deposit new money into your account to meet the call.

Plan your trades so that you never get a margin call. That's the best way. Do it by carefully following the rules outlined in this section, having enough money in your account, never risking more than 10 percent of your equity on any one position (5 percent if your account's small), and calculating your maximum risk while keeping it below the amount that results in a margin call.

Trading Treasury-bill futures

A 13-week T-bill contract is considered a risk-free obligation of the U.S. government. In the cash market, T-bills are sold in $10,000 increments, such that if you paid $9,600 for a T-bill in the cash market, an annualized interest rate of 4 percent is implied. At the end of the three months (13 weeks), you'd get $10,000 in return.

Risk free means that if you buy the T-bills, you're assured of getting paid by the U.S. government. Trading T-bill futures, on the other hand, is not risk free. Instead, T-bill futures trades essentially are governed by the same sort of risk rules that govern Eurodollar trades. T-bill futures

✔ Are 3-month (13-week) contracts based on $10,000 U.S. Treasury bills.

✔ Have a face value at maturity of $1,000,000.

✔ Move in ½-point increments (½ point = 0.005 = $12.50) with trading months of March, June, September, and December.

Trading Bonds and Treasury Notes

The 10-year U.S. Treasury note has been the accepted benchmark for long-term interest rates since the U.S. stopped issuing the long bond (30-year U.S. Treasury bond) in October 2001. Thirty-year bond futures and 30-year T-bonds (issued before 2001) still are actively traded, and the U.S. Treasury announced in August 2005 that new 30-year T-bonds were going to be issued and hit the market in February 2006.

Ten-year T-note yields are the key for setting long-term mortgage rates. By watching this interest rate, you can pinpoint the best entry times for remortgaging, relocating, or buying rental property, and you can keep tabs on whether your broker is quoting you a good rate.

What you're getting into

Bond and note futures are big-time trading vehicles that move fast. Each tick or price quote, especially when you hold more than one contract and the market is moving fast, can be worth several hundred dollars. Some other facts about 10- and 30-year interest-rate futures that you need to know include that they are

✔ Traded under the symbols *TY* for pit trading and *ZN* for electronic trading in the 10-year contract.

✔ Valued at $100,000 per contract, the same as for a 30-year bond contract (which is traded under the symbol *US* for pit trading and *ZB* for electronic trading).

✔ Longer-term debt futures that have higher margin requirements than Eurodollars. As of June 2005, the initial margin for 10-year and 30-year note and bond contracts, respectively, were $1,013 and $1,553. Maintenance margins, respectively, were $750 and $1,150 per contract.

✔ Quoted in terms of 32nds and that one point is $1,000 and one tick must be at least

- ½ of ⅟₃₂, or $15.625, for a ten-year issue.

- ⅟₃₂, or $31.25, for a 30-year issue.

When a price quote is "84-16," it means the price of the contract is 84 and ¹⁶⁄₃₂ for both, and the value is $84,500.

✔ Traded on the CME from 7:20 a.m. to 2 p.m. central time Monday through Friday. Electronic trades can be made from 7 a.m. to 4 p.m. central time Sunday through Friday.

Trading in expiring contracts closes at noon central time (Chicago time) on the *last trading day,* which is the seventh business day before the last business day of the delivery month.

U.S. note and bond futures have no price limits.

What you'll get if you take delivery

If you take delivery, your contract will be wired to you on the last business day of the delivery month via the Federal Reserve book-entry wire-transfer system. What you get delivered to you, as of June 2005, is a series of U.S. Treasury bonds that either cannot be retired for at least 15 years from the first day of the delivery month or that are not callable with a maturity of at least 15 years from the first day of the delivery month. The *invoice price,* or the amount that you'll have to tender, equals the futures settlement price multiplied by a conversion factor with accrued interest added. The *conversion factor* used is the price of the delivered bond ($1 par value) to yield 6 percent.

Bonds that are not callable remain in circulation until full maturity, which means that the holder receives all the interest payments until the bond expires, when the principle is returned. Callable bonds put the holder at risk of receiving less interest because of an earlier retirement of the bond than the holder had planned.

For T-notes, you'd receive a package of U.S. Treasury notes that mature from 6½ to 10 years from the first day of the delivery month. The price is calculated by using a formula that you can find on the CBOE Web site. As a small speculator, your chances of getting a delivery are nil.

Figures 10-4 and 10-5 show the ten-year U.S. T-note futures for December 2005. Figure 10-4 shows a good example of a moving-average trading system during the same time period featured in the Eurodollar sections earlier.

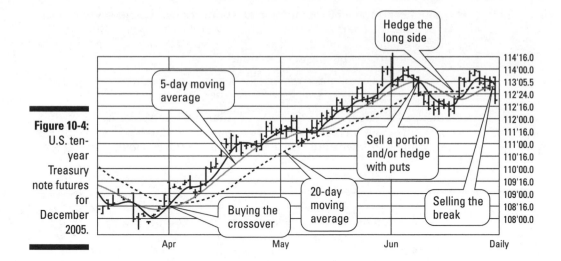

Figure 10-4:
U.S. ten-year Treasury note futures for December 2005.

During the time frame shown in Figure 10-4, even as Eurodollars and short-term instruments fell in price, longer-term instruments rallied because the market continued to believe that higher short-term interest rates eventually would slow down the economy. Elsewhere in the mix were pressures from hedge funds, foreign governments, and big traders setting up huge derivative trades in the options market. The overall effect, however, was to keep long-term interest rates going down and bond prices rising on the long end of the curve.

In June, after the ninth interest rate increase by the Fed, the market decided that the economy was likely to keep strengthening and that the Fed would keep raising rates. According to bond trader rules, rate increases in a strong economy spell a strong sign of inflation and a reason to sell bonds. Other factors that are evident in Figures 10-4 and 10-5 include the following:

- T-note futures rose during the period of interest rate increases until the month of June, when the contract began to struggle. In the cash bond market, long-term rates had been falling until the same time period when they became volatile.

- The trend was above the trio of moving averages — the 5-day, the 20-day, and the 10-day — much of the time.

- An excellent entry point is found in April in Figure 10-4 where the 5-day moving average crosses over the 10-day and the 20-day moving averages. Buying a portion of your position at the first crossover is a common practice when using the moving average crossover as a trading method. You then buy the second portion of the position at the second crossover. You could have bought as the 5-day average crossed over the 10-day average, and again when the 10-day average crossed over the 20-day average.

✔ The uptrend stayed intact until June, so reversing the crossover is just as easy as the chart points out. You can also hedge your position if you're unsure whether the crossover is temporary or you're seeing a significant top by buying a put option.

✔ The break below all three moving averages was clear in late June, giving you an opportunity to sell short.

✔ You need to use trailing stops when trading all futures contracts so that even when you aren't sure whether a top was reached, you nevertheless are stopped out when the price falls below the three moving averages.

Figure 10-5 highlights the use of good trend-line analysis. Take note of the following:

✔ **A double top in bond prices and a key break below the rising trend line.** Note that when the Fed raised interest rates June 30, bond prices failed to close above the previous day's intraday high price, a signal that the market was exhausted. Sure enough, it closed significantly lower the next day.

✔ **The price on July 1.** Closing within the gap is a good example of how gaps become magnets for price reversals at some point in the future.

✔ **The 116 support level.** Your next indicator to watch is when the market tests the 116 key-support area. If you shorted the break in prices below 118, you'd be looking to cover at least some of your short position by buying the contract back and specifying that you are doing so with intent to cover the short position or buying some call options to hedge your position near that area.

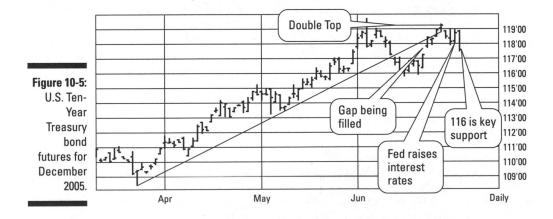

Figure 10-5:
U.S. Ten-Year Treasury bond futures for December 2005.

Chapter 11

Rocking and Rolling: Speculating with Currencies

. . . .

In This Chapter

▶ Exploring foreign exchange rates

▶ Trading the spot market

▶ Weighing in on the U.S. dollar index

▶ Trading the euro, pound, yen, and Swiss franc

▶ Maintaining your sanity in a 24-hour-a-day market

. . . .

*I*n a global economy, investors have come to realize that stocks and bonds are not the only games in town. Currencies are among the fastest growing segments of the capital markets.

Aside from the currency futures, foreign currencies trade in a busy spot market. In fact, explaining how much of the action in currencies takes place in the spot market takes up a good portion of this chapter.

The major goals of this chapter are to introduce you to the currency market, provide a broad overview of the important role it plays in forging relationships between other markets, and give you a good sound base from which to expand your foreign exchange (or as it's known in the business . . . forex) activities.

My first experience in the currency markets was with trading the U.S. dollar index. I broke all the rules and lost some money, but I discovered some valuable lessons that have enabled me to make some profitable trades since then.

These days, because of time commitments and a general distaste for volatility, I still trade currencies, but I do so by using mutual funds, a nice development in the evolution of trading that enables me to participate in a market that I truly love while not having to suffer the hair-raising action that can go along with directly trading currencies and currency futures.

If that sounds like your cup of tea, be sure to check out the currency mutual-fund timing system that I explain on my Web site at `Joe-Duarte.com`, because I use my fund trades as guides for the timing system. For now, though, I'll stick to the currency markets in a more traditional style.

Understanding Foreign Exchange Rates

Foreign exchange rates are influenced by internal and external factors. *Internal factors* can be as simple as determining whether a country has specific controls or limits on its currency. The most current example of a controlled currency is the Chinese yuan, which the Chinese government maintains in a narrow trading band. Other global currencies, especially the ones coming from emerging markets and less developed countries, also are controlled by their respective governments. *External factors* deal mostly with trade issues (disputes) or the market's perception of the political and economic situation in a given country. Of course, wars and natural disasters also qualify as potential market-moving events.

The most important influences on currency values are

- **Interest rates:** As a rule, higher interest rates lead to higher currency prices.

- **Inflation rates:** Higher inflation tends to lead to a weaker currency. This general rule doesn't apply when the rate of inflation is leading a country's central bank to raise interest rates. In that case, despite higher inflation, the markets are likely to bid up that country's currency as they expect interest rates there to continue to rise.

- **Current account status:** Countries that tend to export more than they import tend to have stronger currencies than countries that import more than they export. This relationship is soft, however, because some countries, such as Japan, purposely keep their respective currencies weak by selling them in the open market just to keep their exports high. These countries don't export their currencies; instead, their central banks sell them into the open market by making trades just like any other trading desk. The net effect is to increase the amount of a country's currency that is floating in the markets, thus decreasing its value to indirectly affect the balance of trade.

- **Budget status:** Countries with budget surpluses, again, as a general rule, tend to have stronger currencies than countries with budget deficits. This rule also is soft, because it doesn't hold up all the time. For example, the United States (U.S.) has chronic budget and current-account deficits, but the U.S. dollar experiences long rallies in which its strength is quite impressive.

✔ **Political stability:** Along with interest rates and economic fundamentals, politics are more than likely the most consistent determinants of the exchange rates that are quoted on a regular basis. Despite a fairly strong economy, an otherwise strong dollar during the Clinton administration suffered during the Monica Lewinsky scandal.

Exploring Basic Spot-Market Trading

The *spot market* is where most of the currency trading is done. It's operated nearly exclusively by large banks and corporations. Here's the lowdown on the basics of the spot market:

✔ Trades on the spot market are made continuously Monday through Friday, starting in New Zealand and following the sun to Sydney, Tokyo, Hong Kong, Singapore, Bahrain, Frankfurt, Geneva, Zurich, Paris, London, New York, Chicago, and Los Angeles before starting again.

✔ When big banks and institutions trade currencies on the spot market, they are usually exchanging your currency with another individual party. Both parties usually know and recognize each other.

✔ One third of foreign exchange transactions in the world are done on an over-the-counter basis in the spot forex market, with no exchange being involved. Over-the-counter trades are made directly between two individuals or institutions, usually by phone.

✔ The *interbank market,* where most of the transactions in the spot market take place between banks and corporations, is a network of banks that serve as intermediaries or market makers or wholesalers. Participants buy and sell currencies in the interbank markets, where trades are settled within two days. The two-day settlement is fair to both parties, allowing plenty of time for money to change hands, considering the amount of time it sometimes takes to gather large sums together in one place.

✔ The *retail market* is where the rest of the currency transactions take place. Individual traders conduct these trades over the phone and via the Internet by using brokers as intermediaries. Settlement on the retail market is defined as the transaction day plus one day.

Dabbling in da forex lingo

Like anything else in life, foreign exchange (forex) has its own language, and your currency trading skills will grow faster when you get the terms right early on, that is, before risking your money-making trades in this volatile but mostly sensible market.

Foreign exchange transactions are exchanges between two *pairings* of currencies, with each currency having its own International Standardization Organization (ISO) code. The ISO code identifies the country and its currency using three letters. The pairing uses the ISO codes for each participating currency. For example, USD/GBP pairs the U.S. dollar and the British pound. In this case, the dollar is the *base currency,* and the pound is the *secondary currency.* Displayed the other way, GBP/USD, the pound is the base currency, and the dollar is secondary.

My favorite thing about currencies is the *pip,* the smallest move any currency can make. It means the same thing as a tick for other futures and asset classes. Incidentally, there is no mention of whether Gladys Knight trades currencies anywhere, with or without The Pips.

The four major currency pairings are

- EUR/USD = euro/U.S. dollar

- GBP/USD = British pound sterling/U.S. dollar (also known as *cable*)

- USD/JPY = U.S. dollar/Japanese yen

- USD/CHF = U.S. dollar/Swiss franc

When you read an exchange rate that's quoted on a screen, you're reading how much of one currency can be exchanged for another. If you see GBP/USD = 1.7550, that means you can exchange one British pound for 1.7550 dollars. The base currency is the pound; it's the one that you're either buying or selling.

When you trade currencies, you are, in effect, buying one currency and simultaneously selling another, or vice versa.

When you view a trading screen, you see a frame with two prices. One side is marked "sell" and gives you the selling price, and the other side is marked "buy" and gives you the buying price.

If you want to sell, you click on the sell side. If you want to buy, you click on the buy side. To reverse or close out your trade, you do the opposite of your current position.

Currency on the spot market is bought and sold in groups made up of 100,000 units of the base currency. On the spot market, buyer and seller are required to deposit a margin, which usually is 1 to 5 percent of the entire value of the trade. In other words, if you buy 100,000 GBP/USD at 1.7550, you'd put down the appropriate margin in dollars, while the seller of sterling, who is buying your dollars, would reciprocate by putting down an appropriate margin in sterling.

Location, location, location

Some special currency trading issues are dependent upon where your dealer is located. If you're trading in the spot market, and your dealer is in the U.S., you deposit your margin in dollars. If, however, you're trading through a foreign dealer or using a currency other than the one required by the broker, you have to convert your capital and margin requirements to the currency of the foreign dealer. Each situation is different, but you need to check out all the variables before making any trades.

Here's how it works: If you're trading the USD/JPY (U.S. dollar/Japanese yen) pair, the value of your trade will be calculated in yen, JPY. If your broker uses the dollar as his home currency, then your profits and losses in this trade are converted back to dollars at the relevant USD/JPY offer rate.

Although trading currencies may seem confusing, you can work it out by carefully studying exchange rates and doing some practice trades. Most online currency dealers will enable you to open a practice account so that many of the nuances of trading currencies become self-evident with practice.

Don't get cross over crossrates

Crossrates are the exchange rates between non-U.S. dollar currency pairings. Andy Shearman of Trader House Network, `www.traderhouse.net`, offers a nice example of how *crosses* work. I've adapted it below to show the cross between the pound sterling and the Swiss franc, and your trading screen shows the following crossrates:

- ✔ EUR/USD = 1.0060/65
- ✔ GBP/USD = 1.5847/52
- ✔ USD/JPY = 120.25/30
- ✔ USD/CHF = 1.4554/59

These four pairings are key crossrates. For example, the GBP/USD pairing is the bid (1.5847) and ask (1.5852) price for the British pound sterling and the U.S. dollar exchange rate at the moment. The difference between them, 0.0005, is the *spread,* which amounts to the commission that the dealer collects.

So to calculate the GBP/CHF (British pound for Swiss franc) crossrate, do the following steps:

1. **Find the GBP/USD exchange rate.**

   Bid: 1.5847 Offer (ask): 1.5852

2. **Find the USD/CHF exchange rate.**

   Bid: 1.4554 Offer: 1.4559

3. **Multiply the bid amount for the GBP/USD exchange rate with the same for the USD/CHF exchange rate, and then do the same with the offer amounts.**

   $1.5847 \times 1.4554 = 2.3063$ and $1.5852 \times 1.4559 = 2.3079$

4. **Jot down the answers.**

   GBP/CHF = 2.3063/2.3079

The calculations work for all currencies if you follow these steps. Foreign exchange quotation services and trading software also give you the amounts, but perhaps a little quicker.

Electronic spot trading

Aside from traditional phone-based trading, you can trade currencies in the spot market electronically, but you need to be prepared to sit in front of your screen and manage your trade actively; otherwise, you risk losing large sums rapidly.

You also need to know that you'll pay more for trading currencies in the spot market than the pros do. That's because you're a little guy, and they're not. That's the way of the world, and you need to know that before you get into trading anything.

Something else to keep in mind is that some foreign-currency Web sites and brokers will tell you that trading on their site is commission free. That isn't true. They do collect a fee that amounts to the spread between the bid and ask prices on the currency quotes.

If you keep that in mind, you'll save yourself a lot of grief, and can get on with trading.

Getting your charts together before you trade

If you're going to trade forex, you'll need a good command of technical analysis. You can apply the principles of technical analysis that I discuss in Chapter 7, because the same general principles and indicators apply to foreign exchange rates.

Some particulars about the forex that you need to keep in mind are that currencies tend to trend for a long time, usually months to even years, but within the major long-term trends (see Figure 11-1), countertrend moves usually occur, and a large degree of intraday volatility is common. Some other factors common to long-term currency trends like the one seen in Figure 11-1 include

✔ **Long-term bull (and bear) markets can last for years.** The bull market for the euro seen in Figure 11-1 lasted four years.

✔ **Trend indicators work well in the currency markets.** Note the *intermediate-term tops* marked by the Relative Strength Indicator (RSI) and its nice correlation with the MACD oscillator. See Chapter 7 for more about oscillators.

✔ **Trend lines are especially useful.** Note how the bull market clearly ended when the four-year trend line was broken.

Likewise, note how the double-top failure marked on the chart corresponds with the failure in the RSI and the break below the zero line on the MACD. A momentum failure, coupled with major breaks in the trend indicators and a break below a four-year rising trend line, was a clear sell signal.

Using long-term charts to track currencies is a great way to trade forex instruments. The long-term charts are your guides to the prevailing trend; however, within those long-term trends, you can find significant countertrend ebb and flow, during which you can trade against the long-term trend by

✔ Going long, or buying when the long-term chart is pointing up.

✔ Looking for opportunities to go short when the long-term trend is down.

✔ Using shorter-term charts to guide your shorter-term trades, both long and short.

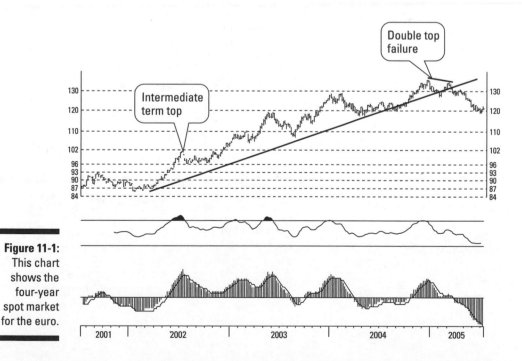

Figure 11-1:
This chart shows the four-year spot market for the euro.

Countertrend moves are an ever-present part of the market that require adjustments. As such, you always need to keep the long-term trend in mind so you don't grow too comfortable trading in the wrong direction, or *counter* to the long-term *trend* line.

When a currency breaks below a long-rising trend line, you must consider that the long-term trend has changed direction. The trend may not change every time this situation occurs. In fact, some markets return to the original trend soon after a break. A countertrend rally is another possible trading scenario. In a countertrend rally, the market remains in a long-term up- or downtrend, but trades in the opposite direction for a short to intermediate period of time can last for days, weeks, or even months before returning to the long-term trend.

You can see a countertrend rally in Figure 11-2, which shows a one-year chart of the euro that focuses on the last year of trading pictured in Figure 11-1.

The vertical line in the middle of the chart connects these three key points:

  ✔ The reversal of the euro

  ✔ A bottom in the RSI indicator

  ✔ A bottom in the MACD indicator

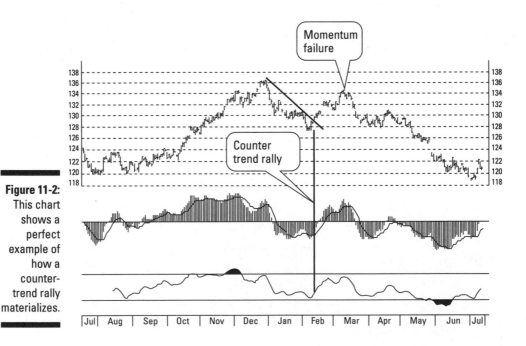

Figure 11-2: This chart shows a perfect example of how a counter-trend rally materializes.

Long-term charts are best used for keeping an eye on the big picture. When you see something that looks small on a long-term chart, use a short-term chart to magnify the time frame. Figure 11-2 magnifies the double top and momentum failure in Figure 11-1. When you look at the shorter-term chart, the momentum failure looks much clearer, and your decision-making therefore is enhanced.

Take your long-term charts seriously. If you've been trading in a certain direction for weeks or months, you're bound to get a fairly good reversal. Any reversal can be big enough to change the long-term trend, so you can play every reversal as one that may be the big one. In Figures 11-1 and 11-2, the long-term charts were correct, even though the one-year chart was less sensitive.

Keep your time frames in perspective. Intraday charts are useful for short-term trading. What looks like a major trend reversal on a three-day chart using 15-minute candlesticks may not amount to much in the big picture. But it's enough of a shift for you to use your short-term strategy.

Setting up your trading rig

Currency trading is heavy metal, so like heavy-metal bands, you need some serious hardware and software to keep your shirt on and your trousers dry.

Top on that list of needs is an electronic brokerage service that enables you to do *straight through processing* (STP), where you trade directly with the dealer through your computer using integrated quotations and transactional and administrative functionality. You can gain access to STP through your online broker, and you can gain access to a decent system through many online brokerage-services providers. You can find other online brokerages that offer STP by using your favorite online search engine.

You need to evaluate different brokers before deciding on one. A good electronic brokerage service gives you access to live, streaming data and enables you to make direct trades through your broker's Web site.

Most online brokers offer plenty of free goodies that you can look at to get a feel for how the forex markets work. They also offer free real-time quotes and a good basic charting service that you can use. Here are a couple of good ones:

- Electronic Brokering Services (EBS — www.ebs.com)
- Pronet Analytics (www.pronetanalytics.com)
- Nostradamus (www.nostradamus.co.uk)

I also maintain a good Web page with currency information on my Web site's directory. You can visit my site at www.joe-duarte.com/free/directory/software-forex.asp.

Here are some other essentials for forex trading:

- A reliable margin account broker. For details on margin and how to choose a broker, see Chapters 3, 4, and 17.

- A fast and reliable Internet connection. You need a good, reliable, broadband connection with your computer terminal dedicated to trading — not instant messaging for your teenager or educational stuff for your homeschooler.

- A big-time computer system on which you can run several big programs at the same time without crashing. You need as much memory and storage as you can muster. A gigabyte of RAM (random access memory) is a good start, but if you're going to run multiple monitors, you may need more, plus the setup for it. You need a good printer for printing your statements and a good backup system. If you plan to take a break and keep a position open, a good Wi-Fi setup for a laptop is a good idea. You also need all the security — antivirus, firewall, and spyware protection — that you can muster to keep your personal data from being stolen.

- Good trading software on which you can open and manage positions and conduct big-time technical analysis.

- Separate computer monitors, so you can

    - Handle market data

    - Submit dealing instructions

    - Look at charts and indicators all at once to keep tabs on all your open positions

    - Adjust your stops and place other orders

    - Keep an eye on how much money you have in your margin account

Two screens is a good number to get you started, but some traders may need more, especially when they trade more than one market at a time.

Using the right orders for your forex trading goals

You can use market orders when trading forex futures and other instruments, but because the forex markets move so fast, you need to set some automatic exit and entry points to manage your risk as part of your armaments.

A *stop loss* is the same kind of order in all markets: It gets you out either at your specified price or the closest possible price depending on market conditions. Same thing's true of a *limit order*, which you use to set your entry point at a predetermined price.

Some other useful orders for the forex market include

✔ **Take profit orders (TPO):** A TPO enables you to get out of your position at a price that you target before you enter the trade. This kind of order specifies that a position needs to be closed out when the current exchange rate crosses a given or set threshold. You can set up a TPO above a long position and below a short position.

✔ **One cancels the other (OCO) orders:** An OCO is an order that has two parts; actually it's made up of two separate orders bundled into one package. An OCO is made up of a stop-loss order and a limit order at opposite ends of a spread. When one order is triggered, no matter which direction the market is trending, the other is terminated. In effect, you enter an entry point and protect your position by limiting your losses immediately. Here's how the OCO works:

  • **Going long:** If you're going long in the market, you set the stop loss below the market spread and the limit-sell order above the market spread. If the base currency rate breaches the limit order threshold, then your position automatically is sold at or near the price at which you set the limit, and you no longer need the stop loss, which then is canceled. Alternatively, if the rate falls to the stop-loss trigger price, then the position is closed out at or near the trigger price, and you no longer have any need for the limit order.

  • **Going short:** If you're shorting the market, you set the stop loss above the market spread and the limit order below — just the opposite of the long position. If the exchange rate rises to the stop-loss trigger price, then the position is closed out, thus canceling the limit order. If the exchange rate falls to the limit-order trigger price, then the limit order is activated, you buy back the position at the predetermined limit-order price, and the stop-loss order is canceled.

Sampling the goods

Here's a simple example of a trade in the spot market:

✔ Buy a 100,000 lot of GBP/USD at the offer price of $1.7550.

The trade is valued at a total of $175,500.

✔ Need to put your broker's margin of 2 percent, or $3,510, in your margin account. You get that amount by multiplying 0.2 × $175,500.

✔ Profit when your trade goes well and the GPB/USD exchange rate rises to $1,760.

Your profit is $500, or 100,000 × (1.760 – 1.7550), or a 14-percent yield.

The U.S. Dollar Index

The Federal Reserve Board introduced the U.S. dollar index in March 2003. The index was the result of the Smithsonian Agreement, which repealed the Bretton Woods Agreement. What does that mean? The Bretton Woods agreement fixed global currency rates 25 years earlier. The Smithsonian agreement, which was viewed as a victory for proponents of free markets, enabled global currencies to float based on market forces.

The U.S. dollar index is used by traders to get the big picture of the overall trend of the dollar and is widely quoted in the press and on quote services. It is similar to the Fed's dollar index, which is a trade-weighted index, meaning that the Fed gives value to each individual currency in the index based on how much it trades within the U.S. However, the value of each index is different, and they shouldn't be confused with one another.

For example, as of July 10, 2005, the Fed's dollar index was quoted at 86.39 on the Fed's Web site. The spot price for the U.S. dollar index on the same day was 90.25. So according to the Fed's index, based on trade, the dollar had lost some 14 percent of its value since March 2003; however, according to the market — in other words, based on traders' perception of the global economy, the geopolitical situation, inflation, and interest rates, among other factors — the dollar had lost only 10 percent of its value (or purchasing power) since the creation of the index.

The U.S. dollar index has traded as high as the 160s and as low as the 70s. Interestingly, though, both the Fed and the trader indexes hit bottom in December 2004.

The U.S. dollar index trades on the New York Board of Trade at Finex and at the Chicago Mercantile Exchange. Here are the particulars of the index:

- A minimum tick is 0.1 and is worth $10.

- Futures contracts expire in March, June, September, and December.

- The overall value of a contract is 1,000 times the value of the index in dollars.

- Delivery is physical, meaning that you receive dollars based on the value of the index on the second business day prior to the third Wednesday during the month of the expiring contract. On the last trading day, trading ceases at 10:16 a.m.

- Delivery day is the third Wednesday of the contract month.

- No trading limits are placed on the U.S. dollar index. Trading hours are from 8:05 a.m. to 3 p.m. with overnight trading from 7 to 10 p.m.

The U.S. dollar index was modified at the inception of the euro and is weighted in a way that's similar to the Fed's trade weighted index, as follows (expressed in percentages):

- Euro's weight: 57.6 percent
- Japanese yen: 13.6 percent
- British pound: 11.9 percent
- Canadian dollar: 9.1 percent
- Swedish krona: 4.2 percent
- Swiss franc: 3.6 percent

The U.S. dollar index is best used as an indicator of trends in the currency markets.

The U.S. dollar index isn't as good of a trading vehicle as the individual currencies. The best way to trade the index is by using currency mutual funds. The Profunds Rising Dollar Fund (RDPIX) and Falling Dollar Funds (FDPIX) are two such funds. Rydex, another mutual fund company, is in the process of registering its own set of dollar trading funds. I use these funds to capitalize on the long-term trends that are possible in the currency markets.

I know that this book isn't about trading mutual funds, but one of the secrets of trading success is understanding what kind of a person you are. If you're overwhelmed by the big expensive trading rig you need to make any money in FOREX and upset (I know I am) because you can't take a coffee or bathroom break for fear the market will move against you and in the blink of an eye you'll end up with a margin call, then you need to consider using these funds. By using the funds, you are, in essence, taking away a good deal of the problems that you can face by directly trading currencies. The funds are priced only once a day. If you check the dollar index a few times during the day, then you have a pretty good idea as to how your fund is going to close that day.

Trading Foreign Currency

Trading currencies can be exciting and lucrative. For me, it's a great market because of the way politics affect the trends. Elections, strikes, and sudden developments, both good and bad, can lead to significant trading profits — if you stand ready to trade.

Trading the euro against the dollar

The euro is a convenient currency, because it encompasses the policies and the economic activity and political environment of a volatile but predictable part of the world — Europe.

Because France, Italy, and Germany, the largest members of the European Union (EU), are socialist countries, they normally operate under high budget deficits and tend to keep their interest rates more stable than the U.S., where the free-market approach and a usually vigilant Federal Reserve make more frequent adjustments on interest rates.

The general tendency of the Fed is to make the dollar trend for very long periods of time in one general direction.

Aside from the technical analysis, here are some general tendencies of the euro on which you need to keep tabs:

- The European Central Bank is almost fanatical about inflation, given German's history of hyperinflation in the first half of the 20th century and the repercussions of that period, namely the rise of Hitler. That means that the European Central Bank raises interest rates more easily than it lowers them.

- The European Central Bank's actions become important when all other factors are equal, meaning politics are equally as stable or unstable in the U.S. and Europe, and the two economies are growing. For example, if the U.S. economy is slowing down, money slowly starts to drift away from the dollar. In the past, that meant money would move toward the Japanese yen; however, because the market knows that Japan's central bank will sell yen, the default currency when the dollar weakens often is now the euro.

- The flip side is that the market often sells the euro during political problems in the region, especially when the European economy is slowing, and the economy in the United Kingdom (UK), which often moves along with the U.S. economy, is showing signs of strength.

As usual, you want to closely monitor major currencies and the crossrates. It's okay to form an opinion and have some expectations, but the final and only truth that should make you trade is what the charts are showing you. The direction that counts is the one in which the market is heading.

The UK pound sterling

The pound is active against the dollar and the euro, offering good opportunities to trade both pairs (GBP/USD and USD/GBP, see the section on "Dabbling in da forex lingo," earlier in this chapter). The UK is a pivotal nation, because it bridges the economical, geographical, and ideological divide between the U.S. and Europe.

Economically, the UK is more free-market oriented than Europe, and it tends to share a more common set of views with the U.S. At the same time, the UK can't totally disassociate itself from Europe, given its history and its geography.

The upshot is a currency that is affected by politics at home and on the two continents to which its destiny — or at least its economy and politics — is so closely related.

 Because the UK is an oil producer, the pound can be affected more directly by oil prices than other currencies. The relationship between oil and the pound is fading, however, because production in the UK's North Sea oil fields is steadily decreasing.

The Japanese yen

The Japanese yen is a manipulated currency, which basically means it is kept low artificially by the Japanese government.

The combination of low interest rates (zero for the last several years — as of the summer of 2005), the lasting economic effects from the bursting of the Japanese real-estate bubble, and the collapse of the stock market and the banking system in Japan have forced its government to keep the yen's value low by selling it in the open market when it reaches a certain level.

The main purpose of maintaining a weak currency is to keep the Japanese export machinery operational. Over the long term, however, a weaker currency will continue to hurt Japan's chance of achieving a lasting recovery.

 The most useful time to trade the yen is when political and potential military problems are taking place in Asia. China's rise as a global power can eventually lead to a major and uncontrolled weakening of the yen. The best way to trade the yen is not against the dollar but rather to use crossrate analysis, especially against the euro and the Swiss franc.

The Swiss franc

The Swiss franc is considered a *reserve currency,* or one that is reliable and tends to hold its value when others don't. It also is a currency to which traders and other investors flow during times of global crisis. Its strength is based on three traditional expectations in the market:

- **Reliable economic fundamentals:** Switzerland has a history of low inflation and current account surpluses. It also is a country whose banking system is well known for holding the deposits of extremely wealthy and stable clients.

- **Gold reserves.** The Swiss franc still is backed by gold, because Switzerland's gold reserves significantly exceed the amount of currency it has placed in circulation. Switzerland has the fourth largest holding of gold in the world. Relative to Gross Domestic Product (GDP), the level of international reserves — with or without gold — is far ahead of all other countries.

- **Little political influence:** Switzerland's political neutrality enables it to set a monetary policy that operates (essentially) in a vacuum and thus enables its central bank to concentrate its effort on price stability. In December 1999, the Swiss National Bank changed the way it manages monetary policy, from one that traditionally targeted the money supply to one that targets inflation. The bank's goal is a 2-percent annual inflation rate.

The two major factors to keep an eye on when trading the franc are

- **Economic data:** The franc can be affected by several key economic reports, including

    - The release of Swiss M3, the broadest measure of money supply

    - The release of Swiss CPI

    - Unemployment data

    - Balance of payments, GDP, and industrial production

- **Crossrates:** Changes in interest rates in the EU or the UK can alter crossrates and have an effect on the U.S. dollar. For example, if the euro or the pound rises and the Swiss franc weakens against them, the franc also is likely to move with regards to the dollar, thus offering traders like you three potential trading vehicles. The general tendency is for a sudden move in EUR/USD — which can be triggered by a major fundamental factor, such as an unexpected change in government, a terrorist attack, or a major economic release — to cause an equally sharp move in USD/CHF in the opposite direction.

The panic response

The Swiss franc often is a financial instrument of refuge for wealthy individuals, corporations, and traders. After the events of September 11, 2001, and the July 2005 bombings in the London Underground, the Swiss franc was the immediate beneficiary of the *flight to quality trade,* as traders acted on reflex, at least initially, and moved money toward traditional safe havens. The U.S. dollar used to be more of a safe haven prior to September 11, 2001, but that distinction has changed, because the markets have adjusted their expectations based on the fact that even though no more major attacks have occurred in the United States, the U.S. nevertheless remains the primary target of Al-Qaeda. Whenever a major terrorist attack occurs, the markets always react as though the attack may be followed by a strike on the United States. Besides the Swiss franc, other safe havens include U.S. Treasury Bonds, U.S. Treasury Bills, and Eurodollars.

Arbitrage Opportunities and Sanity Requirements

The 24-hour trading day in spot currency markets — and its potential for activity whenever any major event occurs and develops — offers great opportunities for *arbitrage,* or trading both on the long and short side by using different currencies. Arbitrage is a sophisticated strategy that you can use when you become experienced at trading.

Here are some basic arbitrage rules to keep in mind:

- **Currencies move in response to news events.** Keeping a calendar of economic releases for Europe, the U.S., the UK, Japan, and Switzerland is a good habit to get into. When a major economic release is outside the realm of expectations, currencies will move, and you can be poised in those situations to make large sums of money in short periods of time.

- **Major events, such as September 11, 2001, hurricanes, and other natural disasters also make the currencies move.** I'm not trying to be morbid, but trading on bad news is a fact of life. As a trader, you can make bad-news decisions that are profitable if you're watching for them.

- **Keep an eye on crossrates and bond markets.** These areas move together, and they often move in opposite directions. After you become comfortable with currencies, you may want to consider setting up trades in interest-rate futures and currencies, which can serve as either a hedge or a profit-making opportunity.

✔ **Research your opportunities in the options markets, and develop a program that includes options.** Currency and interest-rate futures offer option opportunities. By using currency and/or interest-rate options, you can protect your currency positions at a fraction of the cost of owning the direct contract or lot.

✔ **Use the hypothetical trading systems.** Available on the Internet, you can use these Web tools to try different strategies or dissect new charting setups. `ActionForex.com` has some good demos. Get comfortable with the way the currency markets work first, however, before you risk any large sums of money.

✔ **Beware of using mini accounts.** Although mini accounts enable you to trade forex for $300 or less, such trades are a good way to get hurt, given the speed at which these markets can move. Instead, you need to be well capitalized before you make your move into this trading arena.

✔ **Don't give up your day job unless you're a truly gifted trader.** Most people are not gifted traders, and they need to use the currency markets only as part of an overall strategy to build wealth steadily and to protect their overall investment program and goals.

Don't try to trade around the clock. Much of the action in currencies takes place overnight. Europe and Asian trading in currencies can be extremely powerful, and any open position that was profitable when you went to bed can be wiped out by morning. Use your stops wisely, and close out any positions that make you uncomfortable when you're done for the day.

Chapter 12

Stocking Up on Indexes

· ·

In This Chapter

▶ Coming to grips with trading stock-index futures

▶ Establishing fair value for stock futures contracts

▶ Discovering the major types of stock-index futures contracts

▶ Defining strategies for trading stock futures

▶ Trading stock-index futures wisely and successfully

· ·

Stock-index futures came of age October 19, 1987. That's when a major stock market crash was fueled by something known as *portfolio insurance,* or the sale of futures contracts to protect losses in individual stock positions. The most important and lasting influence of the 1987 crash was that the world was awakened to a new era of investing — the era of the one market — in which stock-index futures and the stock market became a single entity.

I remember October 19, 1987, vividly. I had no money and no investments at that time. Boy, was I lucky. But market activity on that day and during the ensuing months is responsible for turning me into a financial-market junky and enabling me not only to save for my retirement but also to earn a living doing something that is exciting and enjoyable — trading and teaching others how to trade.

My first real-life experience with money in a stock-market crash came in 1990, when Saddam Hussein invaded Kuwait. My next experiences came in 1997 and 1998 when the Asian currency crisis hit the markets. Each step of the way, I remember watching the relationship between the cash market and stock-index futures. That interplay sets up the potential strategies for speculation and for hedging that I describe to you in this chapter.

You don't need to trade every major index contract in the world to be successful; you just need to find one or two with which you're comfortable — the ones that enable you to implement your strategies. In this chapter, I focus on the

Standard & Poor's 500 (S&P 500) Stock Index futures, a well-known contract that is central to the markets. Any of the lessons that I describe with respect to the S&P 500 can, however, be applied to just about any contract.

Getting a Grip on the Noise

Stock-index futures are futures contracts based on indexes that are composed of stocks. For example, the S&P 500 futures contract is based on the popular market benchmark of the same name — the S&P 500 Stock Index, a group of 500 commonly traded stocks (see the section "The S&P 500 futures [SP]" later in this chapter).

When you trade stock-index futures, you're betting on the direction of the contract's value, and not on the individual stocks that make up the index.

In a sense, by focusing on the value and general trend of the stocks as a group, you're blocking out a good deal of the noise that often is associated with the daily gyrations in the prices of the individual stocks.

Stock-index futures are an integral part of the stock market's daily activity. As of July 2005, more than 70 stock-index futures contracts traded on at least 20 exchanges around the world. As a percentage of the total number of futures contracts traded, stock-index futures are by far the largest category of futures contracts traded. That dominance clearly speaks of the major role that stock-index futures play in risk management for the entire stock market.

I can think of several major reasons for trading stock-index futures. Here are some of the more common ones:

- ✔ **Speculation:** When you speculate, you're making an educated guess about the direction of a market. I hope you gather from reading this and other chapters of this book that an educated guess is based on careful examination of market history, trends, and key external events that can affect the prices of financial assets. When you speculate, you can deliver trading profits to your accounts by going long or short on index futures, or betting on prices rising or falling, respectively.

- ✔ **Hedging:** A *hedge* is when you use stock-index futures and options to protect either an individual security in your portfolio or in some cases the entire portfolio from losing value. For example, if you own a large number of blue-chip, dividend-paying stocks, and you're getting some nice income from them, you have to think long and hard about selling them. Yet, in a bear market, your portfolio is going to decrease in value.

By using stock-index futures and options, you can sell the market short and protect the overall value of your portfolio, while continuing to receive your dividends.

✔ **Tax consequences:** Gains in the futures markets are taxed at a lower rate than stock-market capital gains. At the top rate, short-term gains (because that's what futures and options traders deal with, primarily) in stocks are taxed at a 39.6 percent rate. Capital gains from successful futures trading are blended by the IRS as follows:

- The IRS has a complex set of rules for taxing gains in the futures markets with specific forms with which you must become familiar, such as IRS Form 4797 Part II for securities or Form 6781 for commodities. I could devote at least a third of a chapter to tax rules, but space restrictions won't allow it, so that means that you need to check with your accountant *before* you start trading.

- The flip side is that you can deduct your losses and get preferential treatment on your gains if you form the right kind of corporation and set up retirement plans and other kinds of shelters. These factors may vary depending on the state in which you reside, and they may change over time as new tax laws are written. Again, be sure to check with your accountant.

- The IRS also taxes stock-index futures at a different rate than commodities, such as soybeans. Short-term gains in the former are taxed up to 35 percent, while short-term gains in the latter average out to 23 percent.

  For example, for every $10,000 you make in short-term gains as a result of trading individual stocks, you may have to pay as much as $3,960 in taxes, but when you trade stock-index futures, every $10,000 short-term gain can be taxed for only $2,784. The $2,784 is based on the blending formula used by the IRS. Again, check with your accountant for the numbers that may apply to you and your tax bracket.

✔ **Lower commission rates:** Many futures brokerages offer lower commission rates. This practice is not as widespread as it was before online discount brokers for stocks became a mainstay of the business. But you still can find low commission rates in the futures markets, a factor that becomes more important as you trade large blocks or quantities of stocks.

✔ **Time factors:** If something happens overnight, when the stock market is closed, and you want to hedge your risk, you can trade futures on Globex while Wall Street sleeps. Globex is a 24-hour electronic trading system for a wide variety of futures contracts (see Chapter 3).

Contracting with the Future: Looking into Fair Value

Fair value is the theoretically correct value for a futures contract at a particular point in time. You calculate fair value using a formula that includes the current index level, index dividends, number of days to contract expiration, and interest rates.

Without getting caught up in the details, the important thing for you to remember about fair value is that it's a benchmark that can be a helpful tool for your analysis of the markets.

For example, when a stock-index futures contract trades below its fair value, it's trading at a *discount*. When it trades above fair value, it's trading at a *premium*.

Knowing the fair value is most helpful in gauging where the market is headed. Because stock-index futures prices are related to spot-index prices, changes in fair value can trigger price changes.

If the spread between the index and cash widens or shrinks far enough, you'll see a rise in activity from computer-trading programs.

Here's how it works:

- ✔ If the futures contract is too far below fair value, the index (cash) is sold and the futures contract is bought.

- ✔ If the futures contract is too high versus its fair value, the futures contract is sold and the index (cash) is bought.

- ✔ If enough sell programs hit the market hard enough over an extended period of time, you can see a *crash,* or a situation where market prices fall dramatically.

- ✔ If enough buy programs kick in, the market tends to rally.

Fair value is the number that the television stock analysts refer to when discussing the action in futures before the market opens.

Major Stock-Index Futures Contracts

You can trade many different stock-index contracts, but they all share the same basic characteristics. I describe many of these general issues in the section that follows, and I address any particular differences with descriptions of other individual contracts throughout the rest of this section.

The S&P 500 futures (SP)

The biggest stock-index futures contract is the S&P 500, which trades on the Chicago Mercantile Exchange (CME). This index is made up of the 500 largest stocks in the United States. It's a weighted index, which means that component companies that have bigger market capitalizations, or market values, can have a much larger impact on the movements of the index than components with smaller market capitalizations. For example, a stock like IBM has a larger market capitalization than the stock of a smaller company in the index, such as retailer Costco.

Some of the particulars about the S&P 500 Index include the following:

- **Composition:** The S&P 500 is made up of 400 industrial companies, 40 financial companies, 40 utilities, and 20 transportation companies, offering a fairly diversified view of the U.S. economy.

- **Valuation:** The S&P 500 Index is valued in ticks worth 0.1 index points or $25.

- **Contracts:** S&P 500 Index futures contracts are worth 250 times the value of the index. That means that when the index value is at 1,250, a contract is worth $250 \times \$1,250$, or $312,500. A move of a full point is worth $250.

- **Trading times:** Regular trading hours for S&P 500 Index futures are from 8:30 a.m. to 3:15 p.m., but S&P 500 Index futures contracts are another example of how 24-hour-a-day trading enables traders to respond to economic news and releases in the premarket and aftermarket sessions. The evening session starts 15 minutes after the close (at 3:30 p.m.) and continues in the overnight until 8:15 a.m. on Globex.

- **Contract limits:** Individual contract holders are limited to no more than 20,000 net long or short contracts at any one time.

- **Price limits:** Price limits should not be confused with circuit breakers (see next list item). *Price limits* halt trading above or below the price specified by the limit. A price limit is how far the S&P 500 Index can rise or fall in a single trading session. The limits are set on a quarterly basis. If the index experiences major declines or increases beyond these limits, a procedure is in place to halt trading. You can find the price limits detailed on the CME's Web site (www.cme.com).

- **Circuit breakers:** Circuit breakers halt trading briefly in a coordinated manner between exchanges. The limits that trigger circuit breakers are calculated and agreed upon on a quarterly basis by the different exchanges.

  The *collar rule* addresses price swings related to program trades that move the Dow Industrial Average more than 2 percent by requiring index arbitrage orders, or orders that bet on the spread between the futures and cash of stock indexes, to be stabilizing. That means that traders using these methods can't pile on orders on the sell or the buy side in an attempt to exaggerate the gains or losses for the market. In effect, what this rule does is decrease the chance for huge gains or losses as a result of futures trading. Details can be found at the Web site for the Securities and Exchange Commission (SEC — www.sec.gov). For this overview chapter, it's good to know that the collar rule exists and that it can have an effect on trading.

✔ **Final settlement:** For all stock-index futures, settlement on the CME is based on a Special Opening Quotations (SOQ) price, which is calculated based on the opening prices for each of the stocks in an index on the day that the contract expires. Don't confuse the SOQ with the opening index value, which is calculated right after the opening. *Note:* Some stocks may take a while to establish opening prices.

✔ **Margin requirements:** Margin values for S&P 500 Index contracts are variable. In July 2005, the initial margin for the S&P 500 contract was $19,688, and the maintenance margin was $15,750.

✔ **Cash settlement:** Stock-index futures are settled with cash, a practice known as, you guessed it, *cash settlement.* That means if you hold your contract until expiration, you have to either pay or receive the amount of money the contract is worth as determined by the SOQ price (see the "Final settlement" list item earlier). Cash settlement applies to all stock-index futures.

Overnight and premarket trading can be thin and dangerous, especially during slow seasons in the stock market, such as in summer, fall, and around winter holidays.

The NASDAQ-100 Futures Index (ND)

The NASDAQ-100 Futures Index contract is similar to the S&P 500 Index futures contract. Here's what you need to know about it:

✔ **Composition:** The NASDAQ-100 Stock Index is made up of the 100 largest stocks traded on the NASDAQ system, including large technology and biotech stocks.

✔ **Valuation:** The ND is valued in minimum ticks of 0.5 that are worth $50.

✔ **Contract limits:** No more than 10,000 net long or short contracts can be held by any individual at any one time.

✔ **Margin requirements:** Margins required for NASDAQ-100 Index futures are similar to the S&P 500 Index futures. In July 2005, the initial margin for the ND contract was $18,750, and the maintenance margin was $15,000.

Minimizing your contract

The e-mini S&P 500 (ES) contract and the e-mini NASDAQ 100 (NQ) are among the most popular stock-index futures contracts, because they enable you to trade the market's trend with only a fifth of the requirement. The e-mini S&P is a favorite of day traders because of its high intraday volatility and major price swings on a daily basis. The mini contracts are marketed to small investors, and they offer some advantages. However, they also carry significant risks, because they're volatile and still have fairly high margin requirements.

The mini contract can be very volatile and can move even more aggressively during extremely volatile market environments. Here are some particulars about the e-mini contracts:

- ✔ **Composition:** The ES and EQ e-mini contracts are based on the same makeup as the respective S&P 500 and NASDAQ 100 index contracts.

- ✔ **Valuation:** One tick on ES is 0.25 of an index point and is worth $12.50. One tick on EQ is 0.50 of an index point and is worth $10.

- ✔ **Contracts:** The value of an ES contract is $50 multiplied by the value of the S&P 500 Index. The value of an EQ contract is $20 multiplied by the value of the NASDAQ-100 Index.

- ✔ **Trading times:** The e-mini contracts trade nearly 24 hours per day, with a 30-minute maintenance break in trading from 4:30 to 5:00 p.m. daily.

- ✔ **Monthly identifiers:** Monthly identifiers for both mini contracts are *H* for March, *M* for June, *U* for September, and *Z* for December.

- ✔ **Margin requirements:** Margins for the ES and EQ contracts are less than for the normal-sized contracts. As of July 2005, the ES requires $3,938 for initial margin and $3,150 for maintenance, and the EQ requires $3,750 and $3,000, respectively.

The day-trading margin is less than the margin to hold an overnight position in S&P 500 e-mini futures. Traders, though, are obligated to pay for the difference between the margins for entry and exit points, which means that if you lose, you're likely to pay up in a big way at the end of the day.

When you own normal-sized contracts and e-mini contracts in one or the other of the underlying indexes, position limits apply to both positions, meaning that each of the contracts is counted as an individual part of the overall position, and the combined number of contracts can't exceed the 20,000 contract limit for the S&P 500-based index and the 10,000 contract limit for the NASDAQ-100-based index.

Trading Strategies

Now that you know the basics of some of the futures contracts that you can trade, the next step is to put this information to use in formulating strategies. As with any other futures trading, you may want to try some of these in paper trading, or by using an online trading simulator. It's always better to get the feel of trading a contract before jumping in with real money.

You can apply every technique described in this book to trading stock-index futures. Moving averages, RSI, MACD, the Swing Rule, pattern recognition, support/resistance levels, and many others (see Chapter 8) — with or without fundamental analysis — all work, and if you applied them properly, you're likely be fairly successful.

Using futures instead of stocks

At the beginning of this chapter, I noted that stock-index futures can be used for hedging or for speculating. Here is a good example of how you can use them as a substitute for individual stocks.

Assume that you have a $500,000 portfolio of Treasury bonds (T-bonds) that are paying you a fairly decent return of 5 percent to 6 percent. You aren't planning to sell any of them, because you want to hold on to those decent yields as long as possible. And based on your knowledge of technical analysis, market sentiment, and your analysis of the economy (see Chapters 6, 7, and 9), suppose that you're looking at a scenario which in the past has led to a market rally, and you'd like to take advantage of that opportunity.

One way to do it is to sell $40,000 of your portfolio and split it into two. For simplicity's sake, assume that the margin, or the amount that you will have to fork over for one S&P 500 futures contract, is $20,000. With that you buy one S&P 500 futures contract, where the margin is roughly $20,000 (Amount 1), while you keep the remaining $20,000 (Amount 2) in your margin account to give you some flexibility, such as leveraging your position with options, considering other strategies, and for protecting you if you're wrong and get a margin call.

Amount 1 ($20,000) should provide enough in your margin account for you to buy one S&P contract, and at the July 15, 2005, closing price of 1230.80, it would give you control of roughly $307,700.

With Amount 2 (the other $20,000), you can invest in and collect interest on Treasury bills and look for other opportunities, perhaps in the options markets, as you look to hedge your S&P 500 contract or to leverage it further, depending on market conditions.

This strategy isn't without risk, but again, it isn't irresponsible either, and it's sensible if your goal is to take advantage of what you think is a coming rally in the stock market. By using stock indexes with a portion of your bond portfolio, you are

- **Simplifying your exposure to stocks.** You don't have to go out and buy 10 or 15 individual stocks to diversify your stock portfolio using the stock indexes.

- **Still leaving most of your money in income-yielding T-bonds.** In other words, you're still guaranteed a reliable rate of return.

- **Taking prudent risks.** If you act responsibly, monitor your position, and follow sound trading rules (see Chapter 17), including prudent profit taking, position hedging, and cutting any sudden and unexpected losses, your risks remain tolerable, even if the market goes against you.

- **Benefiting financially.** The flip side of risk is that if you're correct, you may make a large sum of money in a relatively short period of time.

Protecting your stock portfolio

Another good hedge involves a well-diversified stock portfolio of dividend-paying stocks and the stock-index futures. Using the $500,000 example again, assume your portfolio is made up of stocks rather than bonds.

You can see in Figure 12-1 that the S&P 500 Cash Index made a new high in March, but the relative strength indicator (RSI) failed to match it. That clear divergence was enough cause for concern for you to start monitoring all of your high-yield, dividend-paying stocks. Even though you find that they're actually holding on pretty well, you're still not sure about what will happen if the market starts selling off, because you have no guarantee that even low-volatility stocks won't be sold in a significant price correction.

You have several possible decisions to make. You can

- Take profits on your stock portfolio.

- Sell call options or buy put options on each of your individual stocks. Call options essentially are bets that the underlying stock is going higher. Put options are bets that the underlying stock is going to fall. If you sell a call option, you collect a premium that cushions any losses. If you buy a put option, the appreciation of the value of the put (if your stock falls) cushions any losses. See Chapters 4 and 5 for more about option strategies.

- Look to the futures market for a good way to hedge your stocks.

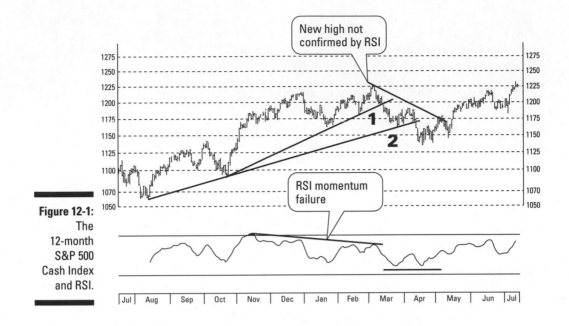

Figure 12-1:
The
12-month
S&P 500
Cash Index
and RSI.

Option strategies on individual stocks may be a good way to go unless you have 10 or 20 positions to hedge, which can take most of your time to monitor and manage.

The idea is to understand that the futures and spot markets are linked, which is what became widely known through the unfortunate circumstances surrounding the market crash in 1987. Since then, this relationship has become widely accepted.

In the example that follows, I look at two charts of the S&P 500. Figure 12-1 is a chart of the S&P 500 Cash Index. Figure 12-2 is a chart of the S&P 500 Index futures. Both are from the same date, July 15, 2005. The object is to find out how futures and cash indexes work in tandem and how you can use this relationship to protect your stock portfolio. For better reference, you need to realize that the futures chart offers a zoomed-in view of the time period.

Using the RSI and cash market in Figure 12-1 as your guide, here is the anatomy of a hedge trade for your stock portfolio using the S&P 500 Stock Index futures:

 ✔ **The indicators:** The RSI's lack of confirmation in the cash market was a caution signal and should have alerted you to a potential change in trend.

 ✔ **The trend-line analysis:** The trend line on the cash index confirmed a major market break. The break below Trend Line 1 by the S&P 500 Cash

Index in Figure 12-1 confirmed your expectations and was your signal to do one of the following:

- Short one S&P futures contract

- Buy an S&P futures put option

Notice how RSI kept falling despite the attempted rally in the S&P 500. The descending trend line above the S&P 500 exhibited resistance in the market, and the failure at the trend line led to another leg down for the S&P 500.

Likewise, note how the RSI bottomed along with the market and how the S&P in the cash and futures contracts broke back above the uptrend line. If you played this trade correctly, you made some money and protected your portfolio (or both).

And notice how the action in the S&P futures was closely mirroring the action in the cash index. If you covered your futures short position in April, you didn't have to do much more to manage your stock portfolio because the market rallied for another two months after that.

The tendency of most traders would be to stay too long in the trading position that I just described — as the market was making a bottom in April. That's what the markets do to fool you. Futures traders don't have the same amount of time to make decisions as someone who's trading only stocks. If you played this trade correctly, you made money. If you weren't sure about what to do, you could have covered the risk to your short position in the futures contract by setting up an options straddle so you could sell the put as the market reversed and ride out the call as the market rallied.

A straddle is when you buy both a put and a call, and it's best used when you're not sure which way the market will break. A successfully executed straddle means that you must sell the side of the straddle (the put or the call) that the market moves against. Check out Chapters 4 and 5 for more about straddles.

Swinging with the rule

A little-used strategy that you sometimes can use to help you know when to take profits is called the *swing rule*. In the example used in the previous section, the swing rule worked well, but you need to take a close look at some six-month indicators. Looking at Figure 12-2, which shows the S&P 500 Index futures, note the "Swing line" label, right at the 1,200 level. A *swing line* is a line that you can draw across the dome formed by the price changes in the futures contract from February to March. As you can tell, the price made a full swing (up and over) during that time frame, ending up right about where it started before it rallied for a few weeks.

To calculate the swing rule, you take the top price of that dome, which is roughly 1,240, and subtract the bottom, or the level across which you drew the swing line (roughly 1,200) to get a 40-point swing. Swing lines serve as guides to how much you can allow the market to fall before you consider taking at least partial profits.

In this case, the swing rule worked perfectly, because the market bottomed near 1,160, just about 40 points below the swing line at 1,200.

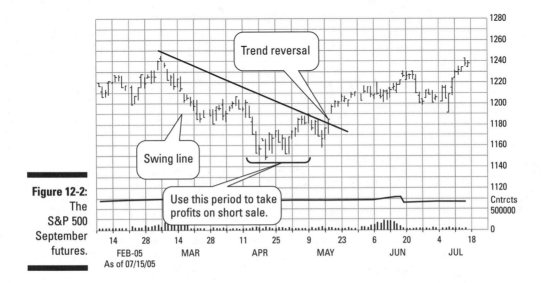

Figure 12-2:
The
S&P 500
September
futures.

Speculating with stock-index futures

Aside from hedging, you can simply speculate with futures contracts just by using technical and fundamental analyses (see Chapters 6 and 7).

Stock-index futures are almost guaranteed to move in response to economic indicators. You can set up positions with both futures and options as you wait for the news to hit. In the last several years, the monthly employment report, which is issued the first Friday of every month, has been an excellent mover for stock-index futures.

Using Your Head to Be Successful

If you're disciplined, you stand a much better chance of being more successful or even extremely successful.

Get real

You can't win every time, and you can't have the same success as a pit trader. Even though the kind of trading, due to the use of different time frames used and strategies, that pit traders and retail investors use are different, it's still unrealistic to expect the same kinds of results.

Most pros will tell you that a large portion of their trades break even, lose a little, or gain a little, and that it's only about 30 percent of the time that they can hit home runs. So if you don't develop a trading plan and prepare yourself for the reality of the game, you're not going to enjoy it.

Get a grip on your money management

Professional traders rely on a few standards, and although the figures change slightly, the principles of those standards remain firm:

- Risk no more than 5 percent of your equity on any one trade.

- Limit your losses to no more than 5 percent per trade. If you only risk 5 percent, it takes 20 trades to wipe you out if you pony up $10,000 in the first place. This is a dynamic process. Adjust your 5-percent loss limit to your current equity level. That means that as your equity rises, the amount risked also gets larger, and as your equity falls, so does the amount risked. That's how you stay in the business, by letting your winners run and keeping a short leash on your losers.

Choose your contracts carefully

The more you know about a particular type of contract, the better off you are. Here are some actions you can take to become a specialist:

- **Figure out how many days a particular contract tends to spend rising or falling along a Bollinger band.** Bollinger bands are flexible bands of price support and resistance levels described fully in Chapter 7. When you find out, you'll have an idea about when that contract is likely to turn around. This tool is particularly useful when you're swing trading near a top or bottom. Although the Bollinger band trends won't be exact, as long as you know that the index usually turns five to ten days after moving along the band, you can then start to follow the index more closely and watch for trading opportunities.

- **Try different sets and combinations of moving averages.** Watching various moving averages, one with the other, you can find out which contracts trade better, for example, with a five-day exponential average, and which ones work best with a nonexponential moving average.

✔ **Try different oscillators and combinations of them.** By trying them out, you can find out which ones work best with each index that you trade. The RSI oscillator works better with some futures contracts, while the MACD and other oscillators work better with others.

✔ **Check out the charts from the past.** Don't be afraid to go back months or even years to look at charts of what some indexes have done in the past. Patterns shown in the charts tend to repeat time and again, which is why pattern recognition becomes so useful.

✔ **Try different option parameters with your index trading.** Find the ones that tend to work best for you and your time frame. Experiment with different strike prices, and consider paper trading with straddles and with individual options. See Chapters 4 and 5.

Take your trading seriously

If you're not up to trading on any given day, that's fine. But if you turn on your screen when your mind is in the clouds and you start making trades, you're going to get hurt. Trust me when I tell you that even if you have only a $5,000 account and you're trading only one contract at a time, a $500 loss amounts to about 10 percent of your entire account. In the futures market, that kind of pitfall can take all of about five minutes' worth of action.

Never be afraid of selling too soon

If you set your targets and they get hit almost immediately after a news release, follow your rules. Your objective got hit; take the money and run. By the same token, don't get greedy. If you're looking at a nice profit, take it before it turns into a loss.

Never let yourself get a margin call

I'll probably get hit by my editor for saying this too many times, but you can't say it, read it, or hear it enough: Never let yourself get a margin call. Set loss limits, no matter what. In the rare case that you do get a margin call, even if you've set up good stops, the markets must have done something remarkable. Meet your margin call. Figure out why you got it. And keep an eye on the market, because other opportunities may soon arise.

Part IV
Commodity Futures

The 5th Wave   By Rich Tennant

"Precious metals? Energy futures? Currency speculation? I say
we stick the money in the ground like always, and then feed
this guy to the sharks."

In this part . . .

Supply rules the roost in the markets that I tell you about in this part, and you'll come away thinking that they make sense for that reason. You'll jump right in with the kings of the hill, oil, and energy futures. Then you'll get into some metal without the leather as you look at gold, copper, and other precious and industrial metals. Finally, I take you down on the farm to fill you in on livestock and agricultural futures.

Chapter 13

Getting Slick and Slimy: Understanding Energy Futures

. . . .

In This Chapter

▶ Understanding the connection between energy (oil) and bond markets

▶ Exploring effects of peak oil and long-term bull markets in energy markets

▶ Balancing energy supplies with demand

▶ Timing the cyclical nature of the energy markets

▶ Coming to grips with markets for crude oil, gasoline, heating oil, and natural gas

▶ Measuring the effects of sentiment on the energy markets

. . . .

*I*never realized that I was going to become an expert in energy until I wrote a book titled *Successful Energy Sector Investing* (Prima-Random House, 2002).

The truth is that I essentially stumbled into what has become my second career. After finishing a book on biotech investments, *Successful Biotech Investing* (Prima Money, 2001), the book company was interested in me writing another book. More than happy to oblige, through my research I discovered that few books had been written about investing in energy, at least at the level most investors could understand, so I put together a proposal, and it was accepted. Although the book got mixed reviews, it nevertheless sold steadily, and it will continue to be available, because I now own the rights, and it has proven to be a pretty good read, even if I do say so myself.

Researching and writing those books opened up a whole new world of possibilities for me as a writer, an analyst, a commentator, and a trader. In a sense, I owe a great deal of my livelihood to the oil markets, which are an interesting bucketful of issues on their own.

What I've discovered about the energy markets can't be fully described in only one chapter, so in this chapter, I provide you with a good summary of the way professionals think about and execute their trades in the energy markets and the way I make recommendations on energy stocks on my Joe Duarte.com Web site (www.joe-duarte.com).

Energy markets are where the action will be for many more years. By focusing on oil futures to figure out their complexities, sensibilities, and basically how they work, you can find out how to use them to make money, especially over the long term.

The emphasis in this chapter is on the entire energy complex from a speculator's standpoint, concentrating on the practical. The goal is understanding how you can use supply and demand, geopolitics, and technical analysis to reach sensible decisions about making good energy market trades.

In this chapter, when I refer to interest rates, unless I specifically say so, I'm referring to both the United States Federal Reserve adjusted rates and the bond-market rates.

Some Easy Background Info

Trading began in energy futures in 1979, and it is centralized at the New York Mercantile Exchange (NYMEX), the world's largest physical commodity futures exchange. The 132-year-old NYMEX trades futures and options contracts for crude oil, natural gas, heating oil, gasoline, coal, electricity, and propane. The NYMEX also is home to trading in metals (see Chapter 14).

Trading is conducted on the NYMEX in two divisions:

- ✔ **The NYMEX division,** which trades energy, platinum, and palladium.
- ✔ **The COMEX division,** which trades the rest of the metals.

NYMEX offers e-mini contracts for oil and natural gas for smaller traders, which also are traded on the Globex network of the Chicago Mercantile Exchange (CME).

The NYMEX Web site, www.nymex.com, offers a good deal of information and is worth a visit. The calendars and margin requirements, which are listed individually for each contract, are especially useful to traders.

Next to interest rates, energy — especially oil — is the center of the universe not only for industry but also for the financial markets.

Completing the Circle of Life: Oil and the Bond Market

Much of what happens in the world — from your mortgage rate to how easy it is to find a job — depends on what I like to call the "Circle of Life" formed by energy prices and interest rates. For the sake of simplicity, the term *oil* (unless I note otherwise) can be used interchangeably with the term *energy* in the rest of this chapter.

This relationship is important because it ties together the two most important aspects of the global economy: energy, the fuel for growth, and interest rates, the catalyst that powers borrowed money to do things. Sometimes the price of oil leads to a rise in interest rates, both in the bond market and through the actions of central banks, and at other times, the opposite happens. In this chapter, when I use interest rates, it means both unless I specify one or the other. The relationship depends on where the economic cycle of supply and demand and politics happen to be at the time. After September 11, 2001, traditional relationships were somewhat changed but not completely abolished.

For example, in mid-2005, one of the major reasons for the Fed to continue to raise interest rates, according to speeches made by Fed governors and Fed Chief Alan Greenspan, was that the rise in oil prices was creating inflation. At the same time, the bond market was struggling with the possibility that high energy prices were increasing the chances of a recession.

As a result, the Fed kept raising interest rates, and the bond market was stuck in a trading range with rates slowly creeping higher.

Here is the way it works. If oil prices rise high enough, one of two things happens: The Fed starts worrying either about inflation or the economy slowing down because oil prices are so high that people can't buy enough of other things.

If inflation is the dominant theory at the Fed, the central bank will raise interest rates. If a slowing economy is more likely, the Fed will start lowering interest rates. The bond market eventually will catch up with whatever the Fed does, and sometimes leads the action of the Fed.

If the Fed worries about inflation enough, its Federal Open Market Committee (FOMC) starts raising the interest rates banks charge for borrowing money. If the opposite is true, such as when the economy slows, then the FOMC starts to consider lowering interest rates to stimulate the economy.

Watching the bond market

You're probably wondering how you can determine — or at least take an educated guess about — how the Fed will act? Your best clue can be found by monitoring the bond market. If bond-market interest rates begin to rise along with oil prices, it's a sign that the bond market is growing concerned about high oil prices triggering inflation. If bond-market rates rise high enough, the Fed is likely to increase bank interest rates. If rates start falling in the bond market, then bond traders are expecting a slowing of the economy, and the Fed is likely to reduce interest rates. As I noted in the previous section, though, sometimes the Fed makes the first move by raising interest rates, and the bond market follows.

This explanation isn't infallible, but it holds true a fair amount of the time. In 2004 and 2005, Federal Reserve Chairman Alan Greenspan called persistently low bond-market interest rates combined with the Fed's continuously high interest rates, a "conundrum."

Nevertheless, when oil prices are rising along with bond yields and/or interest rates from the Fed, then you must look for an *inflection point,* such as where bond yields and overall interest rates have gone high enough to lead to a break in the price of oil, because traders have started factoring in the fact that oil prices have risen to a point where they're becoming a hindrance to economic growth.

Looking for classic signs as oil prices rise

The overall markets are likely to project certain signs as oil prices rise and traders start gauging the effect of the increases on the economy, including

- **Decreasing traffic in stores and malls (and on the highways, for that matter):** By August 2005, as oil prices were reaching all-time record highs, retailers began blaming a slowing of sales on high gasoline prices.

- **Decreasing consumer confidence:** By August 2005, consumer confidence was skidding. Plenty of reasons could be cited for falling consumer confidence and rising gasoline prices. Hurricane Katrina did significant amounts of damage to the Gulf of Mexico's coastline in the United States. The City of New Orleans was rendered nearly useless. The port of New Orleans, a major import hub for oil and export hub for agricultural products, was shut for days. And the oil and gas production and refining infrastructure of the area, which accounts for 20 percent of the gasoline and natural gas used in the United States, was shut down and took several months to be brought back online.

> ✔ **Crazy headlines:** Look for increasing emphasis on oil prices on the evening news and in the media that don't normally cater to business news. A perfect example was the call from Congress for a windfall profit tax on oil companies and repeated calls for hearings on price gouging by gas stations and fuel retailers.

Here's a key to the relationship between oil prices and the economy in general: At some point, interest rates will rise enough to cool off the demand for oil. When that point is reached, oil prices will start to fall, and at some point after that as traders begin to factor in a slower economy, so should bond yields.

The Fed's main goals are to keep prices steady and everyone employed, but achieving them is nearly impossible. So that means the Fed will make mistakes and create inefficiencies in the market that are key to traders making a profit. As a trader, one thing you definitely know is that the Fed will act. As a result, oil always is on the move, and that creates opportunities for you to trade. You have to throw ideology out the door. Regardless of the party you vote for or what you believe, in the oil market, it's what you see that can make you money.

Check out Figure 13-1 (later in this chapter), which shows the relationship between interest rates in the bond market and oil prices, and then notice the following:

> ✔ Oil prices and interest rates generally move in the same direction when viewed over long periods of time. Note the overall upward trend of both charts. Keep in mind that a wide band of movement is involved in this relationship and that I'm discussing only the very big picture. The important point to remember is that rising oil prices can lead to inflation, and that inflation eventually will lead to higher interest rates, both in the bond market and at the bank. See Chapters 2, 6, and 10 for more about bonds, inflation, and the economy.
>
> ✔ Oil prices generally rise enough for interest rates to start to slow down the pace at which they (oil prices) rise as the economy slows from higher borrowing costs. Higher borrowing costs eventually slow demand for fuel.
>
> Note that oil prices made a new high in March 2005, but interest rates in the bond market did not. At that point in time, you needed to be thinking that a top in oil prices was possible because interest rates in the bond market didn't make a new high along with oil prices. Even though you may not have been right, you nevertheless needed to think about it.

Examining the Peak Oil Concept

If you believe in the concept of *peak oil,* you believe that the world is running out of oil. Proponents of this concept assert that global oil production will probably reach a peak during this decade. After the peak, the world's oil production of crude oil will fall, never to rise again.

Although I'm not sure about peak oil, it doesn't matter what I think, because somewhere in the back of just about every oil trader's mind is the thought that the world may just be running out of oil — a thought that now maintains essentially a permanent influence on the oil markets. Needless to say, the concept of peak oil

✔ Gathered steam after the events of September 11, 2001, and it became well established in many corridors of trading during the mega bull market in oil that ensued.

✔ Received support in July 2005 when Saudi Arabia told the world that in ten years, its production wouldn't be able to keep up with global demand if demand continued to grow at rates that were prevalent at the time.

The Post-September 11, 2001, Mega Bull Market in Energy

After September 11, 2001, the world changed. The invasions of Afghanistan and Iraq were only a small part of what happened, not so much in human and political terms, but rather in terms of the financial markets.

Figure 13-1 is a picture of the effect that the events of September 11, 2001, had on energy and related markets. Just prior to September 11, 2001, the U.S. was scrambling to recover from the bursting of the Internet bubble; however, the attacks on the World Trade Center derailed the economic improvement and plunged the country into a deep psychological and logistical nightmare in which businesses closed their doors and job losses began to mount.

The four charts in Figure 13-1 summarize the five-year post-September 11, 2001, period, as of November 1, 2005. When looking at the figure, be sure to note the factors in the list that follows, because they set the stage for the rest of the chapter.

✔ **The U.S. dollar went into a multiyear bear market.** Money left the United States as the Fed lowered interest rates, making the dollar less attractive. Politically, the world also viewed the United States as unstable, unpredictable, and vulnerable because of the attacks. Note also that the U.S. dollar rose out of the bear market as the Fed raised interest rates during the period and that bond rates began to rise. The dollar usually rises when interest rates (bond and/or central bank rates) rise for a long enough period of time.

✔ **Oil and natural gas entered once-in-a-lifetime secular bull markets.** A *secular bull market* is defined as one that lasts years to decades. It didn't take long for traders to start bidding up the price of oil, initially because of the connection of the terrorists who attacked the U.S. to Saudi Arabia, the world's largest oil producer. However, as time passed, a new dynamic developed as money began to flow into China.

In other words, as the U.S. appeared to be entering a period of uncertainty, traders began looking for places where economic growth was not as affected by what happened on September 11, 2001. They found China, whose currency was pegged to the dollar.

As the dollar fell, so did the tendency of the Chinese yuan to remain weak. It solidified even more, because the Chinese government artificially kept the currency at a level that would increase exports to other countries, especially Europe and the United States. As more foreign money flowed into China for those exports, the Chinese economy became more and more able to produce goods and export them to the entire world.

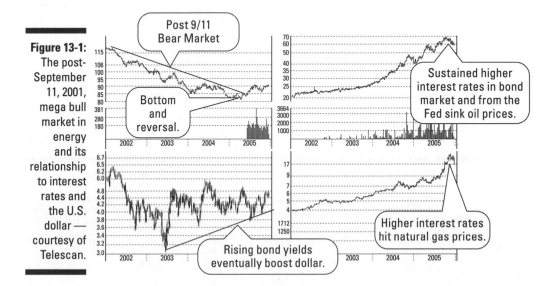

Figure 13-1: The post-September 11, 2001, mega bull market in energy and its relationship to interest rates and the U.S. dollar — courtesy of Telescan.

✔ **Long-term interest rates entered a downward sloping and wide trading range.** The yield on the U.S. ten-year Treasury note initially rose, because traders began to price in the likely collapse of the U.S. economy. By 2003, it was clear that the U.S. economy, although not as strong as it would have been had September 11, 2001, not occurred, was not going to collapse.

As the economy stabilized, interest rates began to rise. Note, though, that the dollar didn't bottom out until 2005, a full two years after bond yields started to rise. That's because these relationships can take significant amounts of time to reach points in which they become evident. In other words, sometimes it takes a large number of interest-rate increases and a long period of rising bond yields to turn a major currency like the dollar around. Don't forget that the politics and general stability of a country play big roles in how strong its currency will be. In the post-September 11, 2001, period, the markets were not immediately convinced that the U.S. would be able to survive the attack and remain a major world power.

Understanding Supply and Demand

Wanna know a secret? Although most people think that demand is what makes prices change, supply rules in the energy markets. As the U.S. economy slowed during the months that followed the World Trade Center attack, the Chinese economy picked up steam, and its demand for oil increased.

The increased Chinese demand, however, was not enough to boost oil prices. Instead, the markets correctly began to price in the possibility of attacks on the oil-producing infrastructure and the increasing challenges of getting oil out of the Middle East. More important, as the U.S. attacked Iraq, the market again correctly factored the loss of Iraq's oil supply into the markets.

Keep these important tidbits about the oil markets in mind:

✔ The world runs on oil, and any threat to the oil supply leads to rising prices.

✔ As an oil trader, your primary goal is to consider the effects of events on supply and to correlate those effects with your charts.

✔ Demand fluctuates, but supply is finite. Weeks are needed to ramp up supply or to turn it back down. Refineries are a bottleneck in the system. So even if plenty of oil is sitting in storage, if the refineries can't turn it into gasoline or heating oil, the supply of those products is impaired.

Charting refinery capacity in the U.S.

The United States has not built a new refinery since the 1970s. The combination of environmental concerns, red tape and paperwork, huge costs in the billions of dollars, and the multiyear time frame needed to finish a new refinery are prohibitive and have prevented any new oil-refining capacity from coming online. In essence, the United States is now in a position in which any increase in demand for oil or oil products cannot be met by domestic refinery capacity. That means that now more than ever, the U.S. depends on foreign resources for its oil and refined products.

Damage to refining and shipping capabilities caused by hurricanes Katrina and Rita brought the U.S. refinery issue to the forefront as gasoline prices skyrocketed. The markets and consumers also reacted as prices reached a level that was high enough to decrease consumption and lead to lower prices.

The net effect of the post-September 11, 2001, bull market in oil, though, was to reset fuel prices at a higher level than prior to that date. I don't think gasoline prices below $1.50 will ever be seen again, barring some truly extraordinary event. If the price goes that low, then I'm wrong — it can happen.

Playing the Sensible Market

The energy markets make sense, regardless of whether you believe in the concept of peak oil.

Real companies have huge trading desks with hundreds of traders all betting on the price of oil. Banks and brokers join oil, trucking, and airline companies in using the oil markets on a daily basis to hedge their future price risks and for pure speculation. Even Goldman Sachs and Merrill Lynch got into the oil storage and distribution business in the early part of the 21st century in the wake of September 11, 2001.

In other words, the oil market is about real people trying to figure out how much oil they're going to need to run their businesses in the next few months to years, regardless of whether they're suppliers or users.

Stock prices are built mostly on analysts' drivel, such as price/earnings ratios and new paradigms, such as the nonsense that sank the Internet stocks. Oil, gasoline, heating oil, and natural gas prices, on the other hand, are based more on real-life circumstances and aren't usually influenced by the kind of fiction spawned by slick Wall Street analysts penning negative e-mails about the stocks they push onto the public.

Supply rules the energy markets, and here are the basics of it:

- ✔ The Organization of Petroleum Exporting Countries (OPEC) supplies 30 to 40 percent of the world's oil. Russia, the next big supplier, and other non-OPEC producers like Mexico, Norway, and the United Kingdom make up the rest of the world's supply. The United States also is an oil and natural gas producer, with Alaska and the Gulf of Mexico being the largest areas. The U.S. ranks above Mexico and Canada in proven oil reserves. The total oil reserves in the U.S. are roughly one-tenth of those in Saudi Arabia.

- ✔ From a practical standpoint, supply is made up of production, or what comes out of the ground, what can be refined, and what can be delivered, both before it gets to the refinery and after it's refined into gasoline, heating oil, and diesel and other fuels.

- ✔ The potential for disruptions in supplies can occur at any of several steps along the route from extraction through the point of sale, and each step has its own unique chance of being the culprit for supply screw-ups that make prices rise.

- ✔ Worker strikes, hurricanes and other natural disasters of all kinds, accidents, spills, sabotage, and even market manipulation by OPEC and other producers all end up affecting supply, not demand.

- ✔ Oil without a doubt is a political tool. The Venezuelan government didn't like President Bush, so it threatened to cut shipments of oil to the United States. Sabotage of oil pipelines was a major weapon in Iraq in the early days of the U.S. invasion.

The one constant in supply, especially in the United States, is that not enough refinery capacity is available to keep up with any more than normal demand. That means when winters are extremely cold, refineries are a key bottleneck in the oil delivery system.

In the new world, with China, India, and the U.S. gobbling up increasing supplies of oil, oil markets in general have to deal with the reality that supplies are going to be tighter than they were even five or ten years ago. That's why prices stayed high in spite of the fact that the war in Iraq settled into a less hectic rhythm and why even if prices fall from levels above $50 per barrel, the days of $10 oil are not likely to return in our lifetimes unless the global economy collapses.

Handling Seasonal Cycles

Energy demand, especially for heating oil, gasoline, and natural gas, is extremely seasonal in nature, and if you look at your own life, you can easily understand how these cycles work.

In winter, you heat your house. If you live on the East Coast of the U.S., that means you use heating oil. Everywhere else you burn natural gas and sometimes coal. Some areas rely on nuclear energy. Likewise, during summer, you drive your car or fly off somewhere colder than where you live to go on vacation.

Traders anticipate the ebb and flow of these cycles and factor them into their bets. A good number of traders work for companies, energy and otherwise, that use the futures market either to have fuel delivered to them for resale or for their own use. Others use energy futures to hedge the cost of the energy they need to run their businesses. Still others like you and me are speculating and trying to make a buck.

All cycles are variable and describe the oil markets only in broad strokes, so you never should expect the course of the oil business to be perfect each time you trade. You will, however, be a better trader if you remain aware of these cycles and watch for their presence. In general, crude oil futures

- Experience a lull in the spring months when refineries convert production from heating oil to gasoline. When that happens, the price of heating oil starts to fall, and gasoline prices firm up.
- Swing up and down during the summer based on gasoline supplies. As the end of the summer nears, another pause occurs when refineries switch over from gasoline back to heating oil production.

This broad cycle became unreliable after September 11, 2001, because prices bucked the cyclical trends and pretty much went higher.

Bear in mind, though, that a seasonal tendency for price action does exist. For example, you don't generally want to look to trade long on gasoline in winter. Instead you want to focus on heating oil during cold-weather months. At the same time, you need to consider natural gas as a potential short sale during the spring and early summer.

Preparing for the Weekly Cycle

A more useful cycle hinges on what happens on Wednesday mornings — or on Thursday mornings after three-day weekends. That's when the American Petroleum Institute (API) and the U.S. Energy Information Agency (EIA) release their weekly supply data reports.

Analysts all pony up their estimates for the reports usually on Monday and Tuesday. They're all focusing on supply, not demand, and they want to know whether inventories are *building* (increasing in supply) or *drawing down* (decreasing in supply).

Making trades based on the API and EIA supply data is a good idea to consider, because you can generate some nice short-term profits if you play it right.

The markets focus mainly on the report from the EIA, because it's a government agency that *requires* companies to provide their supply statistics. The API uses data supplied on a volunteer basis. Thus the API data tends to be less exact because of its information-gathering system.

Analysts almost never get it right. That means that the market usually jumps up or down after the data are released. I do just about everything I can possibly do to rearrange my schedule so I can be in front of my trading screen when that report is released.

A great time for a coffee break is at 10:30 a.m. eastern time Wednesdays so you can watch for the energy supply data. Setting up some potential trades ahead of the release of the reports can help you get a jump on executing them based on the new supply data. Wednesdays can be the most profitable day of the week in the energy pits.

Checking other sources before Wednesday

On Monday and Tuesday, I start scanning news sources for analysts' opinions about the oil market. Doing so gives me a good idea about what may happen if the market is priced wrong regarding current supply levels.

Some good stuff to read before the release of the reports include Myra Saefong's column at MarketWatch.com (www.marketwatch.com). It provides a good summary of expectations. Reuters (www.reuters.com) and Bloomberg (www.bloomberg.com) also provide good summaries of what the market is setting itself up for when the data are released. If your broker gives you access to good news data, Dow Jones Newswires is about as good as any source to get the same data. Dow Jones Newswires is a subscriber service that is accessible online, usually through brokers and financial-service institutions.

How to react to the report

Making trades based on the supply reports isn't an exercise in being exact, because analysts usually are clueless about what's coming up. What you want to look for are instances when they all agree one way or another. For example, if they're all leaning toward a *build* (increased supply) of crude, be ready for the market to go higher if the report even hints of a supply shortage. The same is true for when the market gets set up for a *drawdown* (decreased supply) — be ready for the market to go lower if the report hints of more abundant supplies. Here are a couple of tips for trading the supply reports:

✔ **Be careful when the report comes out.** Give it some time before you jump in. The first few trades can be volatile. After a minute or two, your real-time chart should start to show you the way the market is headed.

✔ **Consider some option strategies.** As with other reports, a straddle is a good potential strategy to consider. Other hedging techniques, such as holding some long positions in blue-chip oil stocks and selling the futures, or buying puts on the futures, also may work.

If the markets are surprised with the supply data in a big way, the move can be huge, and prices are likely to gap up as the figure is released. In this case, three scenarios can apply:

✔ **You're already out of the market.** If you aren't already in the market, you miss a chance to make some money. However, don't go chasing prices trying to get into the market. You'll end up being sorry.

✔ **You have an established position.** You take advantage of the data being in your favor by ratcheting up your sell stops so you can take as much profit as possible if the market happens to turn on you. If you're using a broker, you either gave him instructions on what to do in this situation, or you better have his number on speed dial and hope that you're one of his favorite clients.

✔ **Your position is stopped out.** If you were in the market but were stopped out because you guessed wrong, be glad you're out. Reassess your position and wait for a better opportunity. When you get stopped out, it means that the stop-loss order you placed to limit your losses was triggered as prices dropped to the level you specified.

Forecasting Oil Prices by Using Oil Stocks

One of the most reliable methods of forecasting futures prices is using the action in oil stocks. John Murphy is one of the most prominent promoters of this dynamic, and I've found his approach a very useful starting point.

Changes in oil stocks tend to precede the moves in oil prices and should also confirm them. Sometimes oil stocks also will move along with or just after crude oil futures.

Although oil stock prices may sound unpredictable, under normal circumstances, as a new bull market in oil starts, oil stocks will either start rising along with crude prices before or right after crude oil futures start rising.

Much of the time, although not always, oil stocks will rise or fall before the price of crude oil rises or falls.

Similarly, as the falling trend line of a bear market in oil takes hold, oil stocks will either break sometime before, along with, or just after crude oil futures. Figure 13-2 provides a good example of the dynamic.

Figure 13-2:
The relationship between Exxon Mobil, the oil (XOI) and oil service (OSX) indexes, and December crude oil futures.

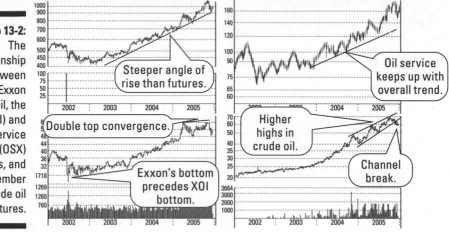

Take note of how

✔ The price of Exxon Mobil stock bottomed out before the oil index (XOI) took off.

✔ The XOI index began to rally at a much steeper rate of rise than the December 2005 crude oil futures (CLZ5) contract. Some of the steeper rise is caused by the fact that the volume of trading in the December 2005 contracts didn't pick up until 2003 and then really started booming in 2004. Nevertheless, oil stocks clearly began to rally before the futures.

✔ Oil service stocks (OSX) kept pace with the XOI and Exxon.

✔ Exxon stopped rallying in February 2005, while oil futures and the rest of the oil stocks continued to move higher. Every time oil futures made a new high, Exxon didn't confirm them — a classic technical divergence that requires confirmation. Figure 13-2 shows a classic double-top pattern in Exxon. A *double top* is when the market reaches a price that's similar to a previous price and then rolls over. A double top is a sign of failing price momentum. Notice how the double top in Exxon was followed by a break-down in the price of oil, which on November 1 dropped below $60.

Figure 13-3 is an enlarged version of Figure 13-2, and it shows in greater detail how the double top in Exxon coincided with the breakdown in the price of the December crude oil contract and how the break in the stock preceded the break in the futures. Be sure to check out these points in Figure 13-3:

- ✔ **Relative strength indicator (RSI) for Exxon and for CLZ5:** Lower highs are found on both charts; however, the Exxon chart also shows clear overhead resistance on the stock's price, a sign that sellers are waiting to unload as soon as Exxon nears $64 per share.

- ✔ **How the crude futures chart continues to make new highs:** The RSI oscillator for crude futures also is cause for concern for the same reason, because it also fails to confirm the new high in crude, a sign of a momentum failure.

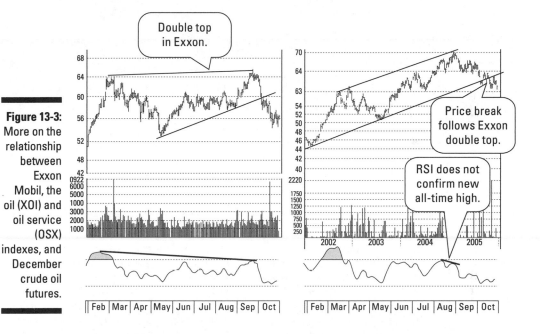

Figure 13-3: More on the relationship between Exxon Mobil, the oil (XOI) and oil service (OSX) indexes, and December crude oil futures.

When the price of Exxon stock no longer confirms the new high in crude oil, it's time to start being careful and monitoring the momentum and trend indicators so you can prepare to sell your crude futures position. In other words, Exxon, in this case, flashed a correct warning sign that oil prices were likely to fall.

As a futures trader, the situation shown in Figure 13-2 gave you little choice but to continue to trade crude futures on the long side. However, in this case, because Exxon was warning you, and the RSI oscillator was not confirming the rallies, you need to be very careful and use tight stop-loss points or consider trading only with options to curb your risk.

Burning the Midnight Oil

Crude oil trades around the world, but New York's Mercantile Exchange (NYMEX) is considered the hub of global oil trading.

Light, sweet crude is high-grade, low-sulfur crude oil that is more easily refined than thicker oils. It also yields better products. When it isn't going by that name, it's called West Texas Intermediate. High-sulfur crude, such as that which comes from Venezuela and certain Saudi Arabian wells, requires special refineries that process only the heavier crudes.

NYMEX also provides trading platforms for futures contracts based on the following:

- Dubai crude oil. This contract is a futures contract for Dubai crude oil.

- The differential between the light, sweet crude oil futures contract and Canadian Bow River crude at Hardisty, Alberta.

- The differentials between the light, sweet crude oil futures contract and four domestic grades of crude oil, including Light Louisiana Sweet, West Texas Intermediate-Midland, West Texas Sour, and Mars Blend.

- Brent North Sea crude oil.

- Oil options.

Crude oil is the world's most actively traded commodity, and the NYMEX contract for light, sweet crude is the most liquid of all crude oil contracts. The NYMEX Web site (www.nymex.com) is well worth a visit.

Here are the particulars of a crude oil contract:

- **Contract:** Each crude oil contract contains 1,000 barrels of oil that will be delivered to Cushing, Oklahoma.

  The e-mini contract trades on the CME Globex electronic platform are cleared at NYMEX and hold 500 barrels of light, sweet crude.

- **Valuation:** A barrel of oil holds 42 gallons and trades in U.S. dollars per barrel worldwide. The minimum tick of $0.01 (1 cent) is equal to $10 per contract.

- **Trading:** NYMEX offers both open-cry trading during regular hours and electronic, Web-based trading after hours. Open outcry trading hours are from 10 a.m. to 2:30 p.m. After-hours futures trading takes place on the NYMEX ACCESS, an Internet-based trading platform, starting at

3:15 p.m. Monday through Thursday and ending at 9:30 a.m. the following day. Sunday trading starts at 7 p.m.

✔ **Margins:** The initial crude oil contract margin for nonmembers as of July 2005 was $4,725 (April 2005 through September 2005), with the maintenance margin for customers at $3,500.

✔ **Settlement:** Contract settlement is physical, and delivery takes place at Cushing, Oklahoma, or similar pipeline or transfer facilities.

Contract listings and termination dates can be found at `www.nymex.com/ lsco_fut_termin.aspx`.

Getting the Lead Out with Gasoline

Gasoline has become a hugely important contract for several reasons. It is the largest-selling refined product sold in the United States and accounts for almost half of the nation's oil consumption. Two important factors that you need to know about the gasoline futures contract are that

✔ **Refinery capacity is limited.** As the global economy continues to grow, the global demand for gasoline also is rising. As is true in the United States, the number of cars in China also is growing, contributing to this increased global demand. For many of the same reasons, environmental and otherwise, gasoline demand outpaced refinery capacity for a good portion of 2005.

✔ **International competition for oil and geopolitical problems in South America are on the rise.** Although a bit more subtle, the importance of Venezuela as a major exporter of oil and gasoline to the United States is becoming a major global market factor. As rhetoric grew more intense between Venezuela's president Hugo Chavez and the United States in 2005, so did the risk of Venezuela cutting off exports.

As I write, no evidence suggests that Venezuela actually is cutting off exports to the United States, but the Chavez government is actively pursuing the development of alternative markets for its oil products, including China and other areas of South America. Indeed, Chavez is making production, exploration, and refinery deals with Russia, Brazil, India, Iran, and Cuba. At some point, if Chavez is successful, the United States may indeed encounter supply problems. I'd expect that the U.S. can buy oil and gasoline from alternative sources. The key is that prices are likely to be higher because of the logistics involved.

Contract specifications

You need a $5,400 initial margin per contract to trade a gasoline futures contract in all months except August and September, when you need $6,750. Market activity for August and September contracts is higher because they are peak months during the summer driving season. Maintenance margins are $4,000 and $5,000, respectively.

A contract gives you control of 1,000 barrels or 42,000 gallons of unleaded gasoline. A 25-cent move in the per-gallon price of gasoline is worth $10,500 per contract, and that amount is the limit move. Each tick of $0.01 (1 cent) is worth $4.20 per barrel. Delivery is physical to the New York harbor.

Trading strategies

Keep the following general tendencies in mind when trading gasoline contracts, but understand that they're not guaranteed to occur or to follow any particular script.

Gasoline prices tend to move along with prices for crude oil; however, gasoline prices are not guaranteed to mirror crude prices, because they move according to their own supply and demand scenario.

Gasoline prices tend to be the highest during summer months when demand is highest. Prices tend to rally for the July, August, and September gasoline futures contracts during April and May. Figure 13-4 shows the start of the rally in the September contract at the beginning of May. The figure also exhibits choppiness in the market as expectations for less driving are incorporated into gasoline prices. This chart is particularly important, because it shows the consistency of the overall seasonal pattern. In 2005, gasoline supplies were below historical stockpiles because of an overall tightness in the market and problems experienced within the refinery industry.

You also need to take note within Figure 13-4 that although Hurricane Katrina pushed gasoline futures prices above $2, the seasonal pattern held. Aside from the usual decrease in demand caused by seasonal factors, in this case, the market was essentially flooded with gasoline imports from Europe, while President Bush also suspended the need for refining a multitude of different grades of gasoline that normally are produced to meet clean-air standards. The combination of these three individual variables led to the decline in gasoline prices.

Keeping the Chill Out with Heating Oil

The price of heating oil has a tendency to rise as the winter months approach. As is true with all energy commodities, supply is the key, and chart watching is as important as keeping up with supply when trading heating oil futures.

After gasoline, *heating oil,* which also is known as No. 2 fuel oil, makes up about 25 percent of the yield from a barrel of crude oil. Here are the particulars of trading heating oil futures:

- **Contract:** Heating oil futures trade in the same units as gasoline: 1,000 barrels of 42 gallons each, or a total of 42,000 gallons. The contract is based on delivery to New York harbor, the principal cash-market trading center.

- **Margins:** Margins for heating oil are quite high, and they're based on a tiered structure that's designed to give a more precise assessment of risk. Each tier consists of at least one futures month, and all of the months within a given tier are consecutive. In general, as of August 2005, the Group 1 margin for nonmembers was $6,075. Groups 2 through 4 initial margins, respectively, were $5,738, $5,063, and $4,388. Maintenance margins, respectively, were $4,500, $4,250, $3,750, and $3,250.

  If you trade *nearby contracts,* contracts that expire in months that are in close proximity to the current month, your margin will be higher, because the volatility and the chance for profit is higher, and you're being charged a premium for that.

- **Valuation:** The price relationship of each tick is identical to gasoline, with 1 cent equaling $4.20 per barrel.

The airline industry, refiners, and others in the oil business use the heating oil futures contract to hedge diesel-fuel and jet-fuel prices, which ultimately means that you're trading against a savvy group of adversaries when you trade heating oil contracts.

Figures 13-4 and 13-5 also show the general tendency of heating oil to rally with oil, gasoline, and natural gas prices. During the time frame depicted in the figure, the contract started to show some price compression in late August and had joined gasoline in diverging from crude oil prices, which suggested that a big move was coming.

Looking for confirmation from different markets is important. As Figures 13-4 and 13-5 show, the energy complex was running into trouble. Crude oil topped out first, followed by gasoline, heating oil, and finally natural gas.

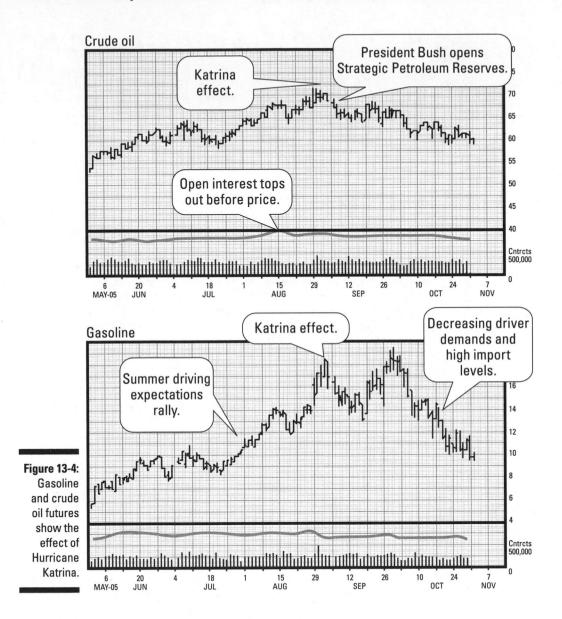

Figure 13-4: Gasoline and crude oil futures show the effect of Hurricane Katrina.

Figure 13-5: Heating oil and natural gas futures after Hurricane Katrina.

Getting Natural with Gas

Natural gas is an increasingly popular fuel. Its reputation for burning cleaner than crude oil and coal has made it the number-one choice of environmentalists and a commodity with a rising demand profile.

Russia has the world's largest natural gas reserves. The United States has roughly a tenth of the reserves of Russia, and Iran has the second-largest natural gas reserves.

Natural gas supplies about 25 percent of the energy used in the United States and is increasingly important in generating electricity, especially during the summer months, when it is used primarily for air conditioning.

Natural gas contracts have nine margin tiers, with initial margin requirements ranging from $10,800 at Tier 1 down to $2,025 at Tier 9. The range of the maintenance margins is from $8,800 at Tier 1 down to $1,650 at Tier 9.

A natural gas contract gives you control of 10,000 million British thermal units (mmBtu), and a 0.1 cent move is equal to $10 per contract.

Aside from the usual supply-and-demand dynamics, natural gas is subject to pressures from the hurricane season, because many major natural gas rigs are located in the Gulf of Mexico. Figure 13-5 shows how natural gas prices held up better than heating oil and gasoline during the week and weekend leading up to the climactic run toward land of Hurricane Katrina.

Getting in Tune with Sentiment and the Energy Markets

Sentiment is a nebulous (unclear) concept. To some it can mean sadness; to others, it means great joy. In the financial markets, it means greed and fear. Greed usually is associated with market tops, while fear usually is the hallmark of market bottoms. These diverging concepts are, of course, what make up the contrarian thesis of investing. (For more information about contrarian thinking, see Chapter 7.)

In the summer of 2005, when oil prices had risen by roughly 50 percent from the previous summer, the huge rise in prices was attributed to a three-pronged combination of refinery problems, significant weather changes, and steady economic growth, compounded by event fear and fanned by the flames of the greatest extension of a bull market in oil that started after September 11, 2001.

It was in this context that I was prompted to start carefully tracking market sentiment.

When I appeared on CNBC on August 24, 2005, the first question I was asked was, "How high can oil go?" My response was that $60 or $70 was possible, but that I wasn't sure. I also said that the market had been going up for some time and that it was due for a pause.

When I returned to my office after the interview, the network pundits were talking to Professor Michael Economides, author of *The Color of Oil* (Round Oak Publishing, 2000), and he was predicting $100 oil, although he didn't say by when. All day long on CNBC and elsewhere in the financial media, coverage of the oil markets was rather dramatic, and so were the perceptions of what was coming.

The next day oil prices fell more than a dollar, and the headline "SCREAMS AT THE PUMP" appeared on the Drudge Report a few days later, signifying that life in the oil markets was about to become even more interesting.

By August 26, 2005, the market was trying to decide what effect Hurricane Katrina was going to have. The market close on that Friday was inconclusive, but by Sunday, August 28, it became clear that Katrina was a major storm and that the oil infrastructure in New Orleans and the Gulf Coast area, which is responsible for a major portion of the energy supply and distribution of the United States, was in peril.

Although oil had traded above $70 per barrel as the storm was brewing overnight August 28, not enough data were available to support prices at that level. As the storm hit on the morning of August 29, damage reports began trickling in, and by August 30, oil finally burst above $70 per barrel during a regular trading session.

As the news of the storm trickled in, and the damage assessment became clear, the oil market took on an entirely new, extremely serious tone that was certain to suddenly make the American public keenly aware of daily price fluctuations.

By the end of trading August 30, crude oil futures for October closed at 69.85, just shy of $70, but nevertheless, still at an all-time record high.

On September 17, I appeared on the *Financial Sense News Hour* radio show with Jim Puplava, and Jim and I both agreed that oil prices were looking as if they were making a top. Few other analysts were on that side of the trade at the time. I submitted an article to Rigzone.com, in which I reported the conversation Jim and I had, and I forwarded the article to CNBC, which was interested enough to call me back for an interview.

I was back on CNBC the week after I made the call on the Jim Puplava show, and told them that if oil fell below $56, it could go to $40. During the next several weeks, the oil market dropped from the $70 area to around $60 by November 1, when Republicans were agreeing with the Democrats in Congress and starting to discuss adding a windfall tax to oil companies for making too much money, another sign that prices could fall further.

A second storm, Hurricane Rita, also hit the Gulf region just a few weeks after Katrina, but the damage, although significant, was not as bad.

By the time this book is released, the full story of Katrina's wrath may be told as events unfold.

What was apparent in November is that at least 50 percent of the oil and natural gas production infrastructure in the Gulf of Mexico was off-line, although refinery capacity was steadily coming back online. The United States was running on imported gasoline from Europe, and yet prices still were going lower, and still people were calling for $100-per-barrel oil.

Some Final Thoughts about Oil

I'll end this chapter with a list of some final thoughts to illustrate several points that you need to know about the oil markets in the summer of 2005:

- ✔ **The bull market in oil was three to four years old.** If you count September 11, 2001, as the date of its birth, or just a little beyond that point in time, that means the bull market was getting old, even by secular, or long-term bull market standards, which are measured in years and sometimes decades.

- ✔ **The prevailing wisdom in August 2005 was that oil prices couldn't go anywhere but up.** The world, after all, was running out of oil, and the global economy could never slow down.

- ✔ **Mainstream media, the majority of the experts, and the tabloids were starting to pick up the chant about impending high oil prices.** The only reasonable conclusion was that oil was ready to make a top. I still get chills when I realize that contrarian analysis worked so well during that period.

Always trade with the trend, but develop a sense of when the market can turn, and don't be afraid to put your money where your mouth is. Don't let what you want to see happen get in the way of what's happening. And don't let what you'd like to happen get in the way of your trading. The market will almost always prove you wrong until you throw in the towel on your beliefs and what your analysis is telling you. Then, if you're not careful, it will swallow you whole.

Chapter 14

Getting Metallic without Getting Heavy

*W*hen I think of heavy metal, I think of loud music, long hair, and fast guitar licks. And if you look hard enough, you may even see me at one of those increasingly popular 1980s metal shows during the summer, because I like to see those old boys still strut their stuff.

The other side of heavy metal has nothing to do with music, but it's still quite industrial and can be just as profitable as record sales and concert grosses for some of the more famous heavy metal bands of the 1980s.

Indeed, metal futures (you knew I'd get around to it, didn't you) experienced a significant revival because the global economy, largely influenced by aggressive growth in China, has brought the luster back into what was a largely faded area of the futures markets.

Metals are divided into two major categories: precious and industrial. The markets of the two different classes look at the same side of the economy but from different angles. Although precious metals are thought of as hedges against inflation, price changes in the industrial metals usually are precursors to the start and often the end of economic cycles.

In this chapter, I focus on gold and copper, but I also tie in enough information about silver, platinum, and the other industrial metals to understand how the markets for each of them work.

From a trading standpoint, especially from that of a beginner, the best way to get started in the metals markets, in general, is to become familiar with the gold and copper markets. They are the two most economically sensitive of all the metals.

Tuning in to the Economy

The prices of precious and industrial metals are linked to economic activity. Gold steals all the headlines, but the industrial metals do much of the work.

Here's what I mean: Rising economic activity leads to increasing demand for industrial metals. When industrial activity reaches the point where demand starts to outstrip supply, inflationary pressures start to build in the system. At that point, gold prices can start to rise.

Industrial metal prices are sensitive to demand. Copper prices, especially, can be a leading indicator of an increase in economic activity, given the wide-spread use of the metal in housing, electronics, and commercial construction. The flip side is that the copper market can start to sag, and prices can start to drop several months ahead of the data, such as Gross Domestic Product numbers (see the section on "Getting into Metal without the Leather: Trading Copper," later in this chapter).

The key word here is *can*. With most of the world's supply of gold in the hands of central banks — whose main goal is fighting inflation — the managers of those central banks know that speculators see rising gold prices as a sign of inflation. When gold rallies tend to get out of hand, central banks start selling the metal from their huge stockpiles, and prices eventually fall.

No one really knows whether central banks are heavy buyers of gold when the price starts to fall; however, it is plausible that when the fears of deflation hit the market or prices continually decline, central banks can become gold buyers of last resort.

The fact that central banks tend to be gold sellers during rallies doesn't mean that gold prices can't rally for significant periods of time. It just means that central banks are a formidable market opponent of the everyday trader and that the days of straight-up advances in gold where smart speculators make or break their lifetime's fortune, although still possible, are not as likely as they once were.

And just so you don't go around thinking that I'm pushing conspiracy theories, you can check out all kinds of extreme and sensible commentaries on central banks and gold anywhere on the Internet.

A good commentary at Financial Sense.com (`www.financialsense.com/fsu/editorials/2004/0308.html`) summarizes a fully disclosed five-year plan of gold sales by central banks.

The highlights are simple. The central banks

- Acknowledge that gold is "an important element of global monetary reserves."

- Set limits of sales over the five-year period of the program to no more than 500 tons per year and no more than 2,500 tons over the entire five-year period.

- Won't sell more gold than they have in reserve.

- Review the agreement in five years.

The bottom line is that gold is a tricky market because of central banks and the role they play in it. On the other hand, industrial metals such as copper offer more transparency in their pricing patterns because of their close relationship with economic expectations and economic activity.

From an investment standpoint, gold still is central to the world's monetary system, no longer because it is a standard for payments, but rather because it is the most strategic holding common to the world's central banks and often is used as a tool to cool off the world's view of inflation.

When you invest in gold, you're swimming against the tide. The world's central banks hold 25 percent of all the gold ever mined. According to the World Gold Council, in 2003, central banks held ten times the amount of gold that was mined in that year — 33,000 metric tons housed in vaults versus 3,200 metric tons mined. I'm not saying that you need to avoid gold completely; I'm simply noting that the average investor is up against a gargantuan market-making opponent in the world's central banks.

Gold Market Fundamentals

South Africa is the world's largest producer of gold, accounting for 25 percent or more of all global production and 50 percent of the accessible reserves. Russia, the United States, Canada, Australia, and Brazil make up the rest of the top-tier producers.

The all-time high in gold prices was set in January 1980, when the price of the October contract hit $1,026 per ounce as the spot-market price rallied to $875. As I write in August 2005, gold is trading near $440 per ounce.

Here are two key factors to keep in mind about the gold market:

✔ **Two major influences have an effect on gold prices.** They are

- **Major political upheaval.** Political crises tend to be the major reason for gold prices to rise.

- **Inflation.** The influence of inflation on gold prices is much less intense than it was in the past because of the management of gold prices by the central banks.

✔ **The most reliable influence in the gold market is its relationship to the U.S. dollar.** Figures 14-1 and 14-2 show how the trends of gold and the U.S. dollar were reversed after the events of September 11, 2001. The Federal Reserve (the Fed) lowered interest rates, in effect printing money and decreasing the value of the dollar, which brought the gold bugs out of hibernation.

Gold prices and the U.S. dollar tend to go in reverse of each other. This relationship is not a perfect one, but it is worth looking for, and over long periods of time, it tends to hold up well.

The price of gold can be confusing, so here's a quick primer.

The international benchmark price for gold is the London Price Fix, which is set in U.S. dollars and is quoted in troy ounces twice daily as the a.m. fix and the p.m. fix. The London exchange summarizes global gold trading as these composite prices.

Gold trades around the world on major exchanges in China, the United Kingdom (UK), and the United States. India and China are countries with expanding demand for gold.

Spot gold and gold futures trade on the New York Mercantile Exchange (NYMEX). Gold futures also trade on the Chicago Board of Trade (CBOT) and have relatively low margin requirements for speculators. That means gold can be an attractive market for small accounts. As of August 2005, initial margin was $1,350, and maintenance was $1,000. The mini contract for gold futures also trades on CBOT.

Mini contracts are smaller versions of the original contract. In the case of gold, a mini contract contains 33.2 troy ounces of gold, compared with a full-sized contract that holds 100 troy ounces. The margin requirements are smaller, but the general characteristics and fundamentals of the market remain the same. The mini contract has a $317 initial margin and a $235 maintenance margin — compared to $952 and $705 for the full-sized contract at the CBOT.

Several reliable information sources for gold can be found on the Internet. Two of the ones I like to use are the World Gold Council (www.gold.org) and Kitco.com (www.kitco.com).

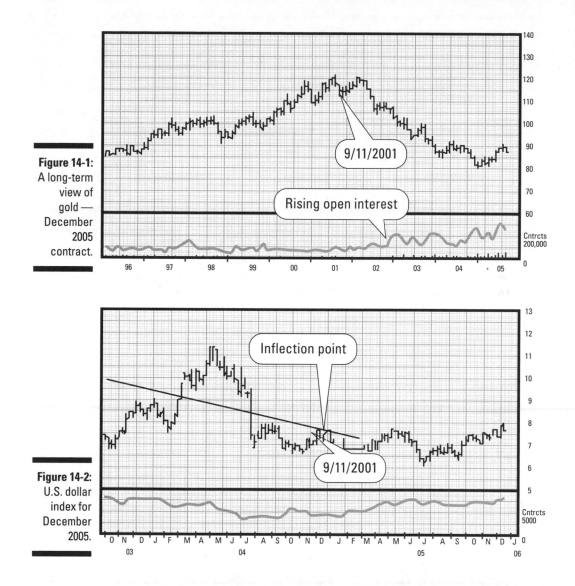

Figure 14-1: A long-term view of gold — December 2005 contract.

Figure 14-2: U.S. dollar index for December 2005.

When trading gold and gold futures, you need to watch the following:

✔ **Actions taken by central banks around the world:** Central banks tend to be net sellers. As a general rule, they either sell or stay out of the markets. See "Tuning in to the Economy," earlier in this chapter.

The Fed, the European Central Bank, the Bank of England, and the National Bank of Switzerland usually are major players in the gold market, but any central bank is a potential seller, especially during periods of heightened inflationary expectations.

- ✔ **The geopolitical situation:** Asia, the Middle East, and South America are global regions full of potential instability. The chance for terrorist attacks is rising on a daily basis and is likely to become something that remains a big influence from time to time during the next several decades.

- ✔ **Wars:** Wars can lead to volatility in the price of gold. The expectations for higher prices during wars is often not met, given the frequency of major regional conflicts around the world and the frequent selling by central banks.

- ✔ **General weakness of the dollar and other major global currencies:** The general relationship is for gold to rise when the dollar weakens. As with other traditional relationships, this rule isn't set in stone, but rather a tendency caused by central-bank intervention in the gold and currency markets.

- ✔ **Inflation:** If the Fed starts talking seriously about inflation and starts raising interest rates aggressively, the gold market is likely to respond with higher prices. For a major rally in gold to develop, the markets have to start believing that central banks can no longer control inflation. That hasn't happened since the 1970s. In 2005, though, the Fed and other global central banks began talking more seriously about inflation. When they did, gold prices began showing some rising power.

- ✔ **Technical analysis indicators:** They can keep you on the right side of the trade. As with other markets (see Chapter 7 for an overview of technical analysis), moving averages, trend lines, and oscillators such as the MACD and RSI work with gold prices and need to be an integral part of your gold trading.

Getting into the habit of looking at long-term commodity charts on a weekly basis makes you better able to deal with any titanic shifts in the long-term trend, such as what occurred September 11, 2001. Figure 14-2 clearly marks the "inflection point" in the gold market's key reversal and subsequent bull run.

Lining the Markets with Silver

Silver is a hybrid metal, because it is used for industrial purposes and as a precious metal in jewelry. The silver market is extremely volatile and can be difficult to trade.

Mexico and the U.S. are the largest producers of silver. Silver mines usually can't be operated profitably when market prices fall below $8 per ounce. As a result, when prices fall below that level, production of silver wanes considerably, with much of it coming as a byproduct of copper, lead, and zinc mining processes.

When trading silver, you need to know these nuts and bolts:

✔ One silver contract contains 5,000 troy ounces, with a 1 cent move being worth $50.

✔ The modern-day trading range for silver is from 35 cents during the Great Depression up to $50 per ounce when the Hunt brothers tried to corner the silver market in the late 1970s.

✔ When copper, lead, and zinc prices rise, especially because of decreased production, the price of silver is likely to rally, because much of the world's silver is a byproduct of mining and processing the other three metals.

Catalyzing Platinum

The platinum market is heavily influenced by Japan, where it's the precious metal of choice. Although a precious metal, platinum also has hybrid qualities. In fact, it is more often used as the key component in making catalytic converters for cars.

The relative economic strengths in Japan, in the automobile market and in the medical and dental fields — where platinum is also in demand — are the major influences on the price of platinum.

Platinum trades on the NYMEX in contracts containing 100 troy ounces. It can be thinly traded, though, and is best avoided by beginning traders. As with gold, South Africa is the world's largest producer, with Russia second, and North America, where some recent finds have occurred, third.

As with any other market, you can apply the usual method of finding out about the fundamentals combined with technical analysis.

Platinum usually trades at a higher price than gold, because supply is much smaller — only 80 tons of the metal reach the market in any given year. For example, on October 28, 2005, platinum futures closed at $941 per troy ounce, while gold futures closed at $474.

Industrializing Your Metals

Technical indicators are the key to predicting future trends in industrial metals, so you need to be on the lookout for the early clues before a trend changes.

The most important industrial metals (copper, aluminum, zinc, nickel, lead, and palladium) start to rally when the market senses that demand is starting to increase, or they start to fall back when it senses supplies starting to stabilize. In general terms, then, at these transition points, trends in the industrial metals markets start to turn. As a trader, you can't get caught in the expectations game, though. You need to wait for the markets to make their moves. No prize is awarded for being the first trader to buy something.

Although gold still is an important asset, the industrial metals complex is a better place for speculators to trade, because it's where supply and demand information and easily measured economic fundamentals (with good correlation to prices) are available and tested by price action and overall response in the markets.

Getting into Metal without the Leather: Trading Copper

Copper is the third most used metal in the world, and it's found virtually everywhere around the globe. The most active copper mines are in the United States, Chile, Mexico, Australia, Indonesia, Zaire, and Zambia.

A beginning trader may be tempted to dive into the gold market, but some good reasons exist for considering copper first, especially its close connection to the economic cycle and the housing market.

Generally, I like to trade markets that have a good correlation to a sector of the stock market where I have access to company earnings and where industry executives are required by law to provide truthful information to the market using widely disseminated means, such as television and major media outlets. You can see what I mean in the next section.

Before that, though, there are few things that you need to know about copper before you start trading it, and they have nothing to do with leather, smoke-filled stages, or headbanging. The keys to trading copper that I tell you about in this list set the stage for the more-involved data that follow.

 ✔ **Uses:** The major uses for copper are in

 • Construction and housing for plumbing and wiring

 • High technology for wiring

 • Semiconductor-related industries for wiring

- ✔ **Markets:** Copper trades at the COMEX, which is a division of the NYMEX in New York, and at the London Metals Exchange. The London contract trades several times more than the U.S. contract in terms of volume, but both are liquid and active contracts.

- ✔ **Contracts:** The COMEX contract is for 25,000 pounds of copper, while the London contract is for 55,000 pounds. New York prices are quoted in dollars and cents per pound, while London prices are quoted in dollars and cents per ton. Thus, a 1-cent move in New York is worth $250, while a $1 move in London in worth $25.

You can use stock prices and trends as predictors of industrial metal prices.

Setting up your copper-trading strategy

Figuring out key relationships within any market is your first step when analyzing it from a technical standpoint. One of my favorites is the relationship between the copper market and the stock of Phelps Dodge, and in turn, its relationship with the bond and housing markets. These interrelationships are as important as any you can find in the futures market, primarily because all the pieces depend on one another for a complete picture of their respective markets to emerge. Here's why:

- ✔ **Phelps Dodge is a leading smelter and producer of copper.** As a result, the stock has an excellent record of predicting the trend in market for the metal. Stock investors start betting on the future trend of earnings for the company based on their expectations for copper demand, and thus, its connection to the company's earnings.

- ✔ **The housing market has a good correlation to the price action of housing stocks.** The key is the information provided in monthly housing reports, especially housing starts and building permits. These two reports are the lifeline of the whole equation, because the Fed looks at them closely as it tries to figure out what to do with interest rates.

The housing stock that you use for this purpose needs to be one that behaves similarly in each cycle. I usually use Centex (NYSE symbol: CTX) or Toll Brothers (NYSE symbol: TOL), because they are large capitalization stocks that service significant portions of the housing market. Toll Brothers is an upscale builder that usually is one of the last to top out because it serves richer customers who can last longer. Centex is a good cross-section builder that also works on commercial properties.

- ✔ **The bond market takes its cues from inflationary indications.** For example, if housing prices rise too rapidly, and signs of bottlenecks appear in commodities markets for copper and lumber, the bond market would start to sell off and interest rates would rise.

Charting the course

Putting copper market interrelationships together requires you to keep a close watch on charts of the components that I explained in the previous section, including copper futures, shares of Phelps Dodge Corporation, housing starts and building permits, and the bond market.

Figures 14-3 and 14-4 show good examples of how these relationships work. Notice the general trends of the metal (Figure 14-3) and the stock (Figure 14-4) and how they usually change directions within a close time frame of each other. Phelps Dodge topped in March, while the metal was drifting lower. Soon after, though, the metal made a new low, and both rallied starting in May and heading into August.

In Figure 14-5, you can see how housing starts started drifting lower in the spring of 2005 after hitting a high point in January. The slowing of housing starts correlates well with an intermediate-term top seen in the price of Phelps Dodge stock. Notice that as housing starts stabilized, Phelps Dodge and copper each staged yet another rally, reaching new highs as it extended into August.

According to Figure 14-7 (later in this section), Centex, a good representative of the housing sector, rallied a full two years before Phelps Dodge took off on its own rally. The reason the rally in Centex led to the rally in Phelps Dodge shows up in Figure 14-6. Copper prices were forming a base in the late 1990s, but only when the market started to price in the fact that demand for the metal would likely outstrip supply did the rally in Phelps Dodge begin.

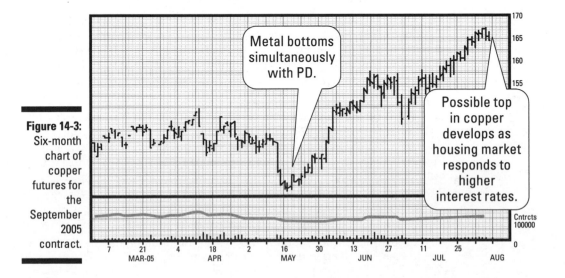

Figure 14-3:
Six-month chart of copper futures for the September 2005 contract.

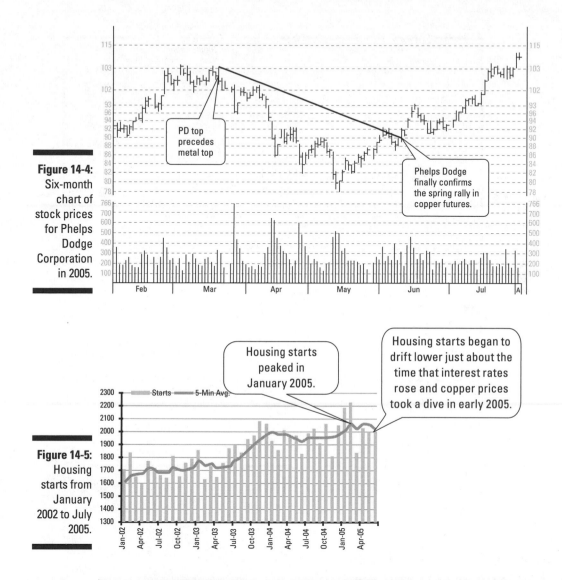

Figure 14-4: Six-month chart of stock prices for Phelps Dodge Corporation in 2005.

PD top precedes metal top

Phelps Dodge finally confirms the spring rally in copper futures.

Housing starts peaked in January 2005.

Housing starts began to drift lower just about the time that interest rates rose and copper prices took a dive in early 2005.

Figure 14-5: Housing starts from January 2002 to July 2005.

Check out Figure 14-7 to see something very important: Centex (right), a major U.S. homebuilder, began to falter at the same time housing starts began to drift. This move is more obvious in Figure 14-8, which shows the U.S. ten-year Treasury note yield rising dramatically on August 6, 2005, in response to a strong U.S. employment report. Note that on the day of the big move up in interest rates, Centex fell apart.

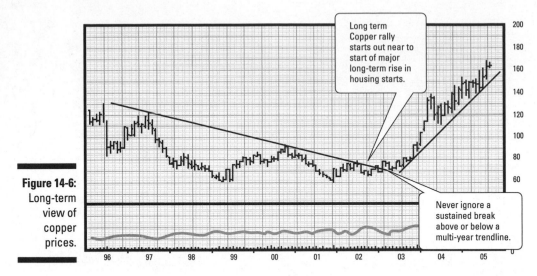

Figure 14-6: Long-term view of copper prices.

By August 16, Phelps Dodge also had fallen, but then something interesting happened in September and October. Hurricanes Katrina and Rita hit the U.S. Gulf of Mexico coast, leading to massive housing and commercial building destruction.

As a result, the market started pricing in a rebound in new construction, driving prices higher.

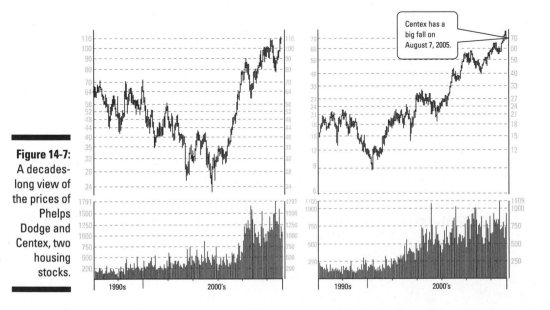

Figure 14-7: A decades-long view of the prices of Phelps Dodge and Centex, two housing stocks.

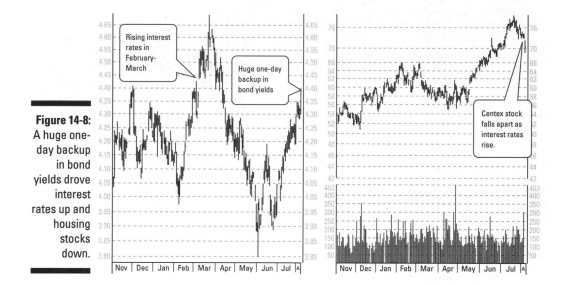

Figure 14-8:
A huge one-day backup in bond yields drove interest rates up and housing stocks down.

At the same time, China's economy, as measured by gross domestic product (GDP), continued to grow at a 9.4-percent clip as the U.S. economy grew at a faster-than-expected rate, and copper prices moved to a slightly new high as the market factored in a rise in demand for copper in the wake of the rebuilding.

My point is that markets react to circumstances as well as perception. A major top in copper was building as the housing market began to respond to higher interest rates, but an intangible set of events — in this case, the hurricanes — and the persistent growth of the Chinese and American economies led to a new leg up in prices. These circumstances give more credence to the relationship between interest rates, the price of copper, and the housing market.

Organizing the charts

I find it useful to organize the way I look at my charts on a time line, and you may benefit from organizing the way you look at charts, too. Here are the steps that I take:

1. **Look at daily charts.**

   Starting with a glimpse of daily charts helps you to get the current picture straight.

2. Look at longer-term charts.

I like to take a step back and view charts spanning years so I can put the current picture (from Step 1) in the right perspective. Orienting the short-term with longer-term charts helps you decide whether the current trading activity is within the long-term trend or a countertrend move.

3. Look at shorter-term charts.

By shorter-term, I mean checking out charts that span either a few days or maybe even only an intraday time period (hours or even minutes) with an eye on optimizing my entry and exit points.

Use a charting program that enables you to look at more than one chart at a time.

Here's what you need to watch for when viewing your charts:

✔ **Differing time lines:** By looking at the same chart using at least three different time lines, you focus in on a much clearer picture of what's happening in the market. With practice, you can compile the trio of time line data in only a few minutes.

✔ **Overall trends:** Using a long-term chart like the one in Figure 14-5 as your guide, you can check out a market's overall trend. You need to plan your trades based on the primary long-term trend. For example, if copper is in a three-year uptrend, you can expect pullbacks. You can short the pullbacks whenever they look like they're going to last. However, as a trader, your main focus needs to be on trading the long side until an irrefutable break to the downside occurs. When that break occurs, you need to turn your sites to short selling, all the time knowing that you'll eventually get short-term opportunities to go long.

✔ **Trend lines:** Never ignore a sustained move above or below a multiyear trend line. Watch trend lines closely. Figure 14-6 shows a new bull market forming in copper, starting in 2003 as the multiyear downtrend line was broken. So just as Pink Floyd sings, "How can you have any pudding if you don't eat your meat?" if you trade futures, keep this in mind: If you don't read your charts, you'll miss important turning points in the market.

✔ **Divergence in your charts:** Make sure copper stocks and copper futures are moving in the same general direction. If they're not, you have a *technical divergence,* a situation that can result in one of two scenarios:

• Futures will turn in the direction of the stocks.

• Stocks will turn in the direction of the futures.

Figures 14-3 and 14-4 show a small divergence between Phelps Dodge and the September futures contract. Although they bottomed in May, the move in copper was stronger than in the stock. It took until June for the full reversal in Phelps Dodge to confirm the rally in the futures.

✔ **Interest-rate trends:** Interest-rate trends are your leading indicator, because the housing market thrives on low interest rates. The big move up in rates in early 2005 was not the top in copper, but it was enough to take the wind out of the rally's sails for quite some time.

Making sure fundamentals are on your side

Success in the futures market depends on how well you know the market in which you're trading, technically and fundamentally. The economically sensitive metal markets are too difficult to trade without using both technical and fundamental analyses.

Here are some key tips for how you can make sense of technical and fundamental information:

✔ **Check housing starts.** This key report shows you whether the current trend in copper is sustainable. For example, housing starts were flat in June 2005, a factor that was reflected in the July 19 report, which you can view at *The Wall Street Journal* online, www.wsj.com, when you subscribe.

✔ **Look beyond the headlines.** The full text of the June housing report contained some important details about single-family home starts being down 2.5 percent from the May report. However, the number of building permits still was rising so that particular number held up the market. Still, as the newspapers flaunted the never-ending housing boom, the June report was cautionary.

✔ **Check supply and demand.** You need to know what supply-and-demand indicators like the Purchasing Manager's (ISM) reports are saying.

A good way to get a grip on supply and demand is to see which industries are reporting growth and which are not from the ISM report, which also is available in full on *The Wall Street Journal* Web site. The July 2005 report was released August 5, 2005, just a few days after the Fed started to set the stage for a more aggressive stance toward higher interest rates and just before the housing stocks began to show signs of weakness. The list of industry sectors that the July ISM report said were growing included "Instruments & Photographic Equipment; Food; Wood & Wood Products; Electronic Components & Equipment; Leather; Miscellaneous*; Industrial & Commercial Equipment & Computers; Transportation & Equipment; Furniture; Chemicals; *Fabricated Metals;* and Textiles."

The sectors that the July ISM said were decreasing in activity included "Printing & Publishing; Glass, Stone & Aggregate; *Primary Metals;* Apparel; Rubber & Plastic Products; and Paper."

A quick glance at these sectors shows these factors:

- Several housing-related sectors were growing, especially the fabricated metals, such as steel and textiles and wood, which are used in furniture. Indeed, furniture also was growing. The overall picture for housing, however, was mixed.

- Primary metals, copper included, were one of the weak sectors.

At a point in the copper market like the one described in the list above, you want to be careful, watch the charts, and wait for the next month's report to confirm your suspicions that the trend may slow.

Getting a handle on the Fed

You must maintain a continued awareness of when the Fed's board of governors and open market committee are meeting.

Nothing happens to interest rates without the Fed getting into the game. So you have to keep an eye on the central bank to watch for clues about whether the Fed is happy with current rates. Remember, the Fed, by design, is paranoid about inflation, and the central banks, as members of the Fed, can control gold prices, thus making the markets wonder about inflation. However, the Fed and the central banks can't sweep rising housing and commodity prices under the rug, so they have to do something about it.

In early 2005, the Fed was getting annoyed with the housing market. Fed Chairman Alan Greenspan had described regional bubbles in selected markets and expressed mixed feelings about them. In July, Greenspan pointed to "signs of froth in some local markets where home prices seem to have risen to unsustainable levels."

The Fed's governors like to make speeches or leak key concepts to the press. And that's clearly what happened in 2005 just before the employment report was to be released August 6, 2005.

On August 3, 2005 (a Wednesday), Greg Ip, a reporter for *The Wall Street Journal* with a pretty good pipeline into the Fed, wrote: "As the Federal Reserve prepares to raise short-term interest rates again next week, officials there increasingly believe the bond market, which sets long-term rates, is diluting their efforts to tighten credit and contain inflation." And it got even scarier: "Some policy makers worry that bond yields are being kept in check by overly complacent investor sentiment, which could rapidly dissipate, pushing up mortgage rates and shaking the housing market. Indeed, some Fed officials see similarities between the attitudes of bond investors today and of stock investors in the late 1990s."

Getting beyond gold and copper

Other metals besides gold and copper trade in the futures markets. After you master — or at least become familiar with — the gold and copper markets, you can try your hand at aluminum, zinc, nickel, lead, and tin.

Most of them are more thinly traded than gold and copper, with the exception of aluminum, which can be very liquid.

The major influences are similar to the economic fundamentals for gold and copper: strikes and wars, individual metal stocks released regularly by the exchanges, and inflation.

Pulling it together

After you determine the long-term trend and check for potential land mines, such as the Fed clearly telling the markets that interest rates are going way up and for a long time, you need to core down your technical analysis toward the short term by doing the following:

- ✔ Use trend lines, moving averages, and oscillators (see Chapters 7 and 8) to look for clear and precise entry points above key resistance when going long and below critical support levels when going short.

- ✔ Always confirm your trades with at least two technical oscillators, such as MACD and RSI, before diving in.

- ✔ Set sell stops or buy-to-cover stops, depending on the direction of your trade, by referring to moving averages or percentages as your guidelines.

Never lose more than 5 percent on any given trade, and you'll stay in the game.

Chapter 15

Getting to the Meat of the Markets: Livestock and More

- -

In This Chapter

▶ Cashing in on meat-market supply and demand

▶ Grilling your understanding of cattle and swine markets

▶ Using meat-market technical and fundamental analyses

▶ Eying big meat-market reports

▶ Checking out the effects of major reports and outside influences

- -

*I*f you're like I was before I began trading, the first image of futures trading that comes to mind is something like pork bellies or orange juice. You probably start chuckling and start shaking your head, saying, "No way man . . . not for me . . . no sir."

Then there's the Hollywood take on commodities traders, usually shown as not too smart, greedy fellows, looking for an edge and a quick buck.

In the movie *Trading Places,* Eddie Murphy and Dan Akroyd turn the tables on two old scoundrels played by Ralph Bellamy and Don Ameche, who were gaming the orange-juice market with inside information before the release of the monthly data hit the wires.

Although the movie was entertaining, and the two old buggers got what they deserved, it unfortunately painted a lopsided picture of the futures market. To be sure, some traders in the futures markets probably would seriously consider trading on insider information, but given the tight surveillance of the markets, and the potential for being caught, finding out just how the markets work and whether you're cut out to trade probably is the best route for you to take.

Trading, after all, is a serious business, and the meat markets are basically about how much you and I have to pay to eat. If you look at it from that standpoint, you start taking it a bit more seriously.

Meat markets are as much about farmers, producers, and other industry-related traders using the markets to hedge their bets against potentially negative outside influences — weather, herds that catch plagues, and even fad diets like the low-carb craze that took hold in the last decade — as they are about people like you and me who look at charts and real-time quotes and try to make money by trading meat.

This chapter is meant to provide a good overview of basic trading strategies. Some excellent and more in-depth information can be found at these Web sites:

- ✔ The Chicago Merchantile Exchange (CME — www.cme.com/files/ LivestockFund.pdf)
- ✔ The Ohio State University (www-agecon.ag.ohio-state.edu/ people/roe.30/livehome.htm)

The best free charting for cattle futures is available from Barchart.com at www.barchart.com, which is a good place to start looking at the meat markets and becoming familiar with the action that takes place in these markets before you decide whether you want to trade in them.

Exploring Meat-Market Supply and Demand, Cycles, and Seasonality

Like all commodities markets, meat markets are based on supply. More than with other commodities markets where supply is key, in the meat markets, a more equitable relationship exists with demand. The two major temporal factors to understand about the meat markets are the longer meat cycle, which is different for cattle than it is for hogs, and the more reliable — although not perfect by any means — aspect of seasonality.

The meat market goes through several phases where herds are built up and subsequently sold. When farmers increase the number of cattle in their herds, it's called the *accumulation phase,* and when they thin the herd for selling, it's called the *liquidation phase.* For hogs, the spectrum starts with *expansion* and ends with *contraction.*

The time that passes from accumulation to liquidation and from expansion to contraction is called the *livestock cycle.* In the past, the cycle for cattle usually lasted 10 to 12 years, and for hogs, it usually was around four years. The actual length of the cycle is measured either from one *trough,* or the low point in inventory, to the next, or from one *peak,* or high point in inventory, until the next. The time that it takes for female swine to reach breeding age has a direct effect on the hog expansion phase.

Seasonality, on the other hand, can be short term or have more of an intermediate duration. During summer months, the demand for certain cuts of beef that can be grilled outside tends to increase. The same is true for the demand for turkeys at Thanksgiving time. When consumers are flocking to one kind of meat at specific times, prices can be affected, and the market reacts and adjusts. For example, some specific times that affect specific meat markets include

- ✔ **January through March:** These three months tend to be strong ones for feeder livestock prices, because grain prices tend to be lower during the same period. *Feeder cattle* are steers, castrated males, and heifers, or females that have not calved. These animals weigh anywhere from 600 to 800 pounds when they arrive at the feedlot, with a goal of reaching 1,000 to 1,300 pounds before they're slaughtered.

- ✔ **April through August:** The spring and summer usually are weak months for feeder prices.

- ✔ **September through December:** These four months are a second season of strength in feeder prices; however, the January through March period historically has been the stronger of the two periods.

Feeder cattle and oat prices sometimes move before live cattle prices. So reliable is this tendency that some traders actually describe this relationship as "Feeders are the leaders."

Understanding Your Steak

Here's a quick-and-dirty overview of the cattle business to get you rolling in the right direction.

Despite increasingly frequent scares about mad cow disease, the steak that everyone loves to eat starts off with a *cow/calf operation,* which in short is a cattle-breeding business that consists of a plot of land that holds a few bulls, some kind of feed, and an average of at least 42 cows, according to government statistics provided by the United States Department of Agriculture (USDA). The cow/calf operations are where natural or artificial insemination takes its course and calves are born.

The breeding process

Producers breed cattle in the late summer or early fall, because nine months are required to birth a calf. Most of the cattle production in the United States takes place in Kansas, Nebraska, Colorado, Oklahoma, Texas, Iowa, Minnesota, and Montana. Many of these areas of the country endure tough winters, so birthing calves in spring gives them a better chance for survival.

Calves spend six months or so with their mothers and then are either released into the feedlot or undergo *backgrounding,* a period where smaller animals catch up in size and weight, essentially a process by which they are fed until they grow to 600 to 800 pounds, which is considered large enough to enter the feedlot and become *feeder cattle.*

Feedlots are where calves, again steers and heifers, are fattened up to become the beef that humans consume. *Cattle hotels* are commercial feedlots that account for only about 5 percent of all lots that are involved in raising feeder cattle, but they produce 80 percent of the cattle sold. Feedlots sometimes buy cattle for their clientele or will charge farmers a fee to custom feed their stock.

Commercial operations offer farmers convenient services, such as boarding and feeding cattle, and often serve as middlemen by setting up deals between farmers and slaughterhouses. In other words, commercial operations fatten up herds and use their industry contacts with packing plants to sell their client/farmer's herds. Sometimes commercial operations combine smaller herds from several farms into one feedlot and then sell them to the slaughterhouses.

Feeder cattle are fed a high-energy diet consisting of grain, protein supplements, and roughage. Putting on weight fast is the idea. The grain portion these cattle are fed usually is made up of corn, milo, or wheat if the price is low enough. Usually, the protein supplement includes soybeans, cottonseed, or linseed meal. The roughage usually is alfalfa hay or even sugar beet pulp, depending on market prices.

The packing plant

When feedlot animals reach specific weights, they are sold to the packing plant. The packing plant is where live cattle and hogs are sent to be slaughtered. Packers sell the meat and by-products, including the hides, bones, and glands, to different customers, including retailers, such as grocery stores and manufacturers of clothing and furniture.

The feeder cattle contract

Feeder cattle contracts are made up of feeder cattle, the precursor to live cattle, and are the province of the feedlot operator. See the section about "Understanding Your Steak," earlier in the chapter, for details about feeder cattle, and the next section for details on live cattle.

The prices of feeder cattle contracts are dependent on two major raw materials, the number of animals on the feedlot and the price of grain.

Feedlot operators increase the number of animals based on the demand for feeder cattle, which is dependent on the demand for live cattle. Corn and other grain prices influence the costs of maintaining an animal on the feedlot. Cheap grain prices usually correlate well with higher feeder cattle prices when you trade this contract. Low supplies of grain stocks, on the other hand, usually lead to weak feeder prices. Here are some of the specifics of feeder cattle contracts:

- ✔ **Composition:** This contract holds 50,000 pounds of feeder cattle, with specifications calling for a 750-pound steer, such that each contract holds an average of 60 animals.

- ✔ **Valuation:** Prices are quoted in either cents per pound or dollars per hundredweight.

- ✔ **Settlement:** Delivery is cash settled and is based on an index, with the final price being the price of the index on the contract's last day.

- ✔ **Price limits:** The price limit is equal to the live contract limit, which is 300 points or 3 cents per pound, or $3 per hundredweight, above or below the closing price for the previous day.

The CME live cattle contract

The main difference between the live cattle contract and the feeder cattle contract is that the animals in the live cattle contract are ready for slaughter.

Buyers of live cattle usually are meat packers who sell the meat and by-products. In general, prices for live cattle tend to rise from January to March, start falling in April, bottom out in July, and then remain below average until October, according to monthly averages on the CME from 1992 through 2003.

This shifting of prices results from the pattern of cattle slaughter. According to USDA data from 1992 through 2003, the number of cattle slaughtered peaks during the period from June through August, making a second but lower peak in October, and then declining into February, when the cycle starts rising again until the June/August top.

Live cattle contracts are much like feeder cattle contracts, with the same daily limits (300 points, 3 cents per pound, or $3 per hundredweight) above or below the previous day's close, but each contract consists of 40,000 pounds of slaughter-ready animals.

Beef prices are susceptible to mad cow disease and other health-related stories — such as being linked to cancer and heart disease — that occasionally appear in the press. These stories can remain in the headlines for several days or weeks. During those periods, avoiding the beef market is best.

Understanding Your Pork Chop

The hog market is similar in many ways to the cattle market, but it has some important distinctions:

- ✔ Pork demand rises in spring because of Easter and in winter because of the holiday season.
- ✔ Hog prices tend to rise in January and peak in May and June, rolling over in July and falling into fall and the holiday season.
- ✔ During the period of rising hog prices, the number of slaughters decreases.

Living a hog's life

Similar to cattle, hogs being raised for the market go through significant stages that traders need to track. The two basic stages are preslaughter and postslaughter. The preslaughter stage is known as the *farrow-to-finish operation,* which means basically the entire process from breeding and rearing a hog to slaughter, because the hog stays on the same farm from birth to finish.

When hogs reach 220 to 240 pounds in a period of about six months, they're sent to market.

Different from beef, a significant amount of pork is processed into smoked, canned, or frozen ham.

Pork bellies

As a frustrated baseball announcer, I love a good slice of bacon, so I thought I'd do the next best thing by shouting out the title of this section as if it were Sammy Sosa striding up to the plate.

Pork bellies, though, are not a laughing matter. Indeed, they are the part of the hog from which bacon is derived. Hogs are cash settled, based on a USDA-calculated index.

Here are the basics of what you need to know about pork-belly contracts:

- ✔ **Contracts:** Pork-belly contracts are traded in lots of 50,000 pounds, compared with 40,000 pounds for the live-hog contract.

- ✔ **Valuation:** When trading hogs and pork bellies, a 1-cent move in hogs is worth plus or minus $400 per contract, while a 1-cent move in pork bellies is worth $500 per contract.

- ✔ **Market makeup:** Speculators make up 85 percent of the trading volume in pork bellies.

Pork bellies are among the most treacherous of futures contracts. The combination of a big move with just a penny's movement in the price and the volatile nature of the contract in general make the pork-belly contract one that you need to be extremely careful about when you trade it.

Matching Technicals with Fundamentals

If you're a livestock producer, you have to be thinking about hedging techniques, because you have real cattle that you must deliver to the market at some point. Thus, futures markets offer you a great opportunity to reduce your risk, and fundamentals combined with technical analysis can help you set up your hedging trades.

Figure 15-1 shows a fairly classic six-month chart for feeder cattle prices. Note how prices rallied in the early part of the year and started to roll over during the summer months.

As a speculator, you want to understand the market from a hedger's point of view, but you need to focus on these keys to the cattle market:

- ✔ **Understanding the seasonal cycle:** Livestock prices tend to be cyclical in nature, but more important, you want to confirm that the cycle is working the way it usually does. In the case of the chart in Figure 15-1, you'd be correct in playing the long side of the market during the early part of the year.

- ✔ **Using technical analysis:** You're not out on the farm, so you must trust the price action. Trend lines, moving averages, and oscillators are useful in trending markets, such as the one shown in Figure 15-1. See Chapter 7 for a full overview of technical analysis.

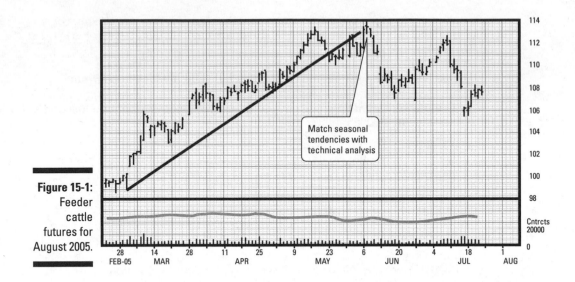

Figure 15-1:
Feeder
cattle
futures for
August 2005.

✔ **Keeping your strategies fluid:** As with other contracts, you need to keep up with government reports that are scheduled for release and hedge your regular positions by buying options or by selling futures contracts if you're long.

✔ **Following your trading rules:** If you set a sell stop or a buy-to-cover stop on a short position, don't change it other than to keep ratcheting it up or down as your position becomes more profitable. And when your rules say the time is right, don't hesitate to take those profits.

If you get stopped out, you either saved yourself a lot of trouble or didn't give yourself enough room. That dilemma is easily remedied. Go back and check the usual price range of the commodity for the specific time frame in which you're trading. If you're trading 15-minute bars and the commodity tends to move one to two ticks during that period, then set your stop just outside of or close to the normal movement. That way, if you get stopped out, it was because of an abnormal movement by the market against your position, and you've likely saved yourself from an even bigger loss.

Watching for Big Reports

As with virtually all other commodities markets, given their connection to supply and demand, meat-market traders need to keep an eye on their own distinct set of key reports. The CME and your broker have calendars that warn you when these key reports are going to be released. You need to take seriously the reports I describe in the sections that follow, because they're the most important inside influence on prices. Many times, the information in one of them is enough to change the overall trend of the particular market for extended periods.

Of course, some reports are more important than others, but you're asking for trouble if you either have an open position or you're trying to set one up without knowing what to expect when one of these potential bombshells hits the street.

Counting the cattle-on-feed reports

Released every month by the USDA's National Agricultural Statistics Service (NASS), the cattle-on-feed report usually moves the market and is made up of these three parts:

- **Cattle on feed:** This part of the report focuses on the actual number of cattle in the feedlots.

- **Placements:** This part of the report focuses on the number of new animals placed into feedlots during the previous month. This number is an important predictor of future supply, because an animal placed in a feedlot can be market ready in 120 to 160 days.

- **Marketings:** This part of the report focuses on the number of animals taken out of the feedlots. This number is a hazier piece of data because it can be affected by an individual operator's feeding methods and particular animal-specific idiosyncrasies.

    For example, depending on demand and how well a particular animal grows, feedlot operators can vary their marketings from month to month.

Playing "This Little Piggy": The Hogs and Pigs Report

The Hogs and Pigs Survey, which is released quarterly by NASS, reports pig crop data from 16 major hog-producing states and is the most important report for the hog and pork-belly markets. Information in it can lead to limit moves that can last for several days whenever surprises are reported.

This report definitely is a market mover, but it can be wrong . . . although you won't be able to verify whether it's right or wrong for six months or so.

Here are the nuts and bolts of the Hogs and Pigs Survey:

- ✔ **Total numbers of pigs:** This figure is the *pig crop,* and it shows where the market volume is at the time the report is released.

- ✔ **Breeding herd numbers:** This figure tells you the total number of hogs not sent to slaughter that are to be kept for breeding purposes.

- ✔ **Farrowing intentions:** This number provides an indication of breeding levels expected in the future.

- ✔ **Market hogs:** This number is the portion of the report that gives you the number of hogs that are being taken to market.

Other meat-market reports to watch

If you want your research to be complete, take note of these reports:

- ✔ **Cattle Inventory Report:** This report is released in January and July and provides the numbers of mature animals and the numbers of calves in the annual crop.

- ✔ **Cold Storage Report:** This report is a monthly release that tells you how much meat is stored in the freezers, including beef, chicken, and pork. It usually moves the pork-belly markets more than anything else.

- ✔ **Out of Town Report:** This report is released after the markets close every Tuesday and, like the Cold Storage Report, is aimed mostly at pork-belly traders. It measures whether pork bellies were put into freezers or taken out of storage. Rising numbers of bellies going into freezers is bearish. Falling numbers of bellies in storage is bullish.

- ✔ **Daily Slaughter Levels:** This report measures the daily activity of meat packers.

Understanding the Effects of Key Reports

Reports in March and June 2005 affected the ebb and flow of the August 2005 pork-belly contract by starting a recovery in the market's recovery and pointing to two trading opportunities you can use to catch this kind of market bottom.

Figure 15-2 shows the pork-belly contract for August 2005 and how it broke above the first trend line and marked a trading bottom and how a second trend line marked a break in the downtrend. The first break in the market occurred soon after the release of the March Cold Storage Report from the USDA, `usda.mannlib.cornell.edu/reports/nassr/other/pcs-bb/2005/`, which contained the following line:

> "Total red meat supplies in freezers were down 1 percent from last month, but up 4 percent from last year. Frozen pork supplies were up 9 percent from last month and up 14 percent from the previous year. Stocks of pork bellies were up 19 percent from last month and up 32 percent from last year."

This reported glut of pork was not worked off until June when the government's Cold Storage Report indicated:

> "Frozen pork supplies were down 9 percent from May, but up 24 percent from the previous year. Stocks of pork bellies were down 9 percent from last month, but up 97 percent from last year."

By July:

> "Frozen pork supplies were down 4 percent from last month, but up 32 percent from the previous year. Stocks of pork bellies were down 14 percent from last month, but up 90 percent from last year."

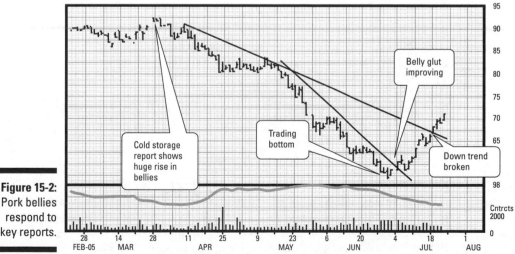

Figure 15-2:
Pork bellies respond to key reports.

That was three months of sequential decreases in the amount of pork in storage, which was good enough for the market to make a bottom. The chart in Figure 15-2 clearly shows how a series of reports can influence the sensible, supply-and-demand driven pork-belly market.

Notice the following key technical developments on the charts in Figure 15-2:

- ✔ Open interest (line on bottom of chart above volume bars) rose as selling accelerated, which is a bearish sign because it shows more people are selling.

- ✔ Open interest declined as the pork-belly contract started to bottom, which is bullish because it shows selling is losing strength.

Outside Influences that Affect Meat Prices

This section presents an important set of background factors that can affect meat prices. Some are short-term influences, but others have been in the pipeline for some time and can suddenly be felt when a certain catalyst hits the news, such as an article that shows that beef is not as healthy for consumption as it was thought to be.

Some longer-term and softer influences on meat prices are

- ✔ **Population changes:** If a demographic shift occurs in which more children are born, more baby food will be sold, which tends to be more vegetable based.

- ✔ **Income changes:** The overall economy affects the kinds of food people buy and whether they will go out to a restaurant and order higher-priced items, such as steaks.

- ✔ **Prices of substitutes:** Higher beef and pork prices are likely to lead to increased use of chicken, that is until the price of chicken gets too high and the potential for a shift back to pork and beef increases.

- ✔ **Prices of complements:** With a sudden increase in the price of barbecue sauce, you can see a decreased demand for beef or pork.

- ✔ **Changing consumer tastes:** This anomaly can be described as the classic Atkins diet effect. Pork, beef, and chicken prices rose when the low-carb craze swept the United States. If a soybean-based diet was to catch on in the same way, you'd likely see a similar phenomenon.

Some shorter-term but more constant influences on meat prices are

- ✔ **Weather:** A tough winter can lead to big animal losses, which, in turn, can affect supply for extended periods of time. Cold winters also tend to make animals eat more but gain less weight. So even if no animal deaths occur, the time to market can be delayed because producers need more time to fatten up animals, in effect delaying their time to market. What then can result is a glut in the market at a later time, lowering prices after the initial rise caused by the short-term shortage.

✔ **Grain prices:** Generally speaking, high feed prices result in liquidation, and low feed prices result in accumulation. The liquidation/accumulation ratio also is affected by the kind of prices producers get for their finished products. If meat prices are high, then producers can spend more money on feed and pass along the added price.

A *forced liquidation,* a period where large numbers of animals are sent to market because of droughts or periods of high feed prices, can lead to a longer-term boom in prices. For example, in 1996, all-time high prices in corn led to forced liquidation of both corn stores and herds. Cattle prices fell, only to rebound strongly after the excess supply was taken off the market.

Chapter 16

The Bumpy Truth about Agricultural Markets

*A*griculture is less popular in modern futures markets than it was in years past. During the first 70 years of futures trading, agriculture was dominant, given its Japanese origin in the rice markets. On the other hand, if weather patterns continue to change in volatility and intensity, and fossil-fuel prices remain above historical price ranges, interest in grain markets is likely to increase among traders.

For entry-level futures traders, the most important agricultural contracts are the corn and soybean contracts. They are the most actively traded and quoted agriculture contracts, so I devote much of this chapter to explaining corn and soybean contracts with regard to the grain and seed complexes.

After you gain a basic understanding of the concepts of seasonality and crop cycles and how external factors influence them, adapting to other contracts becomes relatively easy. In addition to the two major grain contracts, I also briefly touch on coffee, sugar, and lumbers futures in this chapter.

Staying Out of Trouble Down on the Farm

From a real-world economic standpoint, futures contracts in the agricultural markets are important; however, they are not for the fainthearted because of their volatility, the thinness of trading that sometimes accompanies them, and the dependence of prices on the influence of the weather.

Indeed, trading grains and softs can be very challenging, especially during periods of volatile weather, which if recent history is any guide will become a rule more than an exception, especially during hurricane season. *Softs,* by the way, is the name given to a group of commodities that includes cocoa, sugar, cotton, orange juice, and lumber. Here are some characteristics of trading grains and softs that you need to know to stay out of the doghouse and the poorhouse:

- ✔ **Thinly traded contracts:** Grain contracts and softs are not traded as much as stock-index or financial contracts, which leaves traders open to the effects of *decreased liquidity,* or the availability of money in the markets. Decreased liquidity, in turn, can lead to wide price swings in short periods of time, which make trading difficult. See Chapters 7 and 8 for information on technical analysis and details on trading gaps.

- ✔ **Low liquidity:** A lack of cash in these markets can lead to lots of chart gaps and limit moves.

Before you trade any agricultural futures, you need a refined understanding of the fundamentals of the particular sector and market in which you're trading. For example, at the very least, you need to know about growing and harvesting seasons, geopolitical risks in the growing area, and how the weather affects the crop. In other words, these contracts are better left for serious and experienced traders, because they're more adept at collecting information, putting it in the proper context, and managing risk. I'm not saying that you shouldn't trade these markets. I'm just saying that they are not the best ones to start with. As you gain more experience with the general aspects of futures trading, you'll be able to do more in these areas.

Corn, soybeans, and other agricultural futures are excellent contracts to allow someone else to trade for you, either through a commodity fund that specializes in these markets or a good advisor with a good record who knows what he or she is doing.

Agriculture 101: Getting a Handle on the Crop Year

You need to know what the crop year is to be able to understand grain trading. The *crop year* is the time from one crop to the next. It starts with planting and ends with harvesting. During that time, crops are going through what the United States Department of Agriculture and Joint Agricultural Weather facility call the moisture- and temperature-dependent stages of development.

What happens between planting and harvest tends to affect the prices of the crops the most. For example, the weather is a major factor. Drought, flooding, and freezing are the major events. Other external events, such as shipping problems, can also affect delivery at key times, such as when Hurricane Katrina hit the port of New Orleans, from which much of the Midwestern grain makes its way out of the U.S.

Think of the supply of grain brought to market as a rationed situation. By that I mean that although grains are used year round, most of them are replenished only one time during the year. As a result, prices are affected by a combination of current supplies and future supply expectations. The way a grain market perceives future and current supplies and the way that traders predict the effect of internal and external factors on prices is a major set of variables to consider. In other words, in all markets there is a certain fudge factor, or an intangible influence on prices.

Think of it along these terms. In futures markets, as in all markets, perception is as much a part of pricing as reality. The markets are efficient, and that means they react to the information that they have available instantaneously, which leads to short-term price volatility. As with the hog and pig report I discuss in Chapter 15, data in a single quarterly report may be significantly off the mark as slaughter approaches, and thus the reality in any market, grains and softs included, can be different than the original report indicates. So you need to know that markets can retrace major moves as better information becomes available.

As with most other commodities, trading in corn and soybeans is all about supply.

Except during times of extraordinary circumstances, such as dietary fads or major external, political, climactic, or geological events, demand stays within a fairly predictable range.

If under normal circumstances, demand fluctuates within certain bands based on the number of people and animals to be fed at any given time, the market focuses on anything that affects how much grain will be available to feed them from year to year.

That's doesn't mean that demand isn't important. For example, just for the sake of illustration, the markets are used to a certain amount of demand for soybeans from China every year; however, if China's weather changes dramatically and its domestic crop suffers, global demand for soybeans will increase, thus having a direct effect on the markets.

Assuming that U.S. supply remains stable in a year that China's weather changes, you're likely to have an increase in prices caused by the increased demand.

Likewise, if the supply of soybeans is decreased because of a crop plague in the U.S. — which supplies most of the world's soybeans — and global demand remains the same, prices are likely to rise.

The situation is similar in virtually all markets; changes in supply tend to affect prices more strongly than changes in demand. See Chapter 13 for more details about how supply rules the markets.

In general, high levels of current supplies and/or expectations of high supply levels in the future usually lead to lower prices. Conversely, low levels of current supplies and/or expectations of future shortages usually lead to higher prices.

Weathering the highs and lows of weather

Weather plays the main influence on crops, and significant weather developments affect crop markets. Globally, weather is important in grain and seed markets. Some basic points to keep in mind about the weather include

- ✔ Spring weather in the United States (or anywhere for that matter) affects planting season. Too much rain can delay planting.

- ✔ Summer weather affects crop development. Crops need rain to develop appropriately. Droughts play havoc with crop development.

- ✔ During the North American winter, agricultural market watchers and traders concentrate on the weather in South America, because it's summer there. Likewise, dormant winter wheat in North America needs enough snowfall to protect the crop from *winterkill,* or freezing, because not enough snow is on the ground to insulate the crop.

- ✔ A wet harvest can cause delays and decrease crop yields.

These factors all can raise prices.

The U.S. Department of Agriculture (USDA) Weather Bulletin, `www.usda.gov/oce/waob/jawf/wwcb.html`, is an excellent resource for information about weather trends and potential developments. You can subscribe to the report for $60 per year. The USDA releases it on Wednesdays. It may not be worthwhile subscribing to these reports unless you're a farmer who's looking into the small details. As a trader, especially one using charts, you'll be reacting to the market's response anyway.

Weather markets, or periods when crops are being affected by droughts, floods, or freezing temperatures, create possibly the most volatile types of markets, and they're risky to boot. Droughts or unusual snowfall or rainfall patterns are among the more common events that trigger weather markets.

Looking for Goldilocks: The key stages of grain development

Prices for grain and soybean futures can move significantly during three key time frames when seasonal and logistical expectations are the result of the cultivation and growing cycles. At these three times of year, weather conditions can't be too hot, too cold, or certainly not too wet. Like Goldilocks and her porridge, conditions have to be "just right" during

- **Planting season:** When it's time to plant, rainfall is the major influence. Too much rain means a late planting season that can lead to smaller, lower-quality crops, which in turn, can lead to higher prices. A wet planting season offers traders an opportunity to trade on the long side.

- **Pollination or growing season:** Rain and heat are the keys when seeds are pollinating and growing. Too much heat and too little rain lead to lower levels of pollination, which again can lead to smaller crops. Cold temperatures and too much water can have the same effect.

- **Maturation and harvest season:** When plants are maturing and harvest is near, too much heat and too much rain can mean poor crops from difficult field conditions and the spread of fungus among crops.

Cataloging Grains and Beans

The grain complex has multiple components, including soybeans, soybean meal, soybean oil, Canola, palm oil, corn, oats, and wheat. I concentrate on the soybean and corn markets, because they are the most heavily traded markets and offer the best opportunity for small accounts and beginning traders. However, you can apply what you find out about these grains and how these markets work to develop an understanding of other grain markets and to set up strategies.

One caveat is that individual markets have their own subtle sets of parameters, and you'll have to figure them out as you expand your trading horizons.

The soybean complex

The *soybean complex* is made up of three separate futures contracts for delivery of soybeans, soybean meal, and soybean oil. Soybeans are legumes, not grains, but they're traded and cataloged as part of the grain complex. Don't let this weird stuff confuse you. Markets and traders are efficient, and they look for convenience. Besides, can you imagine somebody on TV talking about legume futures? Egads!

Until 2004, the United States was the largest soybean producer with about a 50 percent market share. Until 1980, the U.S. held an 80-percent share, but the Carter administration's grain embargo, a political maneuver in 1980 that was designed to protest the Russian invasion of Afghanistan, cost the U.S. farming industry dearly.

Currently, South America produces most of the other half of the world's soybeans, with China picking up the rest.

Soybeans are the protein source used most by humans and animals around the world. The primary uses of soybeans are for meal for animal feed and oil for human consumption.

Soybean contracts

The soybean contract trades on the Chicago Board of Trade (CBOT). Here are the particulars of a soybean contract:

- ✔ **Contract:** A contract is 5,000 bushels, and prices for soybeans are quoted in dollars and cents per bushel.

- ✔ **Valuation:** A 1-cent move in the price of soybeans is worth $50 per contract, with daily price movements shifting as much as 50 cents per day.

- ✔ **Limits:** Trading limits in soybeans are variable based on prevailing market conditions.

- ✔ **Margins:** As of July 2005, the initial speculative margin requirement was $2,295 per contract, and the maintenance margin requirement was $1,700 per contract.

Soybean meal contracts

Soybean meal (what's left after the extraction of oil from soybeans) can be fed to cattle, hogs, and poultry. A 60-pound bushel of soybeans yields 48 pounds of meal. Forty percent of U.S. meal production is exported. The rest is used domestically. Here are the particulars of the soybean meal contract:

- ✔ **Contract:** A soybean meal contract is 100 short tons (200,000 pounds), with a (short) ton equal to 2,000 pounds. Prices are quoted in dollars and cents per ton.

- ✔ **Valuation:** A $1 move in the per-ton price of soybean meal is worth $100 per contract.

- ✔ **Limits:** Price movements are limited to $20 per day, which is also variable, again depending on market conditions. If the market closes at the limit, the limit is raised for the three subsequent days to accommodate traders. Although this tactic may seem a bit strange, remember that the role of the futures markets, especially in key commodities such as grains, is to enable commerce to take place — capitalism at its finest. If market conditions are such that limits need to be expanded, the exchanges are more than happy to accommodate the markets.

✔ **Margins:** As of July 2005, the initial margin requirement was $1,485, and the maintenance margin was $1,100.

Soybean oil contracts

Soybean oil is the third major soybean product for which futures contracts are bought and sold. A bushel of soybeans produces 11 pounds of oil, and soybean oil competes with olive oil and other edible oils. Soybean oil is extracted by a multistep process that involves steaming, pressing, and percolating (similar to brewing coffee) the beans. If you're really into how soybean oil is extracted, plenty of background info can be found on the Internet. Have at it! Here are the basics of what you need to know:

✔ **Contract:** A soybean oil contract is 60,000 pounds. Prices are quoted in cents per pounds.

✔ **Valuation:** Be careful trading soybean oil. A 1-cent move is equal to 100 points, which is worth $600 per contract.

✔ **Limits:** Trading limits are set at 1 cent, but they can be adjusted, because soybean trading can be very volatile because of the weather and other external factors. Thus, trading limits are variable, meaning that they can be changed if prices continue to be very volatile over a period of time. See Chapter 3 for more about trading limits.

✔ **Margins:** As of July 2005, the initial margin requirement was $1,080, and the maintenance margin requirement was $800.

Getting corny

Corn is the most active commodity among grain contracts, and it is the major crop grown in the U.S. American farmers grow about 50 percent of the world's corn supply, and 70 percent of U.S. production is consumed domestically.

Corn futures are known as *feed corn,* or corn that's fed to livestock — not the same stuff that you and I eat at summer picnics or find behind the Jolly Green Giant label. Here are the particulars of corn futures:

✔ **Contract:** A contract holds 5,000 bushels, and a ¼-cent move is worth $12.50 per contract. Prices are quoted in cents and ¼ cents.

✔ **Limits:** The daily limit is 20 cents, or $1,000. There are no limits in the spot month.

✔ **Margins:** As of July 2005, the initial margin requirement for speculators was $675 per contract, and the maintenance margin requirement was $500 per contract.

The CBOT's Web site (www.cbot.com) can provide you with a great deal of useful background information, charts, and even trade summaries. I highly recommend a good review of the data there.

Culling Some Good Fundamental Data

Although charts are the most useful tools for trading futures, getting a grip on the fundamental expectations of price movements in the particular contract you're trading is important. The fundamentals, of course, are background information, and you need to be aware that even the best guesses can be wrong. The key is to gauge what the expectations are for the market and then find out what prices actually do.

Getting a handle on the reports

You can find plenty of good fundamental information at the USDA's Web site at www.usda.gov. Here is a good sequence of data and market factors to keep in mind for getting a handle on a market's supply and demand:

- **Beginning stocks:** The *beginning stock* is the amount of grain that's left over from the previous year — as reported by the government.

- **Production:** *Production* is the estimated amount of a crop that will be harvested during the current year.

- **Weekly Weather and Crop Report:** The USDA releases a weekly Crop Progress Report that updates the crop and weather conditions. This report usually is released on Wednesday. See the earlier section on "Weathering the highs and lows of weather" for data included in this key report.

- **Import data:** The U.S. is a grain exporter, so this data rarely is significant. If that ever changes — permanently or temporarily — the markets will let everyone know.

- **Total supply:** The *total supply* is the sum of beginning stocks, production, and imports.

- **Crush:** (No, I'm not talking about your favorite orange or grape soda — although a grape would taste great right about now.) *Crush* refers to the amount of demand being exhibited by *crushers,* or businesses that buy raw soybeans and make them into meal and oil.

- **Exports:** Two export reports are released each week; they are

    - Export inspections — released on Monday after the market closes

    - Export sales — released on Thursday before the market opens

✔ **Currency trends:** Trends in the currency markets, especially those of the dollar, can affect export reports.

✔ **Seeds and residual:** Usually 3 to 4 percent of the crop is held for seeding the next year's crop. *Seeds* are important because they're the next season's planting stock. *Residuals* are the portions of soybean oil that are not used in food-related processes. Soybean oil also is used as an additive in pesticides and has biochemical uses, including medications. It's also used as grain spray to prevent dust from settling on stored crops.

✔ **Total demand:** *Total demand* is the sum of exports, seeds, crush, and the residual figure.

✔ **Ending carryover stocks:** Ending carryover stock is a big number that tends to move the markets. It's the total supply minus total demand.

Don't forget the Deliverable Stocks of Grain report

The *Deliverable Stocks of Grain report* is an interesting report that merits its own section, because every Tuesday the CBOT tallies the number of bushels of corn, wheat, soybeans, and oats stored in elevators that are licensed to deliver grains in relation to trades made on the CBOT.

This report is important, because the information contained in it is a good way to determine whether enough grain is in storage for delivery. If not enough grain is in storage, then the market experiences a short squeeze, because traders with short positions don't have any way to make good on their deliveries, so they have to buy futures contracts to make good on their bets. A *short squeeze* happens when large numbers of traders have open short positions, or bets that the market will fall. If the market goes against those short positions, traders have to buy contracts to prevent their losses from getting worse. When large numbers of short positions must cover their positions at the same time, the market rallies.

The Deliverable Stocks of Grain report is issued as a Microsoft Excel spreadsheet and can be found on the CBOT Web site. The best way to use it is to keep track of deliverable stocks and watch how the data are trending over a period of time. In fact, you can view several reports and then construct your own chart on the figures so that the trend becomes visible. Otherwise, you must rely on the market's reaction to the release.

Gauging Spring Crop Risks

The *risk premium* is the influence of future expectations of supply on current prices, and it's the basis for price fluctuations in the futures markets.

As mentioned in the "Looking for Goldilocks: The key stages of grain development" section, earlier in this chapter, crops are most vulnerable during planting, pollination, and harvesting. During these stages, the markets begin to apply a risk premium to prices. This kind of pricing can be an emotional rather than rational process, which is why prices can fluctuate wildly on weather reports, fires, and reports of diseases and insect infestations in the fields.

Corn and soybeans are planted in spring, so they tend to compete for acreage, which makes the price relationship between the two important.

You need to realize that risk is around every corner during each stage of the crop year. Any external news event, such as flooding, drought, crop plagues, or unusual weather developments — late freezes or even the accidental introduction of a foreign beetle that flourished as crops emerged — can shake the markets.

A perfect example of crop risk and its effect on the markets was associated with the rise of orange juice prices in October 2005. Aside from the damage to Florida orange orchards from Hurricane Wilma, an increase was reported in *canker,* a bacterial infection of citrus fruit trees that's spread by wind. Any citrus tree within 1,900 feet of an infected tree had to be cut down.

Planting risk premiums tend to be higher than pollination risk premiums, because of the market's fear that the crop won't ever be planted. Pollination risk tends to be less, because after the crop is planted, there's a greater chance that at least some of the crop will emerge and thus at least some of the crop will be pollinated. The third risk comes at harvest time, when traders begin to fear that crops will wither in the field because of bad weather or other events.

As the market begins pricing in *risk premiums,* futures contracts in corn and soybeans tend to rise during the months of March and April because of the following:

- ✓ Corn planting starts in late March and usually is completed by late May. March and April tend to be months during which corn tends to rally.

- ✓ Corn pollinates in late June or early July. June can be a strong month for corn.

- ✓ Soybeans usually are planted in mid-March through May. March and April can be good rally months for soybeans.

 ✔ Soybean pollination usually takes place in August. August beans can experience a small rally.

 ✔ October and November are harvest months. Rallies during these months usually are not very profitable, because harvest usually takes place, and barring truly extraordinary circumstances, supply and demand find a balance.

During the summer of 1973, the Russians made large purchases of grains. *Supply fear* (the fear that planting, pollination, or harvest won't be successful) truly gripped the market, and the resulting rally was violent, but it didn't last long, because grain prices responded in the absence of major problems with planting, pollination, or harvesting by falling back to their mainstream trend lines, which is rather simple technical analysis.

During May and June, you need to tailor your trades toward going long in corn and soybeans; however, after August, you need to be looking to go short so you can capitalize on the normal trends of the market. The key word is "looking," because external factors like the weather can cause the market to deviate from general seasonal tendencies.

The bumps, rallies, and valleys of the grain markets are only tendencies. Before deciding to make a trade, be sure to

 ✔ Find out from your charts whether the market actually is following seasonal patterns that have tended to happen in the past. In 2005, trading was difficult in the corn market, but it was easier in soybeans because the market tended to trend for longer periods.

 ✔ Look for evidence that confirms what prices are telling you. In the case of corn in 2005, open interest started to rise in conjunction with prices, which is as good a confirmation of a rising trend as there is. Rising open interest means that more buyers are coming into the market. Compare the open interest in soybeans with that of corn, and you can see that the open interest rate for corn actually was flat. Corn contracts had no life in them at that time.

Agriculture 102: Getting Soft

Coffee, sugar, orange juice, and cocoa are known as the *softs*. Some call them the breakfast category of futures. They can deliver some profitable moves if you take the time to become familiar with the standard stuff that goes on in the softs markets.

In contrast to grains and beans, much of the action in softs goes on overseas and often in remote regions of the world, especially in places that from time to time are politically unstable. As a result, trading the softs can be more volatile.

Having coffee at the exchange

Coffee trades in the U.S. and in London, with the U.S. trading the largest amount and most active contract at the New York Board of Trade.

Coffee is all about supply, and the 2001 International Coffee Agreement (ICA), a product of the International Coffee Organization, is meant to provide guidelines with regard to managing the global coffee supply and to encourage consumption. Like all such agreements, the ICA isn't foolproof. It can be circumvented and thus can create controversy in the markets.

Coffee supplies can be affected by smuggling and by quantities of coffee that are not a part of the quota system and arrangements agreed upon by the ICA. Prices can fall whenever the market is hit with data or rumors suggesting that smuggling is on the rise. For details of the 2001 ICA, visit the ICA's Web site at www.ico.org/2001_agreement.asp.

Coffee is produced in two classes, Arabica and Robusta, and thus two coffee contracts are traded. These two classes of coffees can trend differently during short periods of time, but they tend to trade along the same long-term trend line.

Arabica

Arabica beans account for 60 percent of the world's coffee supply. Arabica is a cool-temperature, high-altitude crop. Brazil and Columbia combined produce a third of the world's Arabica coffee. Costa Rica, Mexico, Guatemala, Honduras, and El Salvador also are major producers of Arabica, and Indonesia, Uganda, and Vietnam produce the rest.

Arabica is the more important of the two coffee classes when analyzing the North American markets. Supply, as is usual with commodities, is the key. Weather, blights, moves by big retailers, and political events in Africa, Asia, Brazil, and South America, in general, can cause volatility in the coffee markets.

Robusta

Robusta is a less mild variety of coffee that comes from Africa and Asia. Robusta trades in London and is most often used as instant coffee because of its stronger flavor.

Trading coffee

Coffee trading is centered on the New York Board of Trade (NYBOT, www.nybot.com) for Arabica and the Euronext-LIFFE (www.euronext.com) for Robusta. Euronext consolidated the futures markets in Belgium, France, The Netherlands, and Portugal. LIFFE stands for London International Financial Futures and Options Exchange. Here are the particulars for coffee trading:

- ✔ **Contract:** The contract size for coffee in New York is 37,500 pounds of Arabica, and it trades at the NYBOT. Robusta coffee futures trade at Euronext-LIFFE. A Robusta contract contains five tons of coffee.

- ✔ **Valuation:** A 1-cent move is worth $375 per contract for Arabica. The minimum tick is $1 per ton for Robusta.

- ✔ **Limits:** A 6-cent limit applies only in the back months for Arabica. No limits are in place for the two front months, which makes this contract extremely risky. Colombian coffee gets a 2-cent premium upon delivery. No limits are in place for Robusta.

- ✔ **Trading hours:** The markets are open for trading Arabica in New York from 9:15 a.m. to 12:30 p.m. Trading hours for Robusta in London are from 9:40 to 16:55 London time.

Staying sweet with sugar

Sugar is another breakfast commodity, and it's another volatile commodity that is best left for more experienced traders. As with all commodities, you have to understand the basics of the industry, the key reports that move the market, and how to apply technical analysis to trading. Unlike coffee, most sugar-producing countries produce much of the sugar that they use and then export the rest.

Cuba, India, Thailand, and Brazil are major sugar cane producers. Russia and the European Union are the major sugar beet producers. Russia, China, Europe, the U.S., China, and Japan are the biggest importers, and Cuba, Australia, Thailand, and Brazil are the biggest exporters.

The two sugar contracts are

- ✔ **#14,** which has subsidy-supported sugar.

- ✔ **#11,** which has free-market sugar. The free-market sugar contract is the one to trade. A contract is for 112,000 pounds, and a 1-cent move is worth $1,120.

Sugar trades on the stock-to-usage ratio, which is the level of supplies compared to demand. Sugar traders talk about tightness, which means the state of the supply/demand scenario. A ratio of 20 to 30 percent is low and usually leads to higher prices.

Traders also watch for candy sales and the price of corn, because of competition from high-fructose corn syrup, which competes with sugar as a commercial sweetener.

Building a rapport with lumber

Lumber is another so-called soft. Why that is, I couldn't tell you. Some traders think that it's lumped in with the rest of the softs because another place can't be found for it.

Lumber is used in homebuilding, and the price can be volatile. In some cases, lumber prices peak or trough before housing busts or booms, respectively.

Several months can elapse before a glut or a major shortage finds its way from the futures markets to the housing industry.

The lumber contract calls for 80,000 board feet (construction grade two-by-fours) manufactured in the Pacific Northwest or Canada. Prices are quoted in dollars and cents per board foot. A $1 movement in price equals $80 in the contract. Lumber is another thinly traded contract that you can work your way toward trading as you gain more experience.

Part V
The Trading Plan

The 5th Wave   By Rich Tennant

"Choosing the right investment strategy is like choosing the right hat. You find one that fits you best and then you stick with it."

In this part . . .

In Part V of *Futures & Options For Dummies,* you're getting serious — down to brass tacks. You can't trade without getting organized, so I show you how to set realistic goals and expectations, take inventory of your finances, figure out how to best choose a broker, develop a trading plan, and work through a futures trade in real time.

Chapter 17

Trading with a Plan Today So You Can Do It Again Tomorrow

. . . .

In This Chapter

▶ Coming up with the cash to trade

▶ Choosing who you want to do the trading

▶ Selecting a CTA

▶ Bonding with a broker

. . . .

*I*n this chapter, I help you decide whether you or someone else will do your trading, and I explain how you can go about setting up your trading infrastructure.

Deciding just who will do your trading is as important a decision as you can make, because your success or failure, or how fast you get there, can depend on how you decide to make your trades.

Each side of the aisle has advantages and disadvantages, and much of deciding whether to trade for yourself or have someone do it for you depends on your personality, how much hand-holding you need, and what your expectations are.

If you decide to make your own trades, you must fully commit your time and efforts to the enterprise. In a very real sense, you're starting a new business, and any casual notion you have that becoming a trader will be an easy, effortless road to riches is the way to disaster.

The decisions you make have a direct and usually quick bearing on how much money you make or lose while trading.

Financing Your Habit

The most difficult question that you must answer about trading has to do with where you're going to get the money to trade futures.

A simple rule: If you have to borrow money, you shouldn't trade futures or anything else. Money for trading needs to be money that you can afford to lose, period.

You may have to develop a savings plan over several years that will finance your new endeavor. As a result, you may need to make changes in your spending habits, such as missing a vacation, driving a more modest car, or eating at less fancy restaurants.

Regardless of how you do it, the best way to trade futures is using your own money. When it's your money that you're trading, you're more likely to be extremely careful about what you do with it.

Although most discount brokers enable you to open a self-managed futures trading account for $5,000, most Certified Trading Advisors (CTAs) require a minimum of $50,000, with the range usually being anywhere from $25,000 up to several million dollars. See the next section for more details about choosing a broker or CTA.

Deciding Who's Going to Do the Trading

After you've made up your mind to trade futures, you need to decide who's going to do the actual trading. The choice is pretty simple; either you or someone else will do it, but that also means you have to decide whether to use an advisor, a broker, or a managed account.

Choosing has its subtleties. Keep in mind that when a broker is doing your trading — depending on your agreement — he or she may have to call you and ask your permission to trade on your behalf. That can delay your ability to make short-term profits. Conversely, you may choose to give your broker full trading authority and discretion to make trades for you. If you do, then you have to abide by the results of the broker's decisions, which means you may face some conflict down the line if your broker is either unscrupulous or not very talented.

A managed account is akin to a mutual fund. It is a pooled amount of money that is managed by an individual or a group. Those managers don't have to ask for permission to trade your money, because they trade the entire pool simultaneously, and shareholders make or lose money depending on the results of the pool's trades and the number of shares they respectively hold.

The main advantage of letting someone else do the trading is that you can spend time learning to trade while your account grows, assuming that you find a good firm or broker to manage your account. The main disadvantage is that you have little control of your money, and if you need control, you'll probably be miserable.

Here are your basic trading options:

- ✔ Manage the account yourself based on your own analysis.
- ✔ Manage the account yourself based on advice from newsletters, publications, or even a broker.
- ✔ Have a CTA manage the account.
- ✔ Buy an interest in a limited-partnership pool managed by a professional CTA. Limited-partnership pools also are known as futures funds.

Other advantages of managed futures, either individual accounts or trading pools, are as follows:

- ✔ Good CTAs have more experience than novice traders and therefore have a better chance of making money.
- ✔ Trading pools have more money to invest than individuals and thus can establish better positions in the market.
- ✔ Trading pools can pay lower commissions when they trade and thus save you money on costs.
- ✔ Trading pools are structured as limited partnerships, entities that limit your risk. They spread risk across all the partners, with the managing partner or the manager/management firm assuming the largest part of the risk. You're liable only for losses or any required restitution for fraud and so on, and your liability is limited to the percentage of the partnership that you own. So if you own 2 percent of the shares, and the partnership goes belly up, you'd be at risk of losing only an amount commensurate with what you put in.

Some managed futures funds guarantee the return of your initial investment, if you remain with the fund for a set number of years. The disadvantages of that option are that your return from these funds may be lower, and you usually must hold the fund until maturity, so your money's tied up in the fund, regardless of how well it's doing.

The disadvantages of managed futures accounts are

- ✔ Higher fees, loss of control of your money, and the general illiquidity associated with them.
- ✔ The fact that you have to part with (or give up control of) your money for an extended period of time and be willing to weather some volatility during that holding period.

The Commodity Futures Trading Commission (CFTC) provides an excellent summary of what a CTA is and how the commodities trading system functions at www.cftc.gov/opa/backgrounder/opacpocta.htm. Managed Accounts Reports (MAR), www.marhedge.com, is a good resource for information about managed futures.

Choosing a CTA

A CTA is a professional money manager who must register with the CFTC and undergo a rigorous FBI background check before being allowed to trade other people's money. A knowledgeable CTA can manage your futures trades.

You can find a CTA either through a broker or by subscribing to services such as MAR, which can become expensive.

Reviewing the CTA's track record

After you get a few names of potential CTAs, review their disclosure documents, which by law have to present all their vital information and their track records. Track records (also by law) have to be presented in a way that is easy enough for you to understand, regardless of whether the advisor has made money. They include comparisons with benchmarks such as the S&P 500 and the Lehman Brothers Long-term Government Bond Index.

The track record also has to show

- How much money was being managed
- How much money per month came from trading
- How much came from new deposits or was lost to withdrawals from the fund
- Amounts of fees charged by the fund
- Amounts of fees paid by the fund
- Earnings from interest
- Net return on investment after all fees and trading were taken into account

Be careful in how you look at the posted returns of CTA candidates. Here's an example: Suppose you have two advisors, X and Y, and advisor X's three years of returns are +10 percent, +40 percent, and –20 percent, while advisor Y's returns for the same three years are +15 percent, +10 percent, and +5 percent.

At first glance, you're probably inclined to think that X is the better of the two, but if you do the math, you'll see that if you gave them each $1,000, after three years, X would have $1,232, while Y would have $1,328.

Other CTA characteristics to watch for

Use this checklist to make your best choice of CTAs. Above all, make sure that you match the CTA to your risk tolerance.

- ✔ **Check how long the CTA has been in business.** The longer the advisor has been in business, the better he is likely to be, because he's a survivor.

- ✔ **Find the CTA's largest drawdown or the biggest loss he's ever had.** The two important things to find out are how bad the loss was and how long it took the CTA to get the money back after the loss.

- ✔ **Evaluate the returns of prospective CTAs based on risk.** The CTA who has a lower return but took less risk may be a better choice, because he or she is likely to provide more stable returns, and you may sleep better.

- ✔ **Check out the stability of the business.** Make sure that plenty of signs point to the CTA having a stable business and a stable methodology. Look for consistent but not necessarily high returns.

- ✔ **Ask about risk management.** Look for reasonable answers with regard to money management and risk aversion.

- ✔ **Look for conflicts of interest.** Is the CTA getting paid by certain brokers to use their services? Is that costing you money? What kind of fees is the CTA collecting from other sources as fees and commissions?

Considering a trading manager

Another possible suggestion is employing a trading manager or a middleman when you're trying to choose a CTA. If you're overwhelmed by the thought of having to plow through hundreds of documents while screening your list of potential CTAs, managed funds, and trading pools, a trading manager can act as an investment counselor, serving as an independent resource who can sift through the jungle of paperwork to help you evaluate CTAs, funds, and managers.

Trading managers collect a fee for doing your legwork, and they get a percentage of your profits, which turns out to be a good incentive for them to find someone who is good for your money. Large investors usually employ trading managers.

Choosing a Broker

If you decide to trade for yourself, you need to choose between a full-service and a discount broker. A full-service broker charges you a larger commission but is expected to provide you with good advice about your trades. Some also serve as middlemen between you and CTAs.

Be careful whenever you deal with brokers, CTAs, mutual funds, annuities, and so on, because brokers and advisors sometimes earn large incentives for steering you in certain directions, regardless of whether taking those directions with your money is in your best interest.

Look for full access to the following when you open an account:

- ✔ **All markets:** Even if you're interested in only a handful of markets right now, you may want to consider expanding your horizons in the future, so choosing a broker who can give you all the choices under one roof is best.

- ✔ **Research:** Some brokers offer discounts to newsletters and Web sites, while others offer direct access to their own research departments. Some offer live broadcasts from the trading pits.

- ✔ **The full gamut of technical tools:** You really want an opportunity to get as fancy with your trading as you want to in the future, including having the ability to run multiple real-time charts with oscillators and indicators and receive intermarket analysis.

- ✔ **Intelligent software:** Some brokers offer you access to software and charting packages that enable you to back test, or review, the results of your trading strategies and indicators.

- ✔ **Forward testing your strategy:** Nothing guarantees that you'll match the results predicted by the software, but being able to forward test your trading strategies is a nice tool to have. Back testing shows you how your trades would have worked based on historical data. Forward testing is based on the probability of certain conditions occurring in the future and is more related to how much money you'd make if certain things happened; however, it's a useful tool only in hypothetical settings.

Follow these suggestions when boiling down your choices between brokers:

- ✔ **Test more than one trading platform.** Most brokers will offer you a trial of their software and trading platforms if you register on their Web sites.

- ✔ **Make sure the broker offers a 24-hour customer-service line.** This line of communication is crucial if you decide to exit a position overnight in the face of events that are costing you money. If you have to wait until the morning, your losses can be larger than you'd expect. The 24-hour nature of futures trading is another reason to use stop-loss orders.

✔ **Make sure that you have the choice of entering trades via either the Internet or phone.** If phone lines are busy and you have to make a trade, you want access. If your Internet connection and your backup connection are down, you'd like to have phone access to either check your positions or make trades.

✔ **Check all potential trading fees before you sign up and make a trade.** Check all fees, including whether all the trading bells and whistles are included in the commission or whether extra charges or conditions must be met, such as a minimum number of trades to qualify for certain services.

✔ **Open an account with a well-known firm.** Going with the established broker can be a good idea, at least when you're getting started. If you try to save a few bucks with a smaller firm, you may be sorry later on, especially if you're concerned about order execution, software glitches, and hidden fees. Large firms are not exempt from fraud, but because of their size, information about their practices is more readily available.

✔ **Check for current trading scams:** Look on the CFTC's Web site (www.cftc.gov) under the "Consumer Protection" heading for current trading scams and for disciplinary actions taken against firms and brokers. You'll find important bulletins and helpful Web links to important information about general rules and recent enforcement actions. On the National Futures Association's (NFA) Web site (www.nfa.futures.org/basicnet), you can search for brokers, trading pools, and CTAs.

Falling in the pit of full service

Some of the same criteria that apply for choosing a CTA can be used for choosing a full-service broker (see the earlier sections on "Reviewing the CTA's track record" and "Other CTA characteristics to watch for"). Especially important is whether you're dealing with an experienced broker, who earns his or her keep.

With brokerage firms, many times you meet the lead guy once, but you never see him again. You're left dealing with underlings, and that can be just like Russian roulette. If you get a good one, you'll be mostly okay, if you can handle the larger fees. Much of the time, especially when you have a smaller account, you're relegated to someone just starting out with the firm, and that may or may not be in your best interest.

Choosing a futures and options discount broker

Going the route of the discount broker may be a better alternative if you're adventurous and do your homework, which includes practice trading in simulated accounts.

A large number of discount brokers operate in the futures markets, and you can find most of them by using your favorite search engine on the Internet, or looking at advertisements in *Futures, Active Trader, The Wall Street Journal,* and other publications.

Aside from the important aspects, such as service in general, availability of 24-hour service, commissions, and ease of access to the trading desk, discount brokers offer online trading services. You want to make sure that the trading platform the discount broker provides is easy to use and that the orders you place online are executed in a reasonable amount of time.

Chapter 18

Looking for Balance Between the Sheets

• •

In This Chapter

▶ Finding out what's on your trading mind

▶ Accounting for what's in your wallet

▶ Investigating what you're worth

• •

*T*he futures markets are a zero-sum game. Someone always loses, and someone always wins. In other words, any money that you make trading is money that you've taken away from someone else who's also trading.

Put the shoes on your own feet, and you get a better picture of the situation. Yup, out there in cyberworld or in some crazy trading pit, someone is waiting to take your money away from you. So before you decide to start trading, you need to figure out whether you measure up mentally and financially.

 I'm not talking about your self-esteem or your intellect here, although good measures of both are required for success in trading. More important than how much of those innate qualities you have, you need to know how much money you have and whether you can manage it well enough for continued success in trading futures and options — enough to stay in the game.

In this chapter, I tell you about some basic issues that can help you decide whether you should be a trader or think about doing something else with your money until your finances are in good enough shape to enable you to trade comfortably.

In a sense, you need to keep track of two personal balance sheets, a mental one from which you figure out why you want to trade, and a financial one from which you decide whether you have enough money to finance your trading venture.

Both are equally important, and ignoring one or the other is a recipe for disaster.

Exploring What's on Your Mental Balance Sheet

Your expectations about futures and options shape the role they play in your portfolio. As a general rule, futures and options need to be a part of an overall financial plan that includes stocks, bonds, mutual funds, annuities, real estate, and other assets. Although not a mandatory component, futures can be useful in the portfolio of individuals with large net worths, especially as a hedge against risk. However, the central tenet of your mental balance sheet is understanding why trading futures and options appeals to you.

Why do you want to trade?

Most people look to the excitement often associated with gambling and equate it with trading futures. Unfortunately, trading futures, options, or other assets is not gambling. Trading isn't associated with glitz and shouldn't be associated with liquor or other diversions. In fact, the more aware you are of the current global situation and the current situation in your market, the better off you'll be.

Here's how I answer the question: Trading is a hedge for my life. I have two full-time jobs, my medical practice and my financial business. On occasion, one or the other takes over as a major income producer. When my trading business isn't going well, my medical practice still provides a relatively stable income and vice versa. (I've experienced periods when the opposite has been true.)

I trade for these two reasons:

- ✔ **It's my business.** Trading and the by-products of trading, such as writing books, selling subscriptions to my Web site, and occasionally providing consulting services, are major contributors to my income. By trading, I'm not only making money, I'm also testing strategies in real time that I eventually can pass on to my subscribers (www.joe-duarte.com) in the form of recommendations and insights.

- ✔ **Trading provides income diversification and enables me to maximize the total return on my retirement fund.** I add as much to my IRA every year as is legally possible within my means. I don't miss an opportunity to contribute to it, no matter what. Some years, I fund my IRA entirely from the income that trading and related endeavors produce.

For me, trading is an important source of income and income diversification that I derive from a tremendously enjoyable and agreeable mental and intellectual exercise.

When pondering the question that heads up this section, make sure that your answers are truthful. Just because you're looking for kicks, and you think that trading will fix all your problems, don't fool yourself. Trading is work that requires personal and financial commitment, even if it isn't your primary source of income. If you take it seriously, then you need to think about what you're expecting to get out of it. If you decide that you're not going to take it seriously, don't trade.

Consider the following caveat:

> **Trading is a sporadic way to produce income.** You can experience long stretches during which no matter how you feel or how accurately you follow your trading plan, you'll still have few opportunities to ply your craft, or you'll end up going through a long and steady string of losses. In a good year, I can make as much or more money by trading than I'm allowed to add to my IRA. By adding money every year, I increase the overall rate of accumulation in the account. But in a bad year, I may have to consider taking out a loan to cover my taxes and to fund my IRA.

Trading is a serious game that should not be taken lightly. The key to being a successful trader is to be comfortable with yourself, your motivation, and your ability to formulate a plan and put it into action. Before you start trading, it's important that you understand why you want to trade and look at your own life and situation to make a decision that you can live with when it comes to how much time and effort you can devote to trading and whether you're willing to stick to it.

Trading as part of an overall strategy

Trading futures and options needs to be put into proper perspective. After you've sorted out your mental balance sheet, you can consider where trading fits into your life.

Trading can be a part-time endeavor, or it can be a full-time job. If you're like me, you consider trading as full-time work, but all the same, if you do it part time, it can be a useful source of income.

Say, for example, that you're a buy-and-hold investor in stocks, concentrating on income-producing preferred, blue-chip, and utility stocks. Trading futures can add a more aggressive element to your portfolio.

One ideal way for you to trade to your advantage takes place during times when a market is moving sideways, and you can improve your income by writing call options (see Chapters 4 and 5 for more about options). Another way is when a market is ready to top out, and you can either sell stock-index futures short or buy put options to protect your stock portfolio.

Trading for a living

On the other hand, when you're trading futures for a living, you may want to consider moving to Chicago or New York and looking for a job in the industry. If that is your goal, it probably will take several years to learn the craft and may require significant amounts of capital, guile, risk taking, and effort on your part to accomplish it.

Regardless of what you decide, you can derive at least some benefit from figuring out your mental balance sheet.

The Financial Balance Sheet

The high-risk world of futures trading requires a higher litmus test of your finances than other forms of investing. In the same way that you took the time to explore the reasons why you want to trade and how trading is going to fit into your life, you now must look at your finances with the least amount of flattery possible.

The big question is whether you have enough money to take risks as a trader. If you're struggling to pay your bills every month, and your idea of being solvent is transferring your credit-card balances to a new card every six months to increase your credit line, you're better off not trading futures or options. On the other hand, if you have enough money, you may want to find someone to do the trading for you. And if you're somewhere in between, having no money for trading at all and enough not to worry, you'll probably have to do at least some of the work yourself.

Organizing your financial data

Getting organized may sound elementary, but it's the only place to start. But before you start adding and subtracting, make sure that you have the following matters under control and accounted for within your monthly finances:

- ✔ **Your living expenses, especially food, mortgage, rent, and car payments:** If you can't live the way you want to on what you make, looking for the futures markets to save you from your current situation is not prudent. You have to have enough money for the basic necessities, food, transportation, and rent, before you do anything else.

- ✔ **Your life insurance coverage:** The amount here is variable and needs to be based on your family's expected expenses after your death. Some basic life insurance–need calculators are available online. I recommend a quick Internet search using your favorite search engine.

✔ **Your health insurance needs:** Again, the amount of health coverage you have is based on your family and your individual needs. You need to figure in a worst-case scenario, though.

✔ **Your retirement plan:** This aspect of your finances needs to be one of your highest priorities before any kind of investing. Make sure that you establish one and that you fund it as fully as possible before doing any other kind of investing or trading.

✔ **Your savings plan, including how you're going to pay for your children's college educations:** Start by calculating your savings rate, the percentage of last year's earnings that you didn't spend.

✔ **Your emergency fund:** Set up an emergency fund and don't even think about using it to fund your futures trading. At least three to six months' worth of living expenses is a good start.

When you have the essentials covered, you can turn your sights on reducing or restructuring your debt with a clear and concise end point in mind so you can pay it off and start thinking about accumulating money to trade with. One way is to set yourself up with an allowance every month or every paycheck.

If by some miracle you find that you have enough money left over, congratulations, you can consider trading.

A good place to gather information for preparing this kind of a budget is your tax return or any recent loan application you've filed. You can develop a good inventory of your assets and liabilities by reviewing credit-card statements, your checkbook ledger, and your monthly receipts, especially expenses that are recurring every week or month, such as grocery, cellphone, and utility bills, and car and house payments.

Don't forget to include intangibles, such as car repairs and impromptu medical and dental bills, because they can add up in a hurry, and be sure to categorize your expenses according to their similarities, much like when you're preparing your tax return.

Get a second opinion from a financial planner about the state of your finances. Be careful when your do, because most will tell you that trading futures and options is too risky, and some will try to sell you high front-loaded and back-end-loaded mutual funds instead. If you visit a financial advisor or planner, make sure that you tell him upfront that you're interested only in him checking your work and your calculations.

Setting realistic goals

Set the bar on your finances high enough that you won't be sorry later. Ideally, you need $100,000 or more as an initial trading stake. If you can't come up with that kind of money, wait until you can at least meet the lowest $30,000 to $50,000 trading threshold.

When setting your financial goals, consider the following:

- ✔ **Your age:** How old you are is especially important whenever you're not well capitalized. Make sure that you can make your money back if you happen to have a disastrous start or streak.

- ✔ **The size of your family:** Again, the number of people who rely on you financially is more important when you're not well capitalized. If your income is a significant portion of the family's well-being, then that takes precedence regardless of the circumstances. Never sell your family short.

- ✔ **Job security:** Most traders and would-be traders need a steady infusion of income that's provided by a steady job. If you decide that trading is your job, you still need to find a way to supplement your income during the times when trading won't provide you with enough money.

- ✔ **Your family's attitude toward trading:** If your spouse is going to harass you about trading, or you lose contact with the family because you're up at strange hours trading currencies, you're going to have a major problem at some point.

- ✔ **Your own risk tolerance and emotional status:** If you can't stand the thought of what you'll do if you get a margin call or you get wiped out, find something else to do.

Calculating Your Net Worth

Your net worth can guide you in making your final decision about whether you can actually afford to become a futures trader. The calculation is simple, but it requires attention to detail. Widely used financial computer programs like Quicken can help you do the work. A quick search on your favorite Internet search engine takes you to several Web sites that feature other programs that also can help. You can find a simple free calculator on the Web through a quick search, or ask your bank for a checklist.

You can also do the calculations by hand. If you need a major helping hand with this aspect of getting set up, pick up a copy of Eric Tyson's *Personal Finance For Dummies* (Wiley).

Figure 18-1 shows you a generic personal balance sheet that's self-explanatory. First, you list your assets and add them all up. Next do the same with your liabilities. Finally, you subtract the liabilities from the assets, and you get your net worth.

Cash	15,000
Real Estate	240,000
Car	35,000
Bank Accounts	12,500
Stocks and Bonds	74,000
Mutual Funds	30,000
Retirement Accounts	95,000
Current Values of Businesses	110,000
Others	25,000
Total Assets	636,500
Home Mortgages	200,000
Credit Cards	35,000
Car Loans	28,000
Personal Loans	35,000
Education Loans	12,500
Taxes	13,000
Others	5,000
Total Liabilities	328,500
Net Worth	308,000

Figure 18-1:
A balance sheet to calculate your net worth.

That bottom-line number, your net worth, is the amount you hope that you can get out of all the things you own after you pay off all the debt you owe if for some reason you have to sell everything. And that's the number that can tell you whether trading futures is a good idea.

Pay special attention to the amounts that you have in the following:

✔ **Cash:** Cash means the amount of money you have in money-market funds, your pocket, and even stashed in your secret hiding place.

✔ **Real estate:** Real estate refers to your home and any rental property, second home, or other real property that you may own. As a rule, if you can't sell it tomorrow, it shouldn't count toward this calculation.

✔ **Stocks, bonds, and retirement accounts:** Most people hold stocks, bonds, and mutual funds in their retirement accounts, although some also own them outside of their retirement plans. Any money that's in a retirement account will be subject to tax consequences and early withdrawal penalties, so you need to include those amounts in the calculation. However, you also need to be realistic. You're not likely to cash in your IRA or 401(k) plan to go speculate on soybeans. After reading this book, you better not.

✔ **Business assets:** Consider how much of your business assets are involved in cash flow and inventory. Be careful not to be too generous in this category.

✔ **Credit-card balances, second mortgages, and adjustable-rate mortgages:** Pay special attention to these amounts under liabilities, and be sure to include the latest credit-card balance and make sure the amount includes any big purchases that you've recently made. Don't hesitate to check your account online for the most current, real-time statement on your credit cards.

After you do all of the calculations, here's a useful guideline: If your net worth is less than $200,000, you shouldn't be trading at all, much less trading futures.

Differentiating between trading and investing is important. If you have $200,000 or less, investing in mutual funds is perfectly acceptable, perhaps even in a mixture of stocks and funds, as long as you're careful to follow sound money management and loss management rules and have a long enough time frame to make it profitable. But, if you *are* trading, which by definition means aggressively and actively deploying your money, you'll want to keep the following in mind as a bare-bones set of criteria:

Never risk more than 10 percent of your net worth as a trading stake unless you have a net worth of at least $500,000 to $1 million or more and you're a well-equipped, stable, and experienced trader. If you are, you may want to risk as much as 20 percent of your net worth to trade, provided your expenses and long-term investments are covered. However, risking more than 25 percent of your net worth in any trading venue is a crapshoot and will likely get you into trouble.

Chapter 19

Developing Strategies Now to Avoid Pain Later

A solid trading plan consists of developing a broad understanding of what you'll be trading, getting a handle on your emotions, finding out about different strategies, and tempering your expectations of and interactions with the market. It also takes in the more methodical nuts and bolts of actually putting together a step-by-step detailed plan in which you microscopically map out your strategies and rules.

In this chapter, I give you the background needed to create a more specific trading plan than you ever imagined.

Deciding What You'll Trade

I have no secret here, no magic rules or revelations. I can tell you only that you need to trade what you like and use what you already know to your advantage as much as possible. So when preparing a trading plan, take the following into account:

✔ **Use your experience.** Use what you know to focus on areas in which you're already an expert, but trade what feels right and what you have success in.

✔ **Get specific and get good by applying and refining your knowledge.** It's great to be a one-trick pony. Of all the currencies, I prefer the euro. I find that for me, it makes sense. European monetary policy moves at the pace of molasses, and the European economy usually is slow moving at best. In other words, the news from Europe is less likely to move the markets directly. Instead, the euro is a reactionary currency that tends to move in a slow, steady, one-directional trend, as opposed to other currencies that can be more volatile, such as the Japanese yen, the Swiss franc, and the British pound.

✔ **Study the markets.** See which ones appeal to you the most. If you enjoy trading stocks, you may do well with stock-index futures. If you like a particular sector, such as energy, try a few paper trades (practicing without money) with oil, natural gas, heating oil, or gasoline.

If you're a political junkie like me, the bond and currency markets may suit you well, because they're the markets that move the most with politics and world crises.

If you're in real estate and construction, consider copper and bond futures. Interest rates are the fuel for mortgage rates, while copper is one of the key building materials in home building.

If you own a gas station, you probably have a good understanding of supply and demand in the energy markets.

If you work in produce, you may have a leg up in grains and seeds.

✔ **Remain flexible.** If you discover that you have a penchant for trading well in the soybean markets, even though you're not in the business and you never knew anything about it before, add soybeans to your trading arsenal.

Adapting to the Markets

A major part of your trading success is your ability to adapt. Even if you're a specialist trading one or two markets primarily, you still encounter periods when those markets trade in difficult patterns.

The major point to understand is that no plan works for all situations. However, you can rely on these realities of the markets. They trade in threes:

✔ **Three market directions:** Up, down, or sideways

✔ **Three trading styles:** Trading the reversal, momentum trading, and swing trading

You need to be familiar with the three major trading directions and styles.

Trading the reversal

When trading the reversal, you're looking for the market's turning point, when either a bottom or a top is being made. To find that turning point, you need to keep an eye on the current trend and watch for a significant trend change.

The longer a trend stays in place, the more important the reversal will be, and the longer the new trend is likely to stay in place. Here are some tips for identifying a change in trends:

✔ Use moving averages, trend lines, and oscillators to predict and pinpoint as precisely as possible the meaningful trend changes. I describe how to use these indicators in Chapter 7, which is about technical analysis, and in the numerous examples of individual trades throughout this book.

✔ Set your entry points just above the breakout if you're going long and below the trend breakdown (a switch by the market to a downtrend) if you're going short. See Chapters 7, 8, and 20 for more trading tips. Use a sell stop for long trades and a buy stop to cover your shorts when you're betting on a breakdown.

Trading with momentum

Trading with the trend or with the momentum of the market is a classic style of participating in the markets. In fact, it's something that I always recommend that you do. It works the same way in uptrends that it does in downtrends. Just keep the following in mind:

✔ **If the market is trending up, your position needs to be long.** Even if you're day trading, your primary goal needs to be to look for opportunities to trade when the market is rising.

✔ **If the market is falling (trending down), you need to be short.**

✔ **As with any other trade, protect yourself by using stops.** Stops are preset instructions that direct your broker to sell your position when a certain price is reached and keep your losses from expanding beyond control (see Chapters, 7, 8, and 20).

✔ **Use the market as your guide in momentum trading.** You need to let the market help you make decisions for buying and selling.

✔ **When you're going long, you need to look for breakouts as entry points.** *Breakouts* are signs of market strength.

✔ **When you're going short, you need to look for breakdowns to enter your short position.** *Breakdowns* are signs of market weakness.

A rising channel can be used as an opportunity to swing trade or to trade by using momentum strategies. In this case, every pullback to the lower trend line was yet another opportunity to go long, and every tag of the upper trend line was an opportunity to either take profits and watch for what the market would do next or consider a short-term opportunity by short-selling the market. I tell you more about swing trading in the next section.

Swing trading

Swing trading is the best method for trading in markets in which prices are moving sideways, neither going up nor down. For more information about swing trading, see Chapter 8.

Managing Profitable Positions

One of the most important aspects of trading is deciding what to do when you've earned a nice profit, and you're getting antsy about cashing in. This situation may occur during the course of a normal market or one that is reaching the irrational exuberance, or blow-off, stage.

You must watch for several important indicators during a *blowoff,* or in a market that seems unstoppable and experiences short-term corrections. That can mean that sometimes the market sells off in the middle of the day, and buyers are waiting for the market to drop so they can buy at lower prices.

In this kind of market environment, especially when you've earned big profits, taking profits is a good idea whenever the market drops for two consecutive days.

On the other hand, if the market opens down significantly without news, take it as a sign that worse things may be coming. And if the market fails to set a new high after a short-term correction, it's pointing to an important sign that a significant top is developing.

Whenever the market breaks and you don't sell your position in time, use the snap-back rally, which is when the market bounces after an aggressive period of selling that usually develops so you can move out of your position and into the next.

Building yourself a pyramid (without being a pharaoh)

Futures traders add to profitable positions by *pyramiding,* or adding more contracts to existing profitable positions.

Never use a reverse or inverted pyramid strategy when trading. By that I mean that the first number of contracts you buy needs to be the guideline for your maximum risk. If, for example, you bought three crude-oil contracts, doubled your initial investment in the trade, and the market still looks attractive, you can add to your position, but only by a maximum of three contracts each time you add to your pyramid. The goal is to keep adding contracts as long as the market remains in the same trend or until reality sets in and you run out of the money that you'd set aside for this trade.

When you pyramid a position, you're adding to your existing holdings, not selling your holdings and starting a new position. Check out the example at the end of this section, where I detail how to pyramid a position in which your initial buy is ten contracts.

Use a pyramid strategy only during the early stages of a move, such as the breakout and subsequent early stages of the breakout. If you try it when the market has been moving in one direction for a long time, you're likely to lose money.

Preventing good profits from turning into losses

When you trade and the market turns on you quickly, you obviously have to get out with whatever you have left. But when your positions show nice profits, don't let the market take away your hard-earned gains.

Stay on top of your profits by setting protective sell stops as the market moves. For more details about stops, see the previous section and Chapters 3, 7, 8, and 20. With protective stops, you can (at all costs) make every attempt to at least break even on nice big profits, especially when you're trading markets that move quickly and can change at the drop of a hat if you're not paying attention.

For example, say you establish a position in the euro at 8 a.m., the market rallies, and by 11 a.m. you have a nice profit. In the middle of the day while you take a lunch break away from your trading screen (bad idea), news breaks, and the euro tumbles, taking your profit with it. If you had set a (protective) sell stop and had adjusted it higher as your profits accumulated, you would have gotten stopped out with more money than you started.

Never adding to losing positions

When the market goes against you, it's time to get out. If you *average down,* or add to positions at lower prices in the futures markets, you'll get hurt badly.

Back Testing Your Strategies

Back testing is the practice of using historical data to test how well your indicators work in a particular market. It's a tricky practice, because software programs enable you to look at past markets and test how different methods and indicators have worked in the past. These capabilities amount to a double-edged sword in a chaotic universe, because although your indicators may back test well, you still can get a false sense of security. Similarly, what didn't work in the past may somehow start working.

In other words, no trades ever work exactly the same way twice, so you have to take your back-testing results with a grain of salt. Back testing can, however, help give you a broad feel for how markets behave under certain conditions and help you spot important characteristics of the market, such as the following:

- ✔ **Seasonal trends:** Seasonal trends work best when trading the grain, seed, and livestock markets, because those markets are dependent on well-established planting and harvesting cycles. In other markets, such as bonds and currencies, seasonality is often less reliable, except during short periods of time. For example, stock prices tend to rise at the end of every month and the first few trading days of a new month, because institutions put new money to work during that time frame.

- ✔ **Market tendencies:** The amount of time that a particular market tends to run in a certain direction is a great example. If you look at a long-term chart of the U.S. dollar index, you immediately see that its trend lines tend to last for months to years after they're established (see Chapter 11).

- ✔ **Indicators:** Use your indicators wisely after you confirm their accuracy by back testing them. Get the big picture. For example, if you're testing a moving average crossover method, remember that the one you're studying now may not work as well later. However, if your testing shows that moving average crossovers work in the market you're testing, get a handle on several combinations, and then monitor them in the current market to find out which ones work best.

Setting Your Time Frame for Trading

The aspects of trading that are most often mismatched are the trader's personality and the time frame of the trade. Some people are just more patient than others. To be a good trader, you have to find that delicate balance between your level of patience and the reality of the market. If you try to impose your personality on the market, you're going to get hurt. At the same time, you have to let your general tendencies guide you toward your trading style.

Day trading

Day trading is a misunderstood and oft maligned term. Day trading is the practice of holding positions open for short periods of time during the trading day with the goal of accruing small, but numerous, profits. Usually it means that you exit all positions at the end of the trading day and return to the market with a fresh slate the next day. What it doesn't mean is that you trade every day or that you open positions at the open of the trading day no matter what.

When day trading, you still need to keep basic trading principles in mind, such as picking good entry and exit points, placing protective stops, managing your money, and using technical analysis. And you still need to keep an eye on the news and on the overall trends of the markets.

Intermediate-term trading

Traditionally, intermediate-term trading means that you hold a position for several weeks to several months, which ultimately is impractical in the futures markets, where volatility can lead to margin calls and where leverage makes holding positions for extended periods extremely dangerous.

So in the futures markets, intermediate is more likely to mean several days and is more often referred to as *position trading,* where you use a longer-term time frame as your reference point for keeping a position open.

Long-term trading

Long-term trading is impractical in the futures markets, unless you're extremely well capitalized, and you're hedging your business. When that is the case, however, you can use contracts that are several months to even years ahead as your positions as long as you're mindful of expiration dates and other parameters.

Setting Price Targets

Setting price targets is a useful strategy, especially when you're swing trading, which is where you ease into and out of positions by closely watching a market's trading range. Setting targets in momentum markets, however, may do more harm than good, because you may sell a potentially huge profitable position too soon.

Adapting your strategy to the market's overall trend is the better approach, but Fibonacci levels and support and resistance levels can help you set targets for taking profits.

Reviewing Your Results

After each trade, finding out why you did well or why you failed is a good idea. Checking your trading data from the time you enter a position to the time you exit it on every single trade can be tedious, but it also can be extremely useful. Here is a fairly good overview of the kinds of information and questions you may want to check and answer after good or bad trades:

- **Exit and entry points:** Review your exit and entry points and then ask yourself whether you adapted the right strategy to the right market and whether you used the best possible method to protect yourself.

  Did you give yourself enough room to maneuver? For example, was your sell stop too tight? Should you have given the market more room?

- **Your charts:** Go back and look at the charts you used to make your trade to find out whether the market you were trading is acting similar to the way history shows it has acted in the past. If it isn't, then try to figure out what's different about the market.

- **Fundamentals:** Did you really understand what the fundamentals of the market were telling you? Did you understand the nuts and bolts of the industry? For example, did you pay attention to the part of the livestock cycle that the market was in when you traded hogs? Or did you check the weather reports before you shorted soybeans?.

- **Market suitability:** Are you really suited for trading in a given market? Does it move too fast or too slow for you? If you're trading currencies, for example, can you handle moves that last for several days and keep your positions open overnight? Or does that frighten you and make you lose sleep? If you lose sleep, you'll be flat-footed when you wake up, and you're thus bound to miss something. A 20-minute gap in a chart can be closed in an hour, because the bad or good news that moved your currency turned out to be a false alarm, and the market moved briskly beyond (above) where it was trading before the news hit.

✔ **Technical analysis:** Did you let your own personal judgment ruin your trade because you thought you knew better than the charts? Always trade what you see and not what you think you know. You may eventually be right, and then you can trade the other way, but in the present, trade with the charts, follow the market's response to the news that hit today, and forget what the talking heads are saying.

✔ **Market volume and sentiment:** Did you consider the market's volume and the overall sentiment before you bought that top and got stopped out in a hurry? Low volume and high levels of pessimism often mean that a market has bottomed, while huge volume and a feeling of invincibility are the hallmark of a pending top.

✔ **Subtleties:** Don't miss the subtle stuff. Did you pay attention to your indicators? Did you look at your RSI and MACD oscillators for signs that the market's bottom that you missed came on a lower low on the charts but a higher low on the indicator?

Remember Your Successes and Manage Your Failures

When things go well, you need to remember the moment in your gut, your mind, and your being. If you fail, do the same. That way, if you're ever faced with a similar set of situations, you have a visceral and mental archive that will let you react in the correct manner.

This strategy is tailor-made for trading. For example, when you make a big profit, you need to sear the particulars of that trade into your mind. Try to remember how you did it, what you saw, what you felt, and what decisions you made along the way.

Following your trading plan all the way down to your checklist always is the better approach to trading, because then you already have a road map with which to evaluate your performance.

When managing your failures, avoiding the markets that you just don't understand is best. For example, I don't trade gold. It just doesn't work for me, so I manage it by avoiding it.

In the rare instances when I do consider trading gold stocks or other gold-related instruments, I always ask myself really tough questions, such as whether I can stand the lack of sleep. The result: I rarely trade gold.

Making the Right Adjustments

After evaluating your successes and your failures, you can make changes that keep you out of trouble by

- ✔ Avoiding markets that you don't understand or that make you uncomfortable.

- ✔ Not adding to positions without planning your strategy before pulling the trigger.

- ✔ Having your roadmap ready and not deviating from it unless you've previously decided how you'll do it and how far you're willing to go.

- ✔ Not making the same mistake twice. If you get nailed in the oil market, don't trade oil until you've figured out why you got hammered.

Chapter 20

Executing Successful Trades

*T*his chapter is all about putting together the analysis, the execution, and the management of a trade. Although throughout this chapter, that information generally is hypothetical, it nevertheless relies on real-life examples of trading, starting with your pretrade analysis and then detailing the actual execution of the trade through a phone conversation with your trading desk, managing the position, and then closing out the trade.

The trade I outline chronologically in this chapter obviously is idealized, but it isn't meant to be a Pollyanna-like exercise. Instead, it's an exercise of discovery that uses a real-life example in an active market — the oil market — during a crucial period of time.

Setting the Stage

Here's the scene: The oil market has been in a bull run during the last two months, but a major sell-off took place August 17, 2005.

Following that sell-off, you know that these three scenarios are possible:

✔ A major break in the bullish trend is near, which (in this case) gives you a chance to go short.

✔ The market is about to bounce, which gives you an opportunity to play the countertrend rally, meaning that although you suspect that the primary

> trend is the dominant trend, you can still make money in the coun-
> tertrend by buying a position at a lower price, when the market is over-
> sold in the short term (see Chapter 7 for more about oversold and
> overbought markets) if there are signs of a bottom. You can then ride
> the rising price until it once again turns lower.
>
> ✓ A short-term pullback is occurring in a market that is plenty strong,
>   and by buying on this pullback, you can snag a nice profit as things pick
>   up steam.

If you're trading a short-term pullback, and the rally is a good rally, then it
can carry the market on to new highs. If you're trading a countertrend rally, it
will fail. You'll know which one it is after the fact. The important factors: You
can identify a market that is poised to rally, you know that it can be a rally
that fails or a rally that carries the market to new highs, and you can prepare
yourself to deal with either possibility.

With these three possibilities in mind, you begin analyzing the oil market,
starting August 18, 2005, the day after the big sell-off.

Your three major goals are

> ✓ **Analyzing the situation.** Combine your knowledge of technical and fun-
>   damental analyses with the psychology of a market in the midst of a
>   major bull run.
>
> ✓ **Designing a trading strategy.** Based on your analyses, you must design
>   a well-crafted, step-by-step, careful plan that either makes you some
>   money or gets you out of the position with as little damage as possible
>   (if you're wrong), or the market turns against you.
>
> ✓ **Putting the plan into action.** Make the trade, establish the position, and
>   then manage it as you take the plunge into chaos.

After the sell-off, you wake up the next morning, get your coffee ready as your
computer boots up, and survey the landscape. As you sip coffee while going
through your stretching routine, you scan the latest news on CNBC, in *The
Wall Street Journal,* or on Google News or the Dow Jones Newswires. You
probably ought to check Reuters and Bloomberg, too.

As you scroll through all that information, you have only one goal in mind,
watching the different markets as they set up for trading.

What you know for sure is that the date is August 18, 2005, a bull market is
raging in oil and has been for several years, and the market is clearly at a
critical juncture, because crude oil futures took a tumble the day before after
the release of supply data showed a greater-than-expected fall in gasoline

inventories. Normally that would have been a bullish piece of news, but the sudden downturn, of course, got you thinking that the oil market either is making a major top or may be providing you with a long entry point at a cheaper price.

You take another sip of coffee, and find out that oil is trading near $64 per barrel, the dollar is stable, and stock index futures are flat. Bonds are waiting for the release of the morning's economic data.

You're focused on oil. It's the hot market, and it's the one that suits your style and the one where you've had your share of success.

Getting the Big Picture

As you pour yourself another cup of coffee and grab a roll, you realize that you have some time before heavy trading in crude gets going in a couple of hours, but you note that the price has steadily crept higher in the overnight markets. The economic data of the day include initial jobless claims, July Conference Board leading indicators, the Dow Jones-Bank of Tokyo-Mitsubishi (DJ-BTM) Business Barometer, and the August Philadelphia Fed Business Index, but these releases aren't usually big market movers.

The news is grizzly, but not particularly so, despite the usual and awful body count emanating from Baghdad and the war in Iraq.

One item catches your eye, though. Although not well covered by the media, some of the intelligence services that you subscribe to have commented on the 400 bombs that went off almost simultaneously in Bangladesh. Although an unlikely place for the dramatic, Al-Qaeda is high on the list of suspects in the bombing, and the analysis from the intelligence services suggests that it may be a prelude to an escalation.

So you decide that for now, you'll just be a spectator, watching the oil markets during the next couple of days while sorting through thoughts that the mainstream media hasn't covered the Bangladesh situation well. You ponder the idea that because Bangladesh is in Asia, Asian traders have been paying some attention to it and that may be why oil has stabilized. You're thinking that somebody with some money somewhere may be thinking that some kind of an attack is possible, and as a result, has been building a long position in oil, which is why the market has been steady overnight. You know that big money is also fast money, so you decide to watch and wait and do a little more leg work.

Viewing the long-term picture of the market

You pull up your one-year chart for the December crude-oil contract and note that the August 17 sell-off was preceded by a warning sign from the Relative Strength Index (RSI) oscillator, a reliable indicator for oil. See Chapters 8 and 13 for more about the RSI oscillator.

The RSI oscillator is an important and key indicator that tends to serve as a good early warning system. Your point of view is now narrowed, because you expect that oil will likely bounce, but the bounce may be limited by the long-term overbought nature of the oil market. An overbought market is one that has been rising for an extended period of time, and as the term implies, has gone too far. When markets reach extremely overbought states — for example, when markets have been rising for many years — corrections, or pull-backs, are more likely.

A perfect example is shown in Figure 20-1. The label "RSI sell signal" marks an important momentum failure, because the RSI oscillator failed to make a new high when the crude oil contract made a new high. This situation is called a nonconfirmation and usually is a sign that a top has been made.

You're all set now. You have the background from which you'll approach your trade, albeit with some reservation. Until proven otherwise, a top is possible, but the opportunity for a short-term trade on the long side is worth keeping an eye on.

The oil market still is bullish, and formulating a hypothesis is a good idea. However, the only thing that matters is not whether you were right or wrong; it's whether you make money.

Doing a little technical analysis

Check out the technical status of the oil market by

- **Examining the long-term trend.** The crude oil contract is above its 20-, 50-, and 200-day moving averages. The long- and intermediate-term trends clearly are up, meaning that your focus needs to be on whether those key moving average support levels hold. If key support levels fail, then you'll feel more comfortable about shorting this market. (See Chapter 7 for more about market trends and support.)

- **Watching the behavior of the market in relationship to the Bollinger bands.** All the way up this huge bull run, the Bollinger bands — both upper and lower — have served as support and resistance for crude oil (see Figure 20-1). Notice that every time oil prices tag one or the other of the bands, the result usually and eventually leads to a reversal and a tag of the opposite band.

✔ **Noticing that the 20-day moving average also provided fairly good support for this market.**

In this example, the chance of a bounce is fairly good, based on the technical analysis, because the contract remains above the 20-day moving average, which is roughly at $64 per barrel. A quick Fibonacci check of the current trading range, with a high near $68.16 and a low near $58.23, gives you a trading range of $9.93. By dividing $9.93 by two, you figure that $4.96 is the midpoint of the range and that somewhere around $63.19, crude may make a stand — give or take 50 cents on either side for good measure. The number for the 20-day moving average adds good support and confirmation to the mix (see Chapters 7 and 8).

Now that you have your parameters, you can set up alarms on your trading software to alert you when crude prices fall to $63.19 per barrel.

Stalking the Setup

You're now waiting for the setup, or a key set of developments that need to come together almost simultaneously before you pull the trigger and make the trade.

As you wait for these circumstances to occur, you can set your sights on the short-term chart (see Figure 20-1) and run through the following checklist to get ready for the trade:

✔ Check the status of your account.

✔ Review the key characteristics of your contract.

✔ Hone in on the short-term chart.

✔ Fine-tune your strategy.

✔ Review your plan of attack.

Checking your account

Always know how much money you have in your account. You can check your account status online. Say, for example, that you have $100,000 worth of equity. Your margin check shows that you need an initial margin of $4,725 per December contract and a maintenance margin of $3,375 in the months beyond September. See Chapter 3 for details about margins.

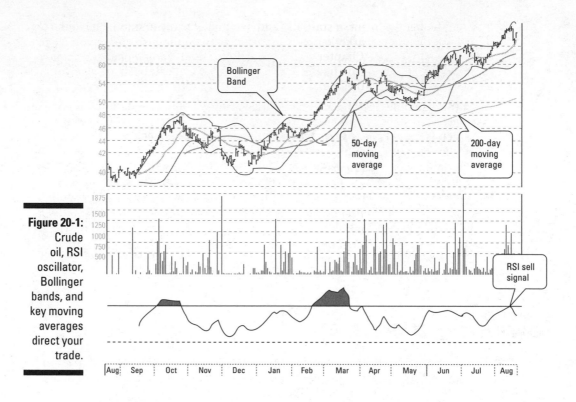

Figure 20-1:
Crude
oil, RSI
oscillator,
Bollinger
bands, and
key moving
averages
direct your
trade.

By consulting the margin requirements for the December contract for crude oil, you quickly calculate that you have enough in your account for going long or short on two contracts, because the margin is $4,725 × 2 = $8,750. You want to figure in how much to limit your losses to, so you have $1,350 per contract that you can play with before you start getting worried about a margin call ($4,725 − $3,375).

Reviewing key characteristics of your contract

As you formulate this trade, reviewing the characteristics of the crude-oil futures contract is a good idea. A barrel of oil holds 42 gallons and trades in U.S. dollars per barrel worldwide. The minimum tick of $0.01 (1 cent) is equal to $10 per contract. A single futures contract for light, sweet crude is in the amount of 1,000 barrels, or 42,000 gallons of oil.

That means that each penny you gain or lose is $10 worth of gain or loss in the contract, so you figure that $1 in price movement in crude oil is $1,000 worth of gain or loss. That means that your loss limit has to be 50 cents per contract, or 5 percent, a standard loss limit used by professional traders that usually gives the market enough room to fluctuate but also steers you clear of huge losses. See Chapter 17 for the details about trading plan and money-management rules. You need to follow the rules you establish, or else you'll eventually get into trouble.

Looking at the short-term chart

Careful observation of Figure 20-2, which covers the 24-hour trading cycle for crude oil over a three-day period from August 17 through August 19, 2005, reveals that the $63.50-per-barrel price range is a key short-term support level. You focus on that level, noting that as the regular trading session ends on August 18, the market breaks below $63 and touches $62.75 per barrel, which is where buyers come out, and by the 2:30 p.m. regular close, they've driven the price back above $64, where it stayed overnight.

Figure 20-2:
A 30-minute chart for crude oil for Aug. 17, 18, and 19, 2005, zooms in on the action shown in less detail on longer-term charts like Figure 20-1.

Date	Open	High	Low	Last	Change
08/19/05	63.86	65.94	63.86	65.79	+2.02
08/18/05	64.40	64.41	62.75	63.77	-0.08
08/17/05	66.70	67.10	63.70	63.85	-2.85
08/16/05	67.02	67.70	66.35	66.70	-0.37
08/15/05	67.10	67.55	66.10	67.07	-0.30

Regular open-cry trading hours at the NYMEX are from 10 a.m. to 2:30 p.m. (14:30) eastern time. After-hours futures trading takes place electronically via NYMEX ACCESS, an Internet-based trading platform, beginning at 3:15 p.m. Monday through Thursday and concluding at 9:30 a.m. the following day. On Sundays, the session begins at 7 p.m.

Now you know that your Fibonacci analysis held up (see the "Doing a little technical analysis" section, earlier in the chapter) and that you have a decent chance to go long if the market holds near $64 in the next trading session — whether overnight or during the regular session — unless something goes awry in the oil market overnight.

Fine-tuning your strategy

You decide that if the oil market holds above $64 per barrel by the morning, you'll place a market order for one contract and watch what happens.

Prepare and then write down your trading strategy in clear terms before you go to bed: For example, you may write: "Buy one contract at $64 or slightly higher, and depending on market conditions, place a sell stop at $63.50. Buy a second contract if market continues to hold."

Reviewing your plan of attack

After you come up with a plan, review it just to be on the safe side. Because you decided to wait to see what happens overnight, you want to make sure that you're up and running in the morning. So going over what's happened, what you've done to prepare, and taking any steps needed to shore up your strategy is a good last step before you go to bed.

Here's what you've accomplished:

✔ You were attracted to the oil market (the right one for you), because it's where the action is. You understand the oil market, so it's okay to trade it.

✔ You've figured out the key trading range (see the earlier section on "Looking at the short-term chart"), and you were able to pick out a major potential bottom using moving averages and Fibonacci retracement-level analysis (see the earlier section on "Doing a little technical analysis").

✔ You've waited patiently for the right setup.

✔ You've calculated your risk, and you've decided on your entry point and your sell-stop placement, as described in the tip under "Fine-tuning your strategy."

Understanding Intermarket Relationships

You're getting ready to trade an oil contract, which means that you're about to put your money up against some very heavy hitters, including hedge-fund traders, traders for Southwest Airlines, Exxon Mobil, the Saudi government, Citigroup, J.P. Morgan, and other dark-cloaked and hooded figures lurking out there.

As you wait for your setup to gel, you need to check what other pertinent markets are doing, including the following:

- ✔ **Gasoline, heating oil, and natural gas:** As of August 18, 2005, these markets were all in recovery mode — the same as crude oil after the selling period earlier in the week. The key is that all of these markets, including oil, were trending in the same direction.

- ✔ **Oil, oil service, and natural gas stocks:** In this real-life example, these sectors also were in the same general trading pattern.

- ✔ **The U.S. dollar:** The dollar was recovering after some selling earlier in the month. That often means that money is looking for refuge, and it was a reassuring sign, if as you originally thought, the smart money was getting concerned about the Bangladesh bombing being a clue that something else may be in the works on the terrorist front.

- ✔ **The bond market:** Again, bond yields were stable and slightly lower than they had been a week earlier, which also was supportive of the idea that money was moving toward safe havens.

You can never have too much information when risking your money in the futures market. Your thorough and methodical analysis of the situation is reassuring and supportive of your overall thesis, which is that oil was due for a bounce and that fear of terror may have been making its way back into the energy market.

Oil always is a politically influenced market. But in 2005, it was the most politically influenced market. That meant that all kinds of interesting strategies may have been lurking, waiting for your two contracts to hit the market so that your stake could be shaved to nothing in a hurry.

Waiting for the Catalyst

Catalysts can always affect the markets, because at some point sellers will overwhelm buyers, or buyers will overwhelm sellers. As a futures trader, the direction of the market doesn't matter as much as your preparation and your reaction.

Waiting for something to jump-start the market is tricky business, because the market can move based on virtually any piece of news, on something purely technical, or just because buyers or sellers overwhelmed the other side at a particular time, and limit orders that were just above or below a key chart point were triggered.

You've done your homework. You have your strategy. The only thing left to do is wait and then put your strategy into play.

Jumping on the Wild Beast: Calling in Your Order

You wake up on August 19, 2005, and see that nothing changed overnight. You checked oil prices just before going to bed, and you know that you never set alarms overnight to wake you up, because the resulting lack of sleep can impair your judgment during the regular trading session.

When you wake up, you check your 30-minute chart, and observe that oil has traded near $64 all night long. So after you do your morning check of the news, events, and the currency and bond markets, you decide to place your trade.

You decide that you want to wait for the regular trading session, and you place the call about 15 minutes after the market opens. That may or may not be enough time to allow for any adjustments from the overnight session to take place, but the charts are telling you that you need to make your decision.

You have good trading software, but you decide to call your broker, because she's been good about giving you good fills, and the guys at the trading desk are good at making sure that you, as a fairly young trader, get the kind of order that you want executed.

So you place the call, using all the correct language. Here's a good template to follow when calling in an order:

1. **Say who you are.**

   "This is Tom Smith."

2. **Say what kind of order you're placing.**

   "This is a futures order." If it was an options order, that's what you'd say at this point.

3. **Give your account number.**

   "My account number is 8648642."

4. **In a clear voice, say what you want done.**

   Buy one October crude oil, $63.39 stop.

5. **Ask for a reading of your order before you agree to have it sent to the floor.**

   The desk usually does this automatically, but it doesn't hurt to remind the person with whom you're working that you need confirmation.

If for any reason you're unsure about your order or unsure whether the desk understood it, make sure that you either cancel it or confirm that the trading desk person knows exactly what you want to do.

You just told the trading desk that you wanted to buy one October crude oil contract at the market price and that you wanted to place a sell stop at $63.39. The desk reads the order back to you, and you agree. The order then gets transmitted to the trading floor, and the desk informs you that you're filled at $64.10 and gives you your order number.

If you wanted to keep the order active indefinitely, you would have told the trading desk that it was a good-'til-canceled (GTC) order. If you wanted to make it a limit order, you would have specified the limit. The fact that you didn't make the order a day order, which would be canceled at the end of the day, makes it a market order, so the point is not that important here. See Chapter 3 for more details about the different types of orders.

When you open an account with a broker, the broker sends you detailed information about how to place orders and what the correct language is. Some have special trading desks for new and inexperienced traders. Most futures brokers are fully aware of the fact that they need your business and will do everything they can to make your life as easy as possible short of guaranteeing that you'll make money.

Riding the Storm

As the day progresses, the market stays fairly quiet, so you decide to put in a second market order that also gets filled at $64.10. At 11:30, the market takes off, and your positions are looking good.

You have some gains after all that waiting — hurrah! And you're still protected by your stop. Now, you raise your stop to $64.50 as the market is starting to take off. As the regular trading close nears, the market is rallying even more, so you raise your stop to $65, and you're nicely ahead now, with a guaranteed paper profit of $900 per contract if your stop gets hit without a major catastrophe knocking prices down so where you get stopped out below your protective stop. A good rule of thumb in a market that is moving rapidly is to raise your stop by 50 cents for every 50-cent rise in the market. You can also place a trailing sell stop and set it at 5 percent. Although I'm giving you guidelines here, the more you trade and the more you become familiar with the way each individual market trades, the more likely you'll develop your own guidelines. The message here is that as the market rises, you need to raise your sell stop to lock in gains.

Now you have a decision to make. Your overall profit is more than $2,000 as the market nears the close on August 19, 2005, a Friday. Your options are

✔ **Selling both contracts and taking stock of your position on Monday.**
This strategy makes sense, because you never know what's going to
happen over the weekend.

✔ **Tightening your stops.** This strategy can get you stopped out of the
market, which means that your sell stop is triggered, your position is
closed, and you're out of the market. That would be good if the market
crashed, or lost ground, and it may cost you some money if you no
longer have a position and the market rallies again. Remember, you want
to let your profits run.

✔ **Selling one contract.** You can take profits on one of your positions,
while you let the other one run.

✔ **Setting up an option position.** By using a put and call straddle, you can
protect yourself. A straddle is when you buy a call option and a put
option at the same time. If the market goes up, your call option goes up
in price. If the market goes down, your put option goes up in price. The
call falls in price in a falling market, and the put falls in price in a rising
market. To make money from a straddle, you sell the losing option and
keep the rising option. In this case, you can keep your oil futures con-
tract(s) and hedge your position with the straddle. If nothing happens,
you can sell both the put and call on Monday and be back to trading only
the oil futures. See Chapters 4 and 5 for more about options strategies.

Knowing When You've Had Enough

Presented with the four trading options in the previous section, I'd choose to
take profits on one contract and see what happens during the weekend. I am
a cautious trader, and I don't like leaving large positions open during the
weekend. By taking profits on one contract and leaving a protective sell stop
on the open contract, I've accomplished two things. First, I took partial profits on a good trade, and second, I've left myself with a reasonable and tolerable risk over the weekend, without having to worry about the straddle, its
commissions, and the added risk that can accompany options trades. You
can choose whichever maneuver suits your personality. The key is that so far
you have a nice profit, and you're not likely to let it turn into a loss.

By the time crude opened Sunday night, August 21, 2005, the October contract was trading above $66, adding to your profit. You can raise your stop
higher overnight by using your trading software or by calling your trading
desk. Most brokerages offer overnight and 24-hour trading desks.

At this point, you can once again take profits by closing out the position or
continue to raise your stops. I'd choose to ride this position out and continue
to manage it by raising the sell stop, keeping a close watch on any resistance
levels that are nearby.

You've done well with this particular trade, but you need to know about some trading mistakes that you want to avoid, including the following:

✔ **Becoming impatient with your stops.** Impatience can get you out of a big win faster than necessary. After you've made a big profit, the natural tendency is to tighten your stops too fast. That's where using a trailing stop will help you. If you set it at 5 percent and leave it alone, the market will take care of the position, meaning that a 5-percent move will stop you out automatically.

✔ **Forgetting that the market has resistance near the $67 level.** You can expect increased volatility as the price of crude approaches that price, which means that your sell stop may get hit nearer the $67 price level.

✔ **Buying more contracts as the price closes in on resistance levels.**

✔ **Applying an options strategy to your position when the price of crude is so close to resistance levels.** Even though the trend still is in your favor, spending money on protection may be more trouble than it's worth. However, if you decide to apply some kind of an option strategy at this point, use extreme care.

✔ **Shorting the market before it breaks to the downside.** Wait for the breakdown.

✔ **Bragging to your friends about how much money you're making in the futures market.**

Reviewing Your Trade

After your trade is completed, you need to review what you did right and what you did wrong. One way to conduct such a review is to answer these questions:

✔ **Was this market the right one for me to trade?** If you understood the fundamentals, and you knew that the action was here, then you traded the right market.

✔ **Should you have bought into this market sooner?** More than likely your answer is no. In a bull market, you bought strength as the crude contract rallied above $64.

✔ **Did you risk the right amount?** You followed your own rules by risking no more than 10 percent of your total equity in one market, and you used the right amount of protection as you set your stops. Best of all, you profited.

✔ **Were you patient enough?** Yes, indeed. You didn't jump into the market until you were convinced that the odds of a bounce back to the top of the range were on your side. Then you waited until the trend was clearly established before adding to your position, and you raised your stops at a steady and patient pace.

Learning the Right Lessons

The trade outlined in this chapter probably is a good prototype for a beginning trader. I tried to make it easy to relate to and used easy-to-follow indicators.

This example is as much about approach as it is about the tools traders use. You can make trading as simple or as sophisticated as you want, but in the end, the only thing that counts is whether you make or lose money using those tools.

Other books may offer different approaches, and as you gain more and more trading experience, you'll develop your own methods. Nevertheless, at the end of the day, trading is all about knowing your market, setting up your strategy, being patient, executing your trading plan, managing your position properly through vigilance, and following your strategy as well as the market will enable you.

Finally, remember that a two- or three-day time frame in the futures markets can be a profitable time if you understand how to trade for short periods of time and how to use technical analysis.

Part VI
The Part of Tens

The 5th Wave   By Rich Tennant

That's the Harrisons. Never have I seen an investment portfolio start so strong and go south so quickly.

In this part . . .

Get ready to put the final touches on your newfound trading abilities. Rules, resources, and strategies are good, but they're a whole lot better when you can use them. That's what The Part of Tens is all about. In this part, I take you through ten or so killer rules and offer more than ten sources of additional information.

Chapter 21

Ten Killer Rules to Keep You Sane and Solvent

Trading is 90 percent head games and 10 percent money. If your head isn't screwed on straight, you're going to lose a lot of money in a hurry. So in this chapter, I help you keep the old noggin atop your shoulders by providing you with a road map to ten of the best trading rules I've discovered during my 17 years of trading. These rules can help you keep your mind and money where they're supposed to be — between your ears and in your pocket, respectively.

Trust in Chaos

Chaos theory rules the markets. By definition, *chaos* is nonlinear order. In other words, what some describe as random actually is orderly in its own peculiar way. Look at the basic tenets of chaos, and then look at a market chart. It isn't hard to see a connection.

Prices follow a nonlinear order. They tend to stay within defined channels or trading ranges. When they rise above or below the range, they enter an area of disorder, but once they enter a new price range, they either go up, down, or sideways, again seeking and eventually finding nonlinear order.

 Big money can be made when you learn to spot the limits of chaos and the transitions from chaos to disorder and back to chaos. By making this concept the basis of your trading, you'll find that working the market is much easier than buying and holding something forever, hoping its price goes up, and much better than having the market work you or (more precisely) work you over.

When you trade with chaos as your guide, you find it easier to accept that the market will do whatever the market wants to do and that your job is to do your best to be on the profitable side (the right side) of the trade and to correct your mistakes as soon as you can.

Avoid Undercapitalization

If you don't have enough money, don't trade, period. It's as simple as that. Many people open futures trading accounts with $5,000 and lose half of it within a month only to run with their tails between their legs back to something safer. I know. That's what happened to me the first time I tried to trade futures.

How much money do you need? Most pros say that you need $100,000 minimum to open a futures trading account. If you whittle at them long enough, they'll come down to $20,000 to $50,000, but few will tell you that you need anything less than $20,000.

More important is the fact that your $20,000 to $100,000 needs to be money that you can afford to lose.

Why do you need so much money? Bluntly, it needs to last long enough for you to endure all the bad trades until you can finally make a good trade that makes you plenty of money.

Be smart with your money. Don't be one of those fools who maxes out his home equity just to be able to trade oil futures. Sure, you may get lucky and make it work, but the odds truly are against that. You can lose your money, and you'll probably lose your spouse, your family, your home, and your shirt.

Be Patient

The two times when you need patience in the financial markets are when you're becoming a good trader and finding good trades.

The problems with today's markets are that you have access to so much information that you can fool yourself into believing that you must trade all the time, and that can get you into big trouble.

In fact, trading for the thrill of it, or because you're bored, is a recipe for disaster. I can remember periods where I haven't traded for days or weeks at a time. These periods of market inactivity occur more often as I've developed my trading skills. When I first started, I overtraded, and I paid the price for it. Luckily, I don't make my entire living by trading and can afford to take my time picking and choosing the right times to trade.

Exercising this kind of patience can be to your advantage, too, because you can pick and choose when and how you trade.

You need to take time to think about your trading life. Some tough choices await you, and here are some important questions to ask before you jump in to the chaotic fray:

- ✔ How much of my livelihood do I intend to make by trading futures and options?
- ✔ How much time am I willing to put into analyzing the markets to improve my chances of delivering profits consistently?
- ✔ How much money am I willing to spend to educate myself and obtain a good trading setup?
- ✔ How long will I give myself to fully develop my trading talents?
- ✔ When will I trade?

Trade with the Trend

Investors are obsessed with the fundamentals. Futures trading isn't investing; it's speculating, so you need to be interested in technical *and* fundamental analyses. But the key here is that technical analysis tells you the direction in which the market you're trading is headed — how it's trending — something you need to know from the get-go.

When trading futures, the market trend, your time frame, your entry and exit points, and the protection of your capital in between are all that matter. If preservation of your capital jibes with the fundamentals of the market and you make money, you can take a few minutes to celebrate and then go right back to worrying about the following:

- ✔ Keeping an eye on your charts
- ✔ Following your trading rules

When trading with the trend, never lower your sell stops just because you think that the market will turn around and you were too tight in setting them. Likewise, when selling short, never raise your stops if the market starts going against you.

Believe in the Charts, Not the Talking Heads

The ultimate truth about trading is the price action. Few sources offer a better view of price action than price charts, especially in the fast-moving world of the futures markets.

Opinions are numerous. Some are going to be right; some are going to be wrong. However, the majority of commentators have their own self-interest in mind. In other words, their goal is to look good in front of the camera or in print so they can keep their jobs. If they traded, they wouldn't have time to talk so much or to write reports.

That isn't to say that when I'm on CNBC, I won't be giving you the benefits of my experience, though, or that CNBC and other television channels don't provide access to good guests and good timely information. My point is that you always need to look at all information through the jaded eyes of a trader, and that means looking at the market's response to a story or an opinion and trading on what the market is doing, not on what the story is telling you.

Remember, Diversification Is Protection

In the stock market, diversification means spreading your risk among a large number of stocks and asset classes. Asset allocation models therefore have become quite handy. An asset allocation model is just a way to divide your investment portfolio and is often depicted as a pie chart. A common asset allocation model calls for a 60-percent exposure to stocks, a 35-percent allocation to bonds, and a 5-percent allocation to cash.

In the futures markets, however, diversification is different. It has more to do with how much cash you have on hand and how you allow seasonal tendencies of the market to affect your trading. What futures diversification boils down to is your ability to manage your capital, your time, and your experience.

If you have more than one or two positions open at the same time in the futures market, you may find yourself in a dilemma, because you have a hard time keeping up with what's happening when the markets move so fast.

The way to get around this problem is to limit the number of markets that you trade at any one time. For some of us, it's one, or maybe two. Much depends on which markets you develop a knack for trading as you progress.

Limit Losses

Limiting your losses while trading is a simple rule that should make sense, but it's a rule that bears repeating.

The 5-percent rule is commonly used by traders and is easy to see and remember. Don't risk any more than 5 percent of your trading capital on any given position, and limit your losses to 5 percent of the value of any given trade.

Get used to limiting your losses early on in your experience so you become disciplined in your approach to trading.

For a futures trader, a 5-percent loss is probably as much as you'll ever want to handle. If you're day trading, you can use period moving averages to identify where to place your stop-loss orders.

Make it a rule never to get a margin call. You'll sleep better.

Trade Small

Trading small goes along with limiting your losses. But above all else, trade within your means. If you have $5,000 equity, which is way too little to think about trading futures, you should never trade contracts that require a $5,000 margin. A bad day can wipe out your entire equity position, and you'll soon be getting a margin call.

For most beginning traders, trading one or two contracts at a time is a good rule of thumb. If you're trading crude oil, your margin is somewhere near $4,700 per contract, which means that you need to have at least $100,000 total equity to be able to trade one contract. See the previous section about how much to risk in any particular market. Your loss limit from that starting point is $235, or 5 percent of $4,700. See the previous section with regard to limiting losses to 5 percent. (Check out Chapter 3 for more about margins and the futures markets.)

A perfect, or nearly perfect, contract for small accounts is the Chicago Mercantile Exchange (CME) Eurodollar contract. Margins for the Eurodollar contract tend to be less than $1,000 per contract, so you're thus at least closer to following the 5-percent rule.

Have Low Expectations

Most good traders are right a third of the time on average and half of the time during periods when they're hot. The way you stay in business is to manage your money so that you cut losses short.

Good traders are masters of the low-expectations game. That's where you think that if you come out even or a few bucks short, it's a good day. Pros readily admit they tend to make a lot of trades just on either side of breaking even. Known as *scratch trades,* they're the most common experience that you're likely to have while trading futures and options.

Having enough money and the sense to be able to continue to trade is key. The longer you stay in the game, the greater your chances of making the occasional big trade.

Set Realistic Goals

After you become well funded, develop a good money-management system, and set your expectations at the right level. The next step is to set realistic goals.

Here are a couple of ideas:

- ✔ **Some pros shoot for a three-to-one reward-to-loss ratio.** If you choose this strategy, that means when things are going well, your goal is to double your money twice over, while (of course) setting prudent stops and managing your money correctly.

- ✔ **Take profits when you've made 20 percent.** I like to take at least partial profits when I make 20 percent on anything. In futures trading, applying this rule is not always possible when you have only one contract, because commissions and fees can eat away at the profit. However, my 20-percent rule works well in the stock market, when I'm trading several hundred shares of stock.

Chapter 22

More Than Ten Additional Resources

. . . .

In This Chapter

▶ Exploring futures and options through government and general-information Web sites

▶ Knowing the commodity exchanges

▶ Reading more books about trading

▶ Checking out the newsletters and magazines

. . . .

*I*f you're going to trade on your own, you need some help, at least in the way of information, so you can apply what you've discovered in this book and in your newfound experiences with trading futures and options.

Literally hundreds of Web sites and publications deal with trading futures and options. This chapter lists and describes some of the more reliable information sources. Although the list may not be large, it is full of useful Web sites, books, and other sources of information that can actually help you become a better trader.

Government Web Sites

The Web sites of the Commodity Futures Trading Commission (CFTC — www.cftc.gov), the United States Department of Agriculture (USDA — www.usda.gov), and the Board of Governors of the Federal Reserve System (www.federalreserve.gov) are useful in their own ways.

✓ **The CFTC** Web site is a great resource for reviewing trading laws and regulations and finding out what kind of recent advisory rulings have been handed down. When laws and regulations change, your trading can be affected. These changes can affect anything from higher fees to what you can and can't trade under certain circumstances.

✔ **The USDA** Web site runs the gamut from important crop and livestock reports to vital weather information. The USDA site can be of great use to you when you trade commodities.

✔ **The Federal Reserve** Web site offers the Fed Beige Book, a great summary of where the Fed thinks the economy has been and is headed. The Beige Book is the Fed's roadmap for interest rates, and it sets the stage for much of the action in the bond and stock markets.

General Investment Information Web Sites

In this section, I list several important Web sites that can serve as libraries of information about trading futures, options, and other securities and financial instruments. Some of these sites require a fee; others don't. I like them all and visit them regularly.

✔ **The "Economy" section of Wall Street Journal.com:** This section of *The Wall Street Journal's* Web site is one of my favorites. It's an excellent resource for catching up on the big picture before you trade. The editorial content is first class, but for a futures trader, the best part is the data library, where you can find charts that chronicle the major economic indicators and enable you to perform a good visual inventory of economic activity.

✔ **Marketwatch.com's "Commodity Summary" (marketwatch.com):** Usually penned by commodities reporter Myra Saefong, this summary provides a great overview of the commodities markets, usually with a pretty heavy emphasis on oil. The best part: It's free, but it works better if you register.

✔ **Reuters.com (reuters.com):** Another excellent free news site, I especially like to check out Reuters early in the morning, because it offers good summaries of the overnight markets.

✔ **Barchart.com (barchart.com):** The most complete Web-based charting service, Barchart.com offers real-time data to subscribers, but its delayed data and charting are excellent for beginners who are trying to get a grip on the knowledge part of trading before they move on to the real thing.

✔ **CandlesExplained.com (candlesexplained.com):** This free site is from Greg Morris, the author of *Candlestick Charting Explained* (McGraw-Hill). It's a good site for anyone who wants an online review or a quick reference to candlestick charting beyond what is available here in *Futures & Options For Dummies*.

Commodity Exchanges

The Web sites of the Chicago Mercantile Exchange (CME — www.cme.com), the Chicago Board of Trade (CBOT — www.cbot.com), and the New York Mercantile Exchange (NYMEX — www.nymex.com) are excellent resources, especially for beginning traders.

All three exchanges provide excellent overviews of the commodities that trade within their jurisdictions, margin requirements, and delayed charting.

Trading Books

Very few high-quality trading books about the futures and options markets are available, given the public's major interest in stocks. Here is a good sampling of some of the better books that I've run across:

- *Trading Commodities and Financial Futures* (Financial Times-Prentice Hall, 2005) is written by George Kleinman, an author with a pure trader's mind-set. It offers an excellent step-by-step guide into the analysis and execution of trading.

- *Starting Out in Futures Trading,* 5th Edition, by Mark J. Powers (Probus Publishing, 1993, largely out of print) offers a trader's point of view, moving between an analyst's and an academic's perspective on the futures markets. You can find used copies at very low prices online.

- *Options as a Strategic Investment,* 4th Edition, by Lawrence G. McMillan (New York Institute of Finance, 2002), is widely accepted as the bible for options trading. It is full of details, offers clear direction, and provides excellent examples about which strategy is best suited for particular situations.

- The Murphy triad: Author John Murphy has compiled and written what some consider a classic trilogy of technical analysis in these three tomes:

   - *Technical Analysis of the Financial Markets: A Comprehensive Guide to Trading Methods and Applications* (New York Institute of Finance, 1999)

   - *Intermarket Analysis: Profiting from Global Market Relationships* (Wiley Trading, 2004)

   - *Technical Analysis of the Futures Markets: A Comprehensive Guide to Trading Methods and Applications* (New York Institute of Finance, 1983)

✔ *Candlestick Charting Explained* by Gregory L. Morris (McGraw-Hill, 1995) is the easy-to-read and use bible for candlestick charting. No trader should be without this one in his or her library.

✔ *Technical Analysis For Dummies* by Barbara Rockefeller (Wiley, 2004) is a pretty good reference book that can be a companion to *Futures & Options For Dummies*. This book offers excellent tutorials for beginners, and it is a great book to read for building a base for more complex fare, such as Murphy's triad.

✔ *Trading For Dummies* by Michael Griffis and Lita Epstein (Wiley, 2004) is another excellent entry-level book that offers the basic principles of trading not only in great detail but also in an easy-to-digest style. This book is great for someone who is interested in trading but isn't quite ready to delve into it.

✔ *Reminiscences of a Stock Operator* by Edwin Lefevre (Fraser Publishing, 1980) is the classic trading book. Although it deals with the stock market during a different era, no other book that I've ever read captures the spirit of speculating better. At the heart of it, this book is about cutting losses at small levels and letting winners run.

Newsletter and Magazine Resources

Many futures publications are available, and many of them can be accessed on the Internet. A few, though, have been around for enough time to have become quite reliable, including the following:

✔ **The Hightower Report (www.futures-research.com):** As Fred Sanford of *Sanford & Son* used to say, "This is the big one, Elizabeth." *The Hightower Report* is the most widely circulated futures newsletter in the United States, and it covers the entire futures complex.

✔ **Consensus National Futures and Financial Weekly (www.consensus-inc.com):** This subscriber-supported service, whose major calling card is its weekly sentiment index, provides a poll of bullish and bearish investors on all commodities and futures, from interest rates to energy and livestock.

✔ **Futures Magazine:** The name says it all; it's the monthly bible of the industry covering all aspects of the trade.

✔ **Technical Analysis of Stocks & Commodities (www.traders.com):** This magazine is written by traders, and it's where I got my start as a writer and an analyst. It's a good resource to scan regularly for good trading ideas.

✔ **Active Trader:** Similar to *Technical Analysis of Stocks and Commodities*, this publication tends to offer more about short-term trading.

Index

BUSINESS, CAREERS & PERSONAL FINANCE

0-7645-5307-0

0-7645-5331-3 *†

Also available:

- Accounting For Dummies †
  0-7645-5314-3
- Business Plans Kit For Dummies †
  0-7645-5365-8
- Cover Letters For Dummies
  0-7645-5224-4
- Frugal Living For Dummies
  0-7645-5403-4
- Leadership For Dummies
  0-7645-5176-0
- Managing For Dummies
  0-7645-1771-6

- Marketing For Dummies
  0-7645-5600-2
- Personal Finance For Dummies *
  0-7645-2590-5
- Project Management For Dummies
  0-7645-5283-X
- Resumes For Dummies †
  0-7645-5471-9
- Selling For Dummies
  0-7645-5363-1
- Small Business Kit For Dummies *†
  0-7645-5093-4

HOME & BUSINESS COMPUTER BASICS

0-7645-4074-2

0-7645-3758-X

Also available:

- ACT! 6 For Dummies
  0-7645-2645-6
- iLife '04 All-in-One Desk Reference
  For Dummies
  0-7645-7347-0
- iPAQ For Dummies
  0-7645-6769-1
- Mac OS X Panther Timesaving
  Techniques For Dummies
  0-7645-5812-9
- Macs For Dummies
  0-7645-5656-8

- Microsoft Money 2004 For Dummies
  0-7645-4195-1
- Office 2003 All-in-One Desk Reference
  For Dummies
  0-7645-3883-7
- Outlook 2003 For Dummies
  0-7645-3759-8
- PCs For Dummies
  0-7645-4074-2
- TiVo For Dummies
  0-7645-6923-6
- Upgrading and Fixing PCs For Dummies
  0-7645-1665-5
- Windows XP Timesaving Techniques
  For Dummies
  0-7645-3748-2

FOOD, HOME, GARDEN, HOBBIES, MUSIC & PETS

0-7645-5295-3

0-7645-5232-5

Also available:

- Bass Guitar For Dummies
  0-7645-2487-9
- Diabetes Cookbook For Dummies
  0-7645-5230-9
- Gardening For Dummies *
  0-7645-5130-2
- Guitar For Dummies
  0-7645-5106-X
- Holiday Decorating For Dummies
  0-7645-2570-0
- Home Improvement All-in-One
  For Dummies
  0-7645-5680-0

- Knitting For Dummies
  0-7645-5395-X
- Piano For Dummies
  0-7645-5105-1
- Puppies For Dummies
  0-7645-5255-4
- Scrapbooking For Dummies
  0-7645-7208-3
- Senior Dogs For Dummies
  0-7645-5818-8
- Singing For Dummies
  0-7645-2475-5
- 30-Minute Meals For Dummies
  0-7645-2589-1

INTERNET & DIGITAL MEDIA

0-7645-1664-7

0-7645-6924-4

Also available:

- 2005 Online Shopping Directory
  For Dummies
  0-7645-7495-7
- CD & DVD Recording For Dummies
  0-7645-5956-7
- eBay For Dummies
  0-7645-5654-1
- Fighting Spam For Dummies
  0-7645-5965-6
- Genealogy Online For Dummies
  0-7645-5964-8
- Google For Dummies
  0-7645-4420-9

- Home Recording For Musicians
  For Dummies
  0-7645-1634-5
- The Internet For Dummies
  0-7645-4173-0
- iPod & iTunes For Dummies
  0-7645-7772-7
- Preventing Identity Theft For Dummies
  0-7645-7336-5
- Pro Tools All-in-One Desk Reference
  For Dummies
  0-7645-5714-9
- Roxio Easy Media Creator For Dummies
  0-7645-7131-1

* Separate Canadian edition also available
† Separate U.K. edition also available

Available wherever books are sold. For more information or to order direct: U.S. customers visit www.dummies.com or call 1-877-762-2974.
U.K. customers visit www.wileyeurope.com or call 0800 243407. Canadian customers visit www.wiley.ca or call 1-800-567-4797.

SPORTS, FITNESS, PARENTING, RELIGION & SPIRITUALITY

0-7645-5146-9

0-7645-5418-2

Also available:
- Adoption For Dummies
  0-7645-5488-3
- Basketball For Dummies
  0-7645-5248-1
- The Bible For Dummies
  0-7645-5296-1
- Buddhism For Dummies
  0-7645-5359-3
- Catholicism For Dummies
  0-7645-5391-7
- Hockey For Dummies
  0-7645-5228-7

- Judaism For Dummies
  0-7645-5299-6
- Martial Arts For Dummies
  0-7645-5358-5
- Pilates For Dummies
  0-7645-5397-6
- Religion For Dummies
  0-7645-5264-3
- Teaching Kids to Read For Dummies
  0-7645-4043-2
- Weight Training For Dummies
  0-7645-5168-X
- Yoga For Dummies
  0-7645-5117-5

TRAVEL

0-7645-5438-7

0-7645-5453-0

Also available:
- Alaska For Dummies
  0-7645-1761-9
- Arizona For Dummies
  0-7645-6938-4
- Cancún and the Yucatán For Dummies
  0-7645-2437-2
- Cruise Vacations For Dummies
  0-7645-6941-4
- Europe For Dummies
  0-7645-5456-5
- Ireland For Dummies
  0-7645-5455-7

- Las Vegas For Dummies
  0-7645-5448-4
- London For Dummies
  0-7645-4277-X
- New York City For Dummies
  0-7645-6945-7
- Paris For Dummies
  0-7645-5494-8
- RV Vacations For Dummies
  0-7645-5443-3
- Walt Disney World & Orlando For Dummies
  0-7645-6943-0

GRAPHICS, DESIGN & WEB DEVELOPMENT

0-7645-4345-8

0-7645-5589-8

Also available:
- Adobe Acrobat 6 PDF For Dummies
  0-7645-3760-1
- Building a Web Site For Dummies
  0-7645-7144-3
- Dreamweaver MX 2004 For Dummies
  0-7645-4342-3
- FrontPage 2003 For Dummies
  0-7645-3882-9
- HTML 4 For Dummies
  0-7645-1995-6
- Illustrator CS For Dummies
  0-7645-4084-X

- Macromedia Flash MX 2004 For Dummies
  0-7645-4358-X
- Photoshop 7 All-in-One Desk Reference For Dummies
  0-7645-1667-1
- Photoshop CS Timesaving Techniques For Dummies
  0-7645-6782-9
- PHP 5 For Dummies
  0-7645-4166-8
- PowerPoint 2003 For Dummies
  0-7645-3908-6
- QuarkXPress 6 For Dummies
  0-7645-2593-X

NETWORKING, SECURITY, PROGRAMMING & DATABASES

0-7645-6852-3

0-7645-5784-X

Also available:
- A+ Certification For Dummies
  0-7645-4187-0
- Access 2003 All-in-One Desk Reference For Dummies
  0-7645-3988-4
- Beginning Programming For Dummies
  0-7645-4997-9
- C For Dummies
  0-7645-7068-4
- Firewalls For Dummies
  0-7645-4048-3
- Home Networking For Dummies
  0-7645-42796

- Network Security For Dummies
  0-7645-1679-5
- Networking For Dummies
  0-7645-1677-9
- TCP/IP For Dummies
  0-7645-1760-0
- VBA For Dummies
  0-7645-3989-2
- Wireless All In-One Desk Reference For Dummies
  0-7645-7496-5
- Wireless Home Networking For Dummies
  0-7645-3910-8